THE SPIRIT AND THE WORD

THE SPIRIT AND THE WORD

Prophecy and Tradition in Ancient Israel

SIGMUND MOWINCKEL

Edited by K. C. Hanson

FORTRESS PRESS
MINNEAPOLIS

THE SPIRIT AND THE WORD
Prophecy and Tradition in Ancient Israel
Copyright © 2002 Augsburg Fortress. All rights reserved. Except for brief quotations in critical articles or reviews, no part of this book may be reproduced in any manner without prior written permission from the publisher. Write: Permissions, Augsburg Fortress, Box 1209, Minneapolis, MN 55440.

Chapters 1–9 were originally published as *Prophecy and Tradition: The Prophetic Books in the Light of the Study of the Growth and History of the Tradition,* ANAO (Oslo: Dybwad, 1946). Chapter 10 was originally published as "The 'Spirit' and the 'Word' in the Pre-exilic Reforming Prophets," *JBL* 53 (1934) 199–227. Copyright Society of Biblical Literature and published by permission. Chapter 11 was originally published as chapter 1 of *Psalmenstudien,* Vol. 3: *Kultprophetie und prophetische Psalmen,* SVAO (Oslo: Dybwad, 1922). It was translated by James Schaaf and published in *Prophecy in Israel,* edited by David L. Peterson, Issues in Theology and Religion (Philadelphia: Fortress Press, 1982).

Scripture is from the Revised Standard Version of the Bible, copyright © 1946, 1952, 1971 by the Division of Christian Education of the National Council of the Churches of Christ in the U.S.A. Used by permission.

Cover art: *The Prophet Jeremiah* (1968) by Marc Chagall (1887–1985). Scala/Art Resource, NY. 2002 Artist Rights Society (ARS), New York /ADAGP, Paris. Used by permission.

Library of Congress Cataloging-in-Publication Data
Mowinckel, Sigmund, 1884–1965.
The Spirit and the Word: prophecy and tradition in ancient Israel / Sigmund Mowinckel ; edited by K. C. Hanson.
p. cm. — (Fortress classics in biblical studies)
Chapters 1–9 originally published as: Prophecy and tradition. 1946.
Includes bibliographical references (p.) and indexes.
Contents: Form, tradition, and literary criticisms — Tradition criticism and literary criticism — The original units of tradition —The form-critical investigation — Tradition and writing — The growth and development of tradition — The transformation of the separate prophetic sayings — The trend of tradition development — The prophets and the tasks of tradition history — The Spirit and the Word in the prophets — The prophets and the temple cult.
ISBN 0-8006-3487-x (alk. paper)
1. Bible. O.T. Prophets—Criticism, interpretation, etc. I. Hanson, K. C. (Kenneth C.) II. Mowinkel, Sigmund, 1884–1965. Prophecy and tradition. III. Title. IV. Series.

BS1505.52 .M69 2002
224'.06—dc21 2002024588

The paper used in this publication meets the minimum requirements of American National Standard for Information Sciences—Permanence of paper for Printed Library Materials, ANSI Z329.48–1984.

Manufactured in the U.S.A.

06 05 04 03 02 1 2 3 4 5 6 7 8 9 10

Contents

Part III: The Prophetic Experience

Abbreviations

AASOR	Annual of the American Schools of Oriental Research
AB	Anchor Bible
ABD	*Anchor Bible Dictionary* (1992)
ABRL	Anchor Bible Reference Library
AcOr	Acta Orientalia
ActaSum	*Acta Sumerologica*
AJSLL	*American Journal of Semitic Languages and Literature*
ANET	*Ancient Near Eastern Texts Relating to the Old Testament*, 3rd ed. (1969)
ANVAO	Avhandlinger utgitt av det Norske Videnskaps-Akademii Oslo
AOAT	Alter Orient und Altes Testament
ASTI	*Annual of the Swedish Theological Institute*
ATR	*Anglican Theological Review*
BASOR	*Bulletin of the American Schools of Oriental Research*
BFCT	Beiträge zur Förderung christlicher Theologie
Bib	*Biblica*
BJRL	*Bulletin of the John Rylands University Library of Manchester*
BWANT	Beiträge zur Wissenschaft vom Alten und Neuen Testament
BWAT	Beiträge zur Wissenschaft vom Alten Testament
BZAW	Beihefte zur ZAW
CANE	*Civilizations of the Ancient Near East* (1995)

CC	Continental Commentaries
D	Deuteronomist
DBI	*Dictionary of Biblical Interpretation* (1999)
DDD[2]	*Dictionary of Deities and Demons in the Bible*, 2nd ed. (1999)
DLZ	*Deutsche Literaturzeitung*
DTT	*Dansk Teologisk Tidsskrift*
E	Elohist
EHPR	Études d'histoire et de philosophie religieuses
ExpT	*Expository Times*
FCBS	Fortress Classics in Biblical Studies
FOTL	Forms of the Old Testament Literature
FRLANT	Forschungen zur Religion und Literatur des Alten und Neuen Testaments
GBS	Guides to Biblical Scholarship
HAT	Handbuch zum Alten Testament
HKAT	Handkommentar zum Alten Testament
HSAT	Die Heilige Schrift des Alten Testaments, E. Kautzsch and A. Bertholet
HSM	Harvard Semitic Monographs
HTIBS	Historic Texts and Interpreters in Biblical Scholarship
HTR	*Harvard Theological Review*
HUCA	*Hebrew Union College Annual*
IBC	Interpretation: A Biblical Commentary
IDB	*Interpreter's Dictionary of the Bible* (1962)
IDBSup	*IDB Supplementary Volume* (1976)
Int	*Interpretation*
IRT	Issues in Religion and Theology
J	Yahwist
JAOS	*Journal of the American Oriental Society*
JAOSSup	JAOS Supplement
JBL	*Journal of Biblical Literature*
JCS	*Journal of Cuneiform Studies*
JHNES	Johns Hopkins Near Eastern Studies
JJS	*Journal of Semitic Studies*
JSOT	*Journal for the Study of the Old Testament*
JSOTSup	JSOT Supplement Series
KAT	Kommentar zum Alten Testament
KHC	Kurzer Hand-Commentar zum Alten Testament
KJV	King James Version (Authorized Version)

LUÅ	Lund Universitets Årsskrift
LXX	Septuagint
LXX[A]	Septuagint: Codex Alexandrinus
MAPS	Memoirs of the American Philosophical Society
MCNES	Modern Classics in Near Eastern Studies
MLBS	Mercer Library of Biblical Studies
MT	Masoretic text
NCBC	New Century Bible Commentary
NedTT	*Nederlandische Theologisch Tijdschrift*
NKZ	*Neue kirchliche Zeitschrift*
NTT	*Norsk Teologisk Tidsskrift*
NTTSup	NTT Supplement
OBO	Orbis biblicus et orientalis
OBT	Overtures to Biblical Theology
OTL	Old Testament Library
OTR	Old Testament Readings
OtSt	Oudtestamentische Studiën
P	Priestly writer/s
PEF	Palestine Exploration Fund
PJB	*Palästinajahrbuch*
Psalmenstudien 1	*Äwän und die individuellen Klagepsalmen* (1921)
Psalmenstudien 2	*Das Thronbesteigungsfest Jahwäs und der Ursprung der Eschatologie* (1922)
Psalmenstudien 3	*Kultprophetie und prophetische Psalmen* (1923)
Psalmenstudien 4	*Die technischen Termini in den Psalmen überschriften* (1923)
Psalmenstudien 5	*Segen und Fluch in Israels Kult und Psalmen dichtung* (1924)
Psalmenstudien 6	*Die Psalmdichter* (1924)
PSBA	*Proceedings of the Society of Biblical Archaeology*
R^{JE}	Redactor of J and E
R^{P}	Priestly Redactor of the Pentateuch
RGG[2]	*Religion in Geschichte und Gegenwart*, 2nd ed. (1909–13)
RHR	*Revue de l'histoire de religion*
RSV	Revised Standard Version of the Bible
RWB	*Religionswissenschaftliche Bibliothek*
SAA	State Archives of Assyria
SAAS	State Archives of Assyria Studies
SATA	Die Schriften des Alten Testament in Auswahl
SBL	Society of Biblical Literature

SBLDS	SBL Dissertation Series
SBLSBS	SBL Sources for Biblical Study
SBLSP	SBL Seminar Papers
SBLSS	SBL Semeia Studies
SBLSymSer	SBL Symposium Series
SBS	Stuttgarter Bibelstudien
SBT	Studies in Biblical Theology
SBTS	Sources for Biblical and Theological Study
SEÅ	*Svensk exegetisk årsbok*
SJOT	*Scandanavian Journal of the Old Testament*
SJT	*Scottish Journal of Theology*
SNVAO	Skrifter utgitt av det Norske Videnskaps-Akademi i Oslo
StTh	*Studia Theologica*
SymBU	*Symbolae Biblicae Upsaliensis*
TAPS	Transactions of the American Philosophical Society
TBT	*The Bible Today*
TDOT	*Theological Dictionary of the Old Testament*
ThBü	Theologische Bücherei
TLOT	*Theological Lexicon of the Old Testament*
TRE	*Theologische Realenzyklopädie*
TUMSR	Trinity University Monographs in the Study of Religion
TZ	*Theologische Zeitschrift*
UUÅ	Uppsala Universitets Årsskrift
VT	*Vetus Testamentum*
VTSup	VT Supplements
YOSR	Yale Oriental Series: Researches
ZA	*Zeitschrift für Assyriologie*
ZAW	*Zeitschrift für die alttestamentliche Wissenschaft*
ZDPV	*Zeitschrift des deutschen Palästina-Vereins*

Editor's Foreword

NORWEGIAN SCHOLAR SIGMUND MOWINCKEL (1884–1965) stands among the major figures in biblical studies during the past hundred years. His published works—written in Norwegian, German, French, and English—cover a broad range of topics, methods, and areas of interest. An accomplished biblical exegete, linguist, and historian, he wrote major studies on the Pentateuch, Joshua, the prophets, Psalms, Job, Ezra and Nehemiah, the history of Israel, the Decalog, and messianism.

Born on April 8, 1884, Mowinckel was a close contemporary of several other renowned Old Testament scholars: Theodore H. Robinson (b. 1881), Johannes Lindblom (b. 1882), Albrecht Alt (b. 1883), Otto Eissfeldt (b. 1887), and W. F. Albright (b. 1891). His parents were Petra and Jørgen, a Lutheran pastor. Mowinckel married his wife, Caroline (Caro), in 1917, and they had two daughters: Wencke and Vibeke. Following in his father's footsteps, he passed his "practical-theological state exam" in 1915 with highest marks; however, he was not ordained in the Lutheran Church of Norway until 1940. After Caro's death and less than a year before his own, Mowinckel married Ingeborg Wilhelmine Wiborg, when he was eighty (1964). He was still actively engaged in research and teaching until his death on June 4, 1965.

Having attended the *Gymnasium* in Bergen, he went on to the University of Kristiania (the city whose name was changed to Oslo in 1925). After his introductory studies in theology, history, and philosophy, he went on to study Old Testament and Assyriology. In addition to his work at Kristiania, in the period of 1911–13 he studied history of religions with Vilhelm Grønbech in Copenhagen, Assyriology with Peter Jensen in Marburg, and Old Testament with Hermann Gunkel in Giessen. He received his doctorate in 1916 based on his volume *Statholderen Nehemia.*

Mowinckel spent his entire teaching career at the University of Kristiania/Oslo, beginning as a research fellow (1915–17), then as an assistant professor (*dosent*) in 1917–22, an associate professor (*professor extraordinarius*, 1922–33), and finally as professor (*professor ordinarius*) from 1933 to his retirement in 1954 at age seventy. He continued teaching seminars until the end of his life.

Methodologically, Mowinckel's work can broadly be identified as tradition history. For him this meant building on the works of earlier literary critics (carefully, and not without critique) but incorporating form criticism, tracing the history of the Israelite cult, and emphasizing the multiple stages—oral and written—through which the tradition moved. He always seemed hesitant to identify himself too closely with any other scholar's methods, but Gunkel and Gressmann obviously loomed large. He was also in dialogue with the "myth and ritual school" (primarily British and American scholars) as well as the "Uppsala school." From the latter, he often strongly disagreed with Ivan Engnell in particular. But early on, the Danish historian of religion, Vilhelm Grønbech, affected him in terms of his views of the cult as a creative drama. And his friend Johannes Pedersen impressed upon him the importance of a social analysis of Israelite culture. Work on Norse sagas and folktales, especially by folklorists Knut Liestøl and Moltke Moe, also had a profound affect on Mowinckel's approach.

Some of his most enduring contributions to biblical studies are his treatments of the Psalms. His six-volume work *Psalmenstudien* appeared in German between 1921 and 1924. It is in this series that he pushed forward the questions on the Psalms: dating (earlier rather than later), Yahweh's enthronement festival (as part of the autumnal New Year festival), and the importance of drama and ritual in the creation and performance of the Psalms (rather than the writings of pious individuals). While in his sixties, he returned to these issues in his Norwegian publication of *Offersang og Sangoffer* (1951). This work was translated as *The Psalms in Israel's Worship* (1962) and continues greatly to influence biblical studies. In all this, he was obviously indebted to Hermann Gunkel's foundational Psalms commentary (1926) and introduction to the Psalms (1933; ET 1998); but he also challenged some of Gunkel's basic assumptions and conclusions. Mowinckel came to identify his approach as "cult-historical" because he was continually asking the question of how the Psalms fit into the social setting and history of ancient Israel's cultic festivals, rituals, and traditions.

Another of his most significant works was his collaboration with (primarily) Simon Michelet and Nils Messel on a translation of and commentary on the entire Old Testament: *Det Gamle Testamente*. This appeared in five volumes (1929–1963), and Mowinckel's contributions were particularly on the prophets and Psalms. In the present volume, the reader will find numerous references in the notes to especially vol. 3 (1944).

Regarding the prophets, Mowinckel's research built upon earlier scholars' works (especially Bernhard Duhm, Karl Marti, Gustav Hölscher), as well as

Gunkel's attention to oral tradition. Mowinckel's key contributions to this discussion are the following:

1. He highlighted the role of religious experience among the prophets.
2. He emphasized the oral basis of prophetic speech and the continuation of that oral tradition alongside written texts.
3. He focused attention on the importance of a prophet's disciples in collecting, preserving, and shaping prophetic sayings in oral and written forms.
4. He interpreted the prophets in relation to the Israelite cultic tradition (see Knight 1975:221–24).

The present volume includes at least brief discussions of all these elements.

For his seventieth birthday, Mowinckel was honored with a Festschrift: *Interpretationes ad Vetus Testamentum Pertinentes: Sigmund Mowinckel Septuagenario Missae* (1955), and his centennial was celebrated in an issue of the *Scandanavian Journal of the Old Testament* (1988). Numerous international awards were bestowed on him throughout his career. He was granted honorary doctorates by the universities of Giessen, Lund, Strasbourg, Amsterdam, and St. Andrews. He was made an honorary member of the Society of Biblical Literature (U.S.) as well as the Society for Old Testament Study (Great Britain). Mowinckel was also awarded the Burkitt Medal for Biblical Studies by the British Academy (1949) and the Commander Cross of the Royal Norwegian Order of St. Olaf (1951); and he was made a Knight of the Swedish Order of the North Star (1951). Among his most famous students are Harris Birkeland and Nils Alstrup Dahl.

The reader should be aware that I have edited Mowinckel's work in a number of ways. Chapters 1–9 required the most editing since the author wrote this work (*Prophecy and Tradition*) in English and published it himself; this meant that no native English speaker had edited the original publication. If a few passages remain obscure, I hope the reader will be tolerant of the difficulties rendering a readable text from an author whose primary writing languages were Norwegian and German. The English texts of chapters 10 and 11 were edited in previous publications, so they required far less work. I have also (1) added footnotes (marked by square brackets) to bring the reader up-to-date in the discussions; (2) employed the RSV for biblical quotations; (3) added bibliographies of Mowinckel's works in English, as well as bibliographies on tradition history, prophecy, and evaluations of Mowinckel's contributions; and (4) created indexes of authors and scripture passages. I have also made occasional modifications in the RSV quotations by changing RSV's "LORD" to "Yahweh" and changing words such as "thou" to "you."

Part I

The Relationship of Methods

1

Form, Tradition, and Literary Criticisms

Introduction

Old Testament research began by taking it for granted that one was dealing with books—with a "scripture" that had always been scripture and that had always been handed down in the form of written documents. Scholars also considered it obvious, without further investigation, that where the biblical authors had been using older sources for their accounts, the sources in question were written documents. And this view could be supported by the fact that the authors themselves—in the Pentateuch, Kings, and Chronicles—frequently refer to "books" as their sources (for example, Exod 17:14; 2 Sam 1:18; 1 Kings 11:41; 1 Chron 9:1). When, therefore, Old Testament scholarship adopted modern critical methods and as a matter of course required that the material should be critically examined and valued, it was the methods of pure literary (source) criticism it came to employ.

Already in the eighteenth century, Jean Astruc spoke of the written sources used by Moses and tried to trace them in Genesis.[1] Pentateuchal criticism developed into the literary analysis of sources. And with respect to the prophetic books, it was an undisputed and untested presupposition for a long time that the "literary prophets" (note this terminology!) had written books, or at any rate "notes," "pamphlets," or the like. Furthermore, it was argued, what might be proved to be secondary—or "not genuine" as the term was used—by historical-critical investigation was due to editorial interference with and interpolations in the written books. "Scribe" and "editor" had replaced the original "author."

For more than a generation this view has been clearly abandoned in principle by almost everyone, particularly concerning the prophetic books. That the prophets were oral preachers, and that their sayings have been transmitted (at least partially) by word of mouth, for some time before they were written down, has been maintained with more or less clarity and consistency. That the historical traditions in the Pentateuch, Judges, Samuel, and so on, had also represented an oral "popular" tradition to a large extent, and that the historical books have had their own oral prehistory, has also been generally recognized for more than a generation by everyone engaged in Old Testament research. All this means that a traditio-historical approach has de facto been utilized alongside the literary one, even though the relation between the two methods and their respective ranges has seldom been discussed in principle.

Quite recently some have demanded that the Old Testament literature should be given a purely traditio-historical treatment. The term "tradition" is then sometimes employed exclusively in conscious opposition to the older method of literary criticism. The latter is declared to be completely inadequate with regard to the transmitted material. Proponents of literary criticism have alleged that it is a purely modern, logical method, and they insist on logic and psychology as well as a purely literary attitude to the material. They consequently are unable to reach a real understanding of the material.

No statement of what is meant, or should be meant, in principle by the traditio-historical method, however, has yet appeared. The label "history of tradition" (or "tradition criticism") seems at the moment to be used primarily as a slogan with all the emotional charge such a slogan is apt to contain. Research, however, is not well served by slogans. They belong to the world of propaganda; and, in most cases, their purpose is to veil or blur the truth. Research needs definitions, facts, principles, and a sense of reality. It requires that principles and methods should be soberly balanced in relation to each other. And it has an unpleasant tendency to view the rise of slogans in their historical connection when considering the history of the research in question. Only then does one see them in their proper perspective.

I belong to those who have always, and to an increasing degree, made use of traditio-historical approaches (form criticism and tradition history) in research, and I am accordingly grateful for any contribution toward the elucidation of the method and its range. I am convinced that it should play a strong role in Old Testament research. On the other hand, however, I am extremely skeptical of any "either/or" attitude in historical or humanities research, particularly the study of religion. I should therefore like to attempt to be clear about what "history of tradition" and a "traditio-historical approach" really are and how far this approach and method really go in Old Testament research.

In all scholarship there is a consensus, even if this consensus manifests itself in antitheses. It is, therefore, undoubtedly necessary to clarify the background of the rise of the traditio-historical approach in our research, which lead us to a deeper understanding.

The purpose of this study is first, then, to demonstrate how the traditio-historical approach to investigating the Old Testament has long been fruitful. This will also clarify what tasks the method has set out to accomplish and what conclusions it has reached up to this point. It will also contribute to explaining its real nature and at what it must now aim. In brief, I want to make a contribution toward the determination of its nature, aims, and limits. By this I want to show that the method has neither taken—nor must necessarily take—an exclusive, alternative attitude toward literary criticism, but that here (as so often with a new methodology) we are not concerned with either/or but both/and. In Part II of this study I shall apply this principle to the problems and tasks of the study of the prophets.

The Historical Background

The traditio-historical approach to Old Testament research is, as mentioned above, nothing new. The reasons it arose—involved in the history of the Old Testament research itself—may be summarized as follows.

1. A fairly far-reaching scholarly consensus had been reached regarding the question of literary criticism, which is the analysis of sources (and especially the analysis of the Pentateuchal sources); it achieved lasting and, in the main, final results.

2. A certain skepticism came to prevail regarding the value and possibility of a continued division of the main Pentateuchal sources into subdivisions (such as P^G, P^S, P^X, P^O), and more interesting possibilities than this dissecting work were anticipated.

3. Scholars realized that the connection between the details of the supposedly detached documents, such as J, E, D, and P, was often poor, and that the separate narratives were really, to a great extent, independent of each other. Furthermore, behind the sources there were smaller, original units that might be supposed to have existed orally before they were collected and edited by the respective authors of the "sources." What then was the character of the supposedly common traditions, of which J and E (according to the prevailing but incorrect view) represent a southern Israelite and northern Israelite record, respectively?

4. It was more or less clear, therefore, that the subject matter of a source might often be much more ancient than the source's period of origin, even if it had only been regarded to a very minor extent as a necessary task to trace this "preliterary" subject matter and articulate its specific details. Such was Julius Wellhausen's attitude toward P, for instance, and even somewhat more that of the real "Wellhausians." They

often pointed out in general terms that there was old material in P; but all the same they drew no conclusions of importance from this recognition.[2] Here, then, was an unsolved task. The feeling for this was kept alive by a certain conservative opposition holding the same fundamental views, most skillfully and energetically represented by Rudolf Kittel,[3] who was interested in maintaining the greater age of the material: a preexilic, partly very old, stratum in P, but who was also partly satisfied with more general postulates.

5. Our knowledge had increased greatly concerning the world surrounding Israel in the ancient Near East, which was the result of the excavations and the numerous discoveries of ancient literatures, and which had become particularly relevant to Israel through the Amarna letters and Syro-Palestinian archaeology.[4] But Wellhausen (and others) had taken surprisingly little account of these developments in his *Israelitisch-jüdische Geschichte* (Israelite-Judean History). These literatures and archaeological discoveries had raised the question whether the older literary criticism had not given its accounts of the history of Israel a too brief and contracted perspective and constructed a purely Israelite "development," not taking into sufficient consideration the possible or certain influences from the much more ancient neighboring cultures. Did not the Assyro-Babylonian literary finds (for example, Hammurabi's stele and many more) show that the "sources" of the Old Testament might be much more ancient than was held by the prevailing evolutionary view of literary criticism?[5] To what extent was Canaan the mediator of influence from Babylonia/Assyria or Egypt on Israel? And what part was played by the nonliterary influence through trade and war? To what extent are we dealing here with oral tradition?

Approach and Purpose

Against this background, the traditio-historical approach pressed forward. It attempted to move beyond the schematization of literary criticism to new problems and further results.

In the history of Old Testament scholarship, these attempts are, in fact, at first connected with form criticism and are associated with the names of Hermann Gunkel and Hugo Gressmann. To begin with, no opposition to the tasks and methods of literary criticism was intended. On the contrary, the representatives of the new school held that literary criticism had now reached such certain results that new tasks could be taken up. Gunkel stated in several places that he believed the source problems of the Hexateuch had, for the most part, been solved. His commentary on Genesis is based on the usual analysis of sources, and throughout he even attempts to reach a still finer distinction between the two supposed primary ancient sources, J and E.[6] The same is true of Gressmann's commentary on the Moses legends in Exodus–Deuteronomy.[7] Both presumed written sources and imagined the whole process of J–E–R^{JE}–D–P–R^{P} as a purely literary process.

But they wanted to penetrate beyond the written literature to the oral tradition and determine its origin, nature, and history before the tradition became literary "sources." Gressmann, for example, tried to show (often with exaggerated logical acuteness) several variants of the separate traditions behind the written narratives of J and E—traditions that had then been united in the form known by or created by J and E, respectively. Form-critical and traditio-historical research then enters Old Testament theology at this point. Gunkel, their predecessor, had placed these tendencies still earlier: in his investigation of the primordial sea and dragon traditions of Genesis 1 and Revelation 12,[8] and in his sketch of the genres and history of Israelite literature.[9] These are the programmatic works of the form-critical and traditio-historical "school."

The form-critical and the traditio-historical methods are closely connected on this point; for there is a real connection between form, style, the contents, and "setting in life" (German: *Sitz im Leben*)—social place and function. A tradition that remains alive and even has a history does so only because it is an expression of some aspect of the life of society and exercises a social function, whether in the cult, public life, or the more private life of the family. The form, together with its contents, points exactly to the social location of this tradition; the form is socially and psychologically given, the one appropriate in the particular situation. Thus, for instance, the form and contents of the burial lamentation are determined by the situation,[10] and the same applies to the ritual lamentation,[11] the tale of the sacred sites, and the cultic legend. The same is also true of the heroic tale, the tribal tale, and the historical tradition. They also have their own life governed by "laws," however. They are transmitted, transformed, or preserved according to the laws governing all oral tradition, which again are determined by social, psychological, and artistic concerns, making themselves consciously or unconsciously felt.

The task of investigating the tradition in the historical books of the Old Testament, then, had only just begun with the literary analysis of sources. The older critics were naïve in their belief that when the most ancient sources had been found through literary analysis, then the real history had virtually been ascertained; this is illusory. For behind the written document is the oral tradition, and the latter has had a life of its own, perhaps for many centuries. But centuries, or even decades, are not needed before a certain transformation of a tradition sets in, depending upon what interests are associated with it. And in itself there is nothing to prevent an old tradition from being accidentally preserved by a late source. Apart from this, however, only a very small part of the work has been done when it is realized what a tradition means in the context in which it has been placed by a later chronicler. The method of literary source criticism, which had long ago gone beyond operating with only such external criteria as the different divine names, constantly refined its analysis of sources; and this threatened to dissolve it as a method.[12] In fact, it had shown more than once that the connections between the separate narratives and tradition complexes of a source were completely secondary; with regard to both form and content there was often no necessary connection between the separate narratives or cycles of narratives. Indeed these were very often opposed to each other within one and the same source.

Thus, in 1 Samuel 9, Saul is quite a young boy who lets himself be led by the old domestic slave. Shortly afterwards, in 1 Samuel 11 and 13–14, we encounter him as an experienced warrior with an almost grown son. But all the same, both these narratives are ascribed to the J source. Should the same method be adopted in this case as elsewhere in the disentanglement of J and E (viz., to build our list of "contradictions"), then these two narratives would have to be distributed between two sources. It is therefore logically correct, according to the method gradually developed by the literary critics, when Kittel assigns chapters 13–14 to his K source, whereas he takes chapter 9 and possibly chapter 11 to be from a sub-source or secondary source K^2 or K^J. A constant division of sources into new sub-sources seemed unavoidable.[13]

From this the literary critics themselves had already begun to perceive that the original datum is the separate tradition, the separate narrative, the separate local story, the separate stanza. Binding together the individual traditions into larger units constituted a later stage in the history of tradition.

And it was on this point that the new school began. The first task is to separate the individual units of tradition from the secondary contexts in which they are now placed. Here literary criticism had, to a certain extent, done good preparatory work. Then the nature of the separate traditions has to be determined: What kind of tradition is it that we are faced with? A historical narrative? A local story? A cult etiology? And so forth. Furthermore, the "motifs" have to be analyzed, following the possible traces of a growth or transformation of the tradition. One must follow the growth of the separate traditions into larger units, "cycles" of stories, for example. In brief, the history of the tradition must be traced leading up to the written sources. This also contributes to the understanding of the origin and milieu of the sources, and of their interests. Here, however, investigations of style will make new contributions to the determination of the separate real sources—oral tradition or literary—in a more reliable way than the linguistic and phraseological statistics with which literary criticism has so far often been satisfied.[14]

In addition to this, one must attend to the study of larger compositions as well. What means are available to decide whether we are dealing with a source, in the sense of a larger connected composition of originally independent units? Source criticism according to its dogma of (on the whole) literary sources and its formal criteria—such as the use of the divine names and similar linguistic-statistical characteristics—often had to rest content with recording that story "A" might well be connected with the preceding narrative "B." But proof of a conscious artistic composition only exists when the transmitted units have been formed and adapted to each other, so that the one story in some way or other continues the preceding one and points forward to the next, demanding it as its continuation, as is the case, for instance, in 2 Samuel 9–20. We also are dealing here with originally independent traditional units, such as the narrative about the Ammonite war, David and Bathsheba, and so on; but they have now been molded together into an artistically rounded and connected composition. An example of a really thorough analysis is Leonhard Rost's treatment of just this composition.[15] When such an actual composition has been proved—or rather as a part of this proof—the question arises concerning a precise stylistic analysis of all the means of language, sentence structure, phraseology, elements of speech, and elements of narration that the narrator has employed to reach the aim: to form a cohesive unit out of the transmitted elements and motifs. An example of such planned and comprehensive stylistic analysis, which must replace the more casual separate observations and indistinct impressions but from another part of the Old Testament canon, is Köhler's investigation of the style of Deutero-Isaiah (Isaiah 40–55).[16]

From the understanding of these larger units of tradition, research must then proceed to the final aim of exegesis, which cannot be its starting point: to understand from all aspects the final result of the history of tradition represented by the existing form of the books. These books are the result of the working up of all the traditional material. Here is one of the weakest points of the older exegesis by the literary critics. The commentaries often lost themselves in analysis of sources and had nothing to say about what all these details and elements had come to mean within the new entity that the edited text—or developed tradition—constituted. Finally, this procedure threatened to become a consciously followed principle, whether the exegete in question was of a more or less "radical" or "conservative" disposition. Both Hermann Gunkel's and Otto Procksch's commentaries on Genesis are commentaries on the separate (real or supposed) sources in Genesis, not on the final form of the book.[17] Traditio-historical research failed to reach the final synthesis in these works.

The new view had important consequences for the interpretation of the legal material of the Pentateuch as well. The form-critical principle of research also asked about the place of the *torah* in life and tried to solve this issue as it interacted with formal and stylistic peculiarities. It began to consider the separate *torahs*—the original and separate, small, law complexes—as independent units, which had no original and necessary literary connection with the sources within whose frames they chanced to have been transmitted;[18] but these in their turn had often been pieced together into larger and also once independent complexes. Gressmann had already pointed to the priestly oracle and the priestly sacral legal verdict or legal instruction as the origin of sacred law, and to the connection of what he calls, somewhat misleadingly, the "lay law" (*das Laienrecht*) with other Near Eastern legislation, with Hammurabi and the ancient Sumerian, Assyrian, and Hittite laws, and presumed that Canaanite law to have served as an intermediary.[19]

Albrecht Alt articulated a clearer understanding of these matters. With a form-critical approach, he established a concrete picture of the nature, origin, and social connection of both case law and "sacral law" proper. He also realized the independence in principle of the legal tradition and its independence from the historical tradition, with which it became connected only at a comparatively late stage.[20] I, for one, have attempted to demonstrate through form-critical and cult-historical investigations that this combination of laws also has its own setting in life. It is not a purely literary process but has a cultic background.[21]

From the very beginning, an important aspect of this form-critical and traditio-historical method was the broader basis it tried to establish by placing its investigations in the light of comparative narrative and motif research from all other regions and peoples. Characteristic in this respect is the important part played by Axel Olrik's essay on the fundamental epic "laws," both for Gunkel and many of his successors.[22] In that connection the movement emerged at the same time as the so-called *Religionsgeschichtliche Schule* ("History of Religion School").[23] On a broadly comprehensive basis, it took up a series of mythical motifs in the Israelite tradition for treatment and wanted to trace their origin in non-Israelite religions and milieus. The excavations from the world surrounding Israel had brought to the surface a colossal amount of material, which threw new light on the Old Testament, particularly on the laws, and which demanded to be taken into account and was also fairly quickly exploited by the scholars of the new school.[24] Gunkel's *Schöpfung und Chaos in Urzeit und Endzeit* (Creation and Chaos in Primaltime and Endtime) got the new school started.[25] The valuable impulses and views of the school have influenced all Old Testament research. Its defects have gradually been shed—for example its one-sided interest in the *origin* of an idea and neglect of what Israel had made out of it, whatever its origin.[26]

The cult pattern, partially of foreign origin—which formed the background of, for example, the Psalms—was completely realized. Gunkel proved this already in his first papers on the Psalms. It was exactly on the basis of the form-critical approach that he came to the problem of the ritual pattern.[27] This approach has also been a leading one for me, and I have never considered myself as belonging to the History of Religion School in the proper sense. I would refer here to my *Psalmenstudien* (Psalms Studies), particularly Volume 2: *Das Thronbesteigungsfest Jahwäs und der Ursprung der Eschatologie* (Yahweh's Enthronement Festival and the Origin of Eschatology). There I attempted to reconstruct the Israelite epiphany and enthronement festival, partially on the basis of general Near Eastern myth and ritual, particularly the Babylonian New Year Festival. The latter was supposed to be the ritual prototype that is also reflected in many ways in Israel's great festival and the psalms that were associated with it.[28]

The results of archaeological research proper, which have now attained such importance, especially in American and English research,[29] were also taken into account by the representatives of the new school. This is shown by several of the works of Gressmann, primarily his volume *Altorientalische Texte und Bilder zum Alten Testament* (Ancient Oriental Texts and Images Relating to the Old Testament).[30]

The Emphasis on Oral Tradition

The assumption on which all this work rested was a clear realization for Gunkel that everywhere we are dealing with an *originally oral tradition*. The separate stories or cycles of stories, the separate ditties and folksongs, the separate laws or smaller complexes of laws, had to have existed as oral tradition, handed down from generation to generation within the milieu and with the social function relative to the original setting in life (*Sitz im Leben*) of the genre (*Gattung*) in question. The history of the genres, the outlines of which Gunkel often believed to be able to glimpse, was thought to be a history that had taken place initially within the oral tradition. The changes to which the original motifs and separate stories had been subject, and the development they had accordingly gone through before they had the form in which they now exist, were changes within the oral tradition. The history of this development is accordingly, in a very real sense of the term, a "history of tradition." The different variants that Gressmann—rightly or wrongly—believed to be able to prove in his analysis of the Moses stories in J's and E's rendering of the separate stories are all thought to be variants within the oral tradition. This is so even if the methods employed by Gressmann to disentangle the variants from one another are still often influenced by the formal criteria of a "literary criticism."[31] Gressmann is fully aware that behind the question of literary criticism looms that of "content analysis" (*Sachkritik*), motif criticism, and the history of tradition (or whatever one chooses to call it).[32] In Gunkel's Genesis commentary, most of his discussion actually concerns the preliterary stage of the material and is his primary interest. It may be said with some justification that his exegesis and the exposition of the meaning and ideas attached to the old traditions by the final literary author or authors is very often unsatisfactory.[33]

Regarding the transmission of the sayings of the prophets, it is also the form critics and tradition historians (along with Gunkel) who have clearly realized and emphasized the originally oral character of the prophetic word. This is true even if the older interpretation of the prophets as authors of "books" is still too prominent even in Gunkel.[34] I recognized in principle already in 1916 that both the prophetic tradition and the prophetic "books" were originally collected and transmitted by word of mouth in oral tradition.[35] The original prophetic sayings were not speeches in the modern sense but short "oracular words," as Gunkel demonstrated by means of the form-critical method. A classic work in this field is Gressmann's analysis of Deutero-Isaiah's sayings.[36]

The influence from the new impulses of the form-critical and traditio-historical school accordingly became more and more marked within Old Testament research and without its being felt as a distancing in principle from literary criticism itself.[37] The importance of the method in principle was still pointed out by Adolphe Lods; compare also Willy Staerk's paper on literary criticism and tradition criticism.[38] A conscious successor of Gunkel is, for example, Antonin Causse in his treatment of the oldest poetry of ancient Israel.[39] The same is the case with my popular outline of the literary history of Israel and Judaism.[40] This point of view is even more prominent in H. M. Chadwick and his history of Hebrew literature,[41] and in Frederick C. Grant, who agrees for the most part with Chadwick.[42] Even Otto Eissfeldt, one of the most consistent literary critics, could not avoid considering the preliterary stage of the material.[43] The same is true of Gunnar Hylmö's treatment of Old Testament literature,[44] as well as the most recent Scandinavian introduction to the Old Testament by Aage Bentzen.[45]

A full understanding of the importance of the oral transmission and its continued importance even after the traditions were written down, however, was obtained through the work of H. S. Nyberg.[46] Starting from the conditions of transmission within the Muslim civilization from ancient to modern times, Nyberg maintains (with good reason) that the transmission of canonical and authoritative "literature" in the ancient Near East in principle occurs by word of mouth—whether sources, commentaries, or systematic interpretation. Writing is used only to aid memory. The written word is not the primary authority; that rank is given to the tradition of the "wise men"—"the tradition" supported by the connected series of authorities: A transmitted to B, and B to

C, and so on, this event, this saying, or this interpretation.[47] Should discrepancies arise between the manuscript/s and tradition, then the oral tradition of the wise men is right; where the "chain of transmission" is found to be in order, the written text must be corrected to conform to the tradition.

There are many indications that this was the case with Jewish traditions. Its interest in the assured chain of transmission of learned authorities—from A to B to C, etc.—is well known from the Mishnah tractate *Pirqe 'Abot* (Sayings of the Fathers). And in the synagogue the rule long prevailed that the Torah should not be read at the worship service from a manuscript but be reproduced from memory.[48] The Masoretic system of writing demonstrates that in cases of doubt the decision rests with the tradition of the learned: "that which is written" (*kethib*) must yield to "that which is spoken" (*qerê*). Classic evidence of this are the "scribal emendations" (*tiqqunê sopherîm*): places where the "original" written text has been emended by the scribes, primarily based upon dogmatic considerations. The supposed tradition is accordingly not always a real tradition but learned theory.[49]

Nyberg's point of view has been taken up by Harris Birkeland, who showed that it was also valid for prophetic literature.[50] The only logical conclusion —both from the form-critical and tradition-critical research of Gunkel's "school" and from the insight of recent times into the psychological and religious nature of prophecy—is that the entire prophetic transmission was initially by word of mouth, and that the prophetic books are all collections and later recordings of separate sayings or complexes of sayings from oral tradition.[51] Birkeland now wants to show how the original, brief, separate sayings in the oral tradition were collected by association into "tradition complexes," and the latter are joined together into larger compositions and "books." I have carried these views further, partly by pointing out the religious interests and the religio-social conditions that have led to transmission and collection of the prophetic sayings and finally to the rise of a written prophetic literature,[52] and partly by showing how the collection process gradually took place in specific cases.[53]

The last phase of the traditio-historical approach is represented by Ivan Engnell, who has proclaimed most strongly and exclusively the complete bankruptcy of literary criticism and its inadequacy with regard to the material.[54] He identifies the method he wants to employ as "consistently traditio-historical," without, however, providing any further definition or further articulation of the methodology. It seems, however, to include two axioms, as he carries it out in his programmatic book.

1. Agreeing with Nyberg, he maintains that the transmission of Old Testament literature is in principle by word of mouth. Oral traditions of

> many kinds (historical traditions, myths, stories, legends, prophetic sayings, laws, ritual rules, etc.) and poetic products have been transmitted from one generation to another in the course of the ages and have gradually been joined together into larger compositions by an oral process. Even after this tradition had been recorded, the recorded matter has mostly been handed on (and combined) by word of mouth.
>
> 2. This process of growth makes it dangerous in principle—and at any rate practically impossible—to get behind the tradition as it now exists. Attempts to analyze tradition, whether by literary analysis of sources or motif analysis, and to discover several strata of tradition, are usually made in vain. Even if they are not dismissed as marginal, they are judged as western evolutionism. The sayings of the prophets, for instance, are only available as they have been formed, possibly transformed, and joined together by tradition; it is of no use to try to reach the exact words (*ipsissima verba*) of the prophets.

Even if one may largely agree with the first of these axioms, the logical necessity of the second following the first is unclear to me. It is also unclear how this capitulation in principle with respect to all attempts to penetrate into the origin and history of the tradition may be reconciled with the slogan "consistently traditio-historical."

In Engnell's terminology, the term "traditio-historical" seems to have lost much of its original relation to history: the study and explanation of the origin, growth, and development of the different traditions and the tradition complex. It refers, above all, to the mere stressing of the fact that the composition of the original units (separate traditions) and the compilation and elaboration of the present books have been the oral—not literary—work by the transmitting circles. So for Engnell, for example, P does not appear as a separate source, but as the last author and editor of the Pentateuchal traditions. He makes no real attempt to distinguish between earlier and later traditions or between earlier and later strata in the traditions. The interest is primarily directed antithetically against the literary point of view and method.

Engnell repeatedly expresses an excessive rejection in principle of the treatment of the Old Testament scriptures according to the method of literary criticism. But he has not provided a picture of how the oral formation of the traditions and processes of transmission—the joining together of separate traditions and motifs, and so on—have taken place. And his sketch of the religious and inner-historical development of Israel often appears to represent an abandonment of the attempt to achieve clarity through a penetrating historical criticism of tradition.[55] Tradition sometimes appears to be understood as something static rather than a dynamic process, as a real *history*.

Conclusion

These new research methods and approaches, as represented by Gunkel and his followers, also quickly came to have fatal consequences for the old "literary criticism" as "source criticism," the so-called "higher criticism." I hope to be able to discuss this in more detail in another connection. The form-critical and tradition-critical school as such, however, did not intend a breach with the method. While the new tendencies were represented by scholars who themselves sprang from literary criticism and accepted some or many of its fundamental positions (and who also practiced literary criticism of the transmitted documents), it is possible to speak of self-revision within the historical-critical scholarship of the Old Testament. Where the latter continued to be research, it also continued to be historical-critical. It is outside the scope of this historical statement to discuss in detail the separate consequences of the older school of literary criticism.

2

Tradition Criticism and Literary Criticism

The Necessity of Literary Criticism

Tatian's Diatessaron

It may be useful to make some remarks of a more general character about literary criticism and the history of tradition. Although Old Testament scholars did not invent literary criticism and its methods, it is a legitimate and often necessary and useful methodology. Although this is not the place to address this question in detail, I hope I shall be able to return to it in a broader context. Tatian's *Diatessaron* is sufficient proof that source analysis may be necessary in itself and lead to results.[1] Is it unlikely then that it should be applicable to Old Testament literature? A purely literary procedure like that of Tatian, it is maintained, is unthinkable in the ancient Near East, with its emphasis on oral transmission, until Hellenism had produced a milieu working with literary categories.[2] But our knowledge of the mentality and literary activity of the ancient Near East must also be built on the study of available literary sources. The latter are even primary sources compared to analogies based on, for example, conditions in Islam. An unprejudiced study of one of the Old Testament books, in spite of all allowances for the originally oral character of the tradition, may lead to the result that we are dealing with a technique bearing fundamental similarities to Tatian's procedures. If so, then one must recognize this fact and admit that in ancient Israel traditions could have, in certain cases, been passed down and literary work carried out in this way.

Chronicles

In this connection, it should be pointed out that the author of First and Second Chronicles has notoriously drawn on the written Book of First and Second Kings. The same is true of his drawing on Nehemiah's memoir, which he has edited along with other traditions, some of which may have been oral. But the Chronicler himself cites these traditions as "books," and he knew them in written form: "The Chronicle of Solomon," "The Chronicles of the Kings of Judah," "The Chronicle of the Kings of Israel," and so on. We have the Book of Kings; so disentangling this source from Chronicles can consequently be done by any clever school child. If Kings had not come down to us, however, the source problem itself and the necessity of its solution would have presented itself all the same. There is no doubt at all then that this procedure might have succeeded to a great extent. The Chronicler and his late sources are in fact so different from the more ancient source of First and Second Kings—in terms of style, linguistics, and religious and theological ideas—that it is not very difficult to determine where he himself is speaking as opposed to the more ancient source.[3]

Regarding Nehemiah's memoir, it exists at present only as a fairly large part of the Chronicler's historical work. Scholars agree unanimously, however, that the stylistic and (to some extent) ideological indications are sufficiently clear to enable one to disentangle the source from the editor's work. We simply have to employ the stylistic criteria consistently that we can discern in the undisputed Nehemiah passages. And we should not blunt our critical judgment out of some misguided apologetic in order to "save" as much as possible for the Nehemiah source. The Chronicler has tried to put his own stamp on the sources through interpolations in the case of Nehemiah's memoir as much as he did with Kings, expressing his own religious views. This is not solely an assumption but is demonstrable in a number of cases.

The "author" or "editor" of the Ezra-Nehemiah books (based on the extant Hebrew text) worked in a literary way. This may be established beyond question from the fact that in Nehemiah 7 he has not only repeated the census lists of Ezra 2, but also included part of the Chronicler's story of the first return from Babylon, which frames the list in Ezra 2 (Ezra 2:68-72 = Neh 7:70-72a).[4]

Jeremiah

Finally, I want to point out a third example: the convincing case of Jeremiah's sayings. For twenty-three years they existed solely in oral tradition. Then Baruch wrote them down at the dictation of the prophet (Jeremiah 36). Subsequently, "many similar words were added to them" (36:32). But besides this reference in Baruch's first (or, if we like, second) Book of Jeremiah (see 36:23), several Jeremiah sayings also circulated in oral tradition, as well as stories about him. It is indeed a fact that some of the longer, strongly deuteronomistic prose speeches of Jeremiah included in the book are actually parallels to (variants of) metrically formed sayings that were obviously part of Baruch's scroll.[5]

These speeches certainly represent a secondary tradition, in terms of both form and content, compared with the sayings in the Baruch scroll, which have kept their original metrical form. The speeches (partially) provide us Jeremiah's thoughts but not his own words. Jeremiah's sayings also continued to survive as oral tradition beside Baruch's scroll and, in a way, independent of it. In certain deuteronomistic circles, such Jeremiah sayings were used as starting points for, and leading words in, hortatory speeches within the circle; by this means they have undergone a transformation in a deuteronomistic spirit.

This tradition process represents an example (one of many) of the continued life and actualization of the prophetic sayings in the religious history of Israel. Whether they existed in oral form, written form, or both, the "deuteronomized" words of Jeremiah were assimilated into Baruch's book (either gradually or at a particular time) in either a more or less unaltered or altered shape. Oral and written tradition have flowed side by side and finally also influenced each other. In this case it is the written form, Baruch's recordings, which has best preserved the original; it is important to stress this in order to modify the views of Nyberg and Engnell on the fixity of verbal tradition. In this definite case, the parallel oral tradition is a further development and a transformation of the original Jeremiah sayings.

The insertion of these speeches in the Baruch scroll (already more or less altered) must have been a piece of literary work. It is evident that the speech in Jer 44:1-14, for example, has been inserted into the Baruch tale (Jer 43:8-13; 44:15b-30). And Jer 44:15a is a redactional connecting verse.

The Book of Jeremiah, therefore, presents us with a double task. First, we must discover, if possible, what the Baruch scroll was and what the "many similar words" were that "were added" to it; this is the task of literary criticism. Second, we must try to discover what constituted the original Jeremian nucleus in the deuteronomistic prose tales. This is a task of tradition history, where we have to deal with (among other things) the religious interests and forces at work in the transformation of the original Jeremiah tradition.

On the whole, the tradition of the Old Testament was not only written down but became written in principle and became "sacred scripture." Subsequently it has been transmitted in copies, sharing the conditions and limitations of all copies. What is important in this connection, however, is that the recording of the tradition did not take place all at once, as a recording of a tradition that had taken on fixed form, but gradually and sometimes as part of the creation and life of the process of transmission itself. Oral and written transmission interacted constantly. That fact alone makes the use of the methods and views of literary criticism justified and necessary, while still granting its limitations. Literature must be treated with the means and methods of literary analysis. We shall examine several instances of this interaction between oral and written "literary activity" in what follows.

The Traditio-Historical Method

So far we have provided a sketch of the rise of the traditio-historical approach from Gunkel and Gressmann to the present. It will appear from this that the method itself has full and far-reaching justification. If we want to understand the origin and development of the Old Testament we must reckon to a great extent with the oral tradition. Large parts of the Old Testament are "preliterary" literature. Even in the transmission of the written parts the transmission and further evolution by word of mouth may have played an important part. It is important, then, to realize how far this approach will assist us.

The term "history of tradition" necessarily implies not only that the idea of a transmission through copies is replaced by the idea of transmission through inculcation and further learning, or that one stops reckoning with literary personalities as sources but rather is content to believe that the material has reached the final author (for example, of the Pentateuch) as oral tradition. That may be well and good, but it neither extends our knowledge of the real character of the material nor provides any greater certainty regarding the originality or reliability of the tradition. The problem of the material's value as source still remains a problem demanding a solution. One might maintain, with Kapelrud, that the Chronicler wrote down the narrative of Ezra from oral tradition in "Chronicler circles."[6] Or one could follow me in an earlier study in believing that the Chronicler has taken up a written narrative deriving from "an eyewitness in an extended sense," one who has perhaps witnessed the events without having taken an active part in them or seen them from within.[7] It makes no difference which approach ones takes with regard to what primarily interests us: the literary character of the narrative and its value as an historical source. The fact is that in both views a displacement has taken place in relation to the real events; this is necessarily the result of those events having been seen, selected, and formed according to definite religious ideas and interests, and transmitted for a particular purpose. Indeed all tradition has a purpose, a tendency influencing it. To find what interests and what purpose the tradition is expressing in a particular case is a task that is exactly the same no matter how we consider the question of authorship.

Of course traditio-historical research attempts to investigate the *history* of tradition. That is, one attempts to trace the origin and development of the separate traditions and complexes of traditions down to the form they obtained when included in literary histories, and in that way both an understanding of the nature of the separate materials and a valuation of them as historical sources.

The first task, then, is really that of the analysis of forms and genres (German: *Form-* and *Gattungsforschung*; *Form-* and *Gattungsgeschichte*). On the basis of stylistic form-elements, characteristic content, and the interest it expresses, one may define the detached original tradition-units, for example: the local tale, the detached cult etiology, the detached Moses tradition. Then one must recognize them separately for what they are: a cult etiology, a local etiology, a heroic tale, a historical tale, a mythical motif, a legend, etc. In other words, one must determine the literary character and social function of each tradition—in brief, its classification or genre (*Gattung*, in Gunkel's sense of the term). In this sense, it is Gunkel who is the founder of the traditio-historical method. This name is indeed more apt for Gunkel's method than the one he gave it himself: the form-historical or form-critical method. One should note, however, that he exaggerated the importance of formal definitions (particularly in the study of the Psalms). And, regarding the cultic setting of the Psalms, he neglected (to some degree) the very essential contribution made by ideas and concepts to the determination of the cultic setting of the Psalms.[8]

The tasks of the history of tradition, however, are not exhausted. The traditio-historical understanding of the Pentateuch, for example, has not been reached when the various complexes and kinds of tradition have been disentangled and the connections pointed out between the following:

- the Primeval History and ancient Near Eastern myths and cosmogonies;
- the peaceful relations with the neighboring peoples reflected in the patriarchal narratives in contrast to the Exodus and the heroic tales;
- the character of the heroic tales as recollections from a period of national struggles and their inherent difference from the Genesis traditions;
- the possible connection of the Exodus stories with the Passover cult.

Not only are all these complexes and details to be connected with their respective settings in life: the cult, tribal life, warrior life, the royal court, the scribal school, and so on. But we must also ascertain whether they exist in their original form, whether we may identify indications allowing conclusions concerning a more ancient or an original form, whether and in what manner the tradition has changed (developed) in the course of time, and what basic narrative motifs comprise the tradition in question.

To mention a concrete example, we must find out by means of a traditio-historical approach and motif analysis whether the story of Joshua's victory over the southern Canaanite kings at Gibeon is a real heroic tale (Josh 9:1-27). In other words, does it have a historical core focused on a historical figure? Or is it a tale that has been formed from scattered traditional materials, chiefly local tales, and has only secondarily been attached to Joshua and the period of conquest?[9] We are concerned with *motif-historical* research (motif criticism); this too belongs to the "history of tradition."

Once more it must be emphasized that in this fuller sense of the term it is Gunkel and Gressmann who have been the pioneers of the history of tradition. They are tradition historians fully as much as many recent advocates of oral tradition at the expense of the literary activity, even if the pioneers should have been mistaken in many of their individual conclusions. In reality, what Gunkel and Gressmann call the "preliterary stage of the material" plays a much more important part in their works than the subdivision of the text into written sources. For them, the latter is never more than a (supposed, perhaps also exaggerated and overestimated) means of reaching a more important aim: to understand the material itself, the "tradition" in its original and continued life.[10]

Certainly Gunkel and Gressmann's traditio-historical approach is not opposed or antagonistic to literary source criticism in principle. The same is true about the strong traditio-historical element in my own treatment of Joshua and Samuel in *Det Gamla Testamente* (The Old Testament), both in the introduction and the notes.[11] Conceptualizing the traditio-historical method as an exclusive alternative to literary criticism is, in reality, very far from being a consistently traditio-historical method.[12] It is a narrowing and deprecation of the method that can only lead to leaving much of the real research undone.

Oral Tradition and Its Conditions

As tradition criticism becomes established as the leading methodology, it will also become necessary to understand the *"laws" governing oral tradition* and the consequences this has for evaluating the final text of scripture. First, it is necessary to say something about the implication of Nyberg's recognition that the transmission even of the written books took place to a great extent by word of mouth. Nyberg bases this, as we remember, on the conditions of transmission (what Birkeland calls *Traditionswesen*) in the Islamic world, with the learned men's literal, oral transmission of even voluminous works that also exist in a written form, primarily the Qur'an and Qur'anic interpretation. Here we can also point to the attitude of the Jewish learned men to the Law: it should be known by heart, and the same also originally applies to the Mishnah and Talmud. But the implication of this fact for the understanding of the earlier stages of the biblical tradition must not be exaggerated. The condition and presupposition for all this literal learning by heart and transmission is, in the case of the Arabs, the existence of a holy scripture that precisely from the first moment was valued as "scripture." Mohammed regarded one of the great results of his mission that the Arabs had become a "people of the Book." Every word and every letter of this scripture was considered inspired and immovable. Only such a religious and dogmatic fundamentalism gives a real motive and an approximate guarantee for a tradition that, above all, endeavors to be literal and without loss of the "smallest iota."[13]

At an earlier stage or in circumstances where such a pure fundamentalist view is still lacking, one cannot expect the ideal of transmission to be understood in the same way. This is true particularly in a more popular tradition like that represented by itinerant narrators, such as the Arabic *rawis*, or the storytellers from India so often encountered in the pages of Rudyard Kipling's stories, or perhaps also the Israelite "men of God on the road."[14] The ancient historical traditions of Israel concerning their ancestors, Moses, the conquest of Canaan, the heroes during the period of the judges, the first kings, and so on, were of course regarded as true and reliable but by no means as "inspired," let alone literally inspired.

When only the facts themselves were "correctly" related, the manner of telling, the details with which the narrative was embellished, and other issues were, to some extent, obviously left to the artistic ability of the narrator. But the selection and form of the traditions were also influenced by the unconscious (but strict) demands made by the popularity of the story and the consideration of what the listeners care to hear or not. They had no norms prescribing how and in what words the story was to be told and transmitted. The many variations of the same stories (for example, those in Genesis)[15] show, on the contrary, that each narrator felt a certain liberty to narrate in such a way that: (a) the "truth" of the story was stressed as much as possible and as his poetic gifts and imagination made him see the matter, (b) as it accorded with his religious and moral opinions of the ideal characters, and (c) so that he could arouse and keep the interest of his audience to the best of his ability. No fundamentalist dogma prohibited him from adding an explanation where he deemed one necessary,[16] a further description, a retarding point he believed might increase the attention, or a repetition of a scene that suited the taste of the audience. Nor was there a prohibition against leaving out, abbreviating, or (unconsciously) altering things he believed had no interest or which he himself no longer understood. In such circumstances, oral transmission becomes no mechanical matter but a *living process* during which the tradition is created or, at any rate, constantly taking new forms and making new or additional combinations.

The stage of fundamentalist "authority of the letter" and "unchangeability of the letter" (which the Qur'an had from the beginning, and which was consequently possessed also by its authoritative interpretation) was only gradually reached by the Israelite-Judean tradition. And this occurred at different periods in the case of different kinds of tradition. In prophetic circles, they attempted to transmit literally the *separate* prophetic sayings (certainly to begin with). This is shown both by the metrical form of the sayings and the frequent use of the first-person singular forms, for example in the vision narratives. In certain connections, however, it was not considered in any way objectionable to transmit the prophetic words in an abbreviated, contracted form, provided that this was of importance to the course of the story (for example, when the prophetic saying was transmitted as a detached part of a more or less legendary tale about the prophet). This is seen from both the Elijah and Elisha stories and from several of Baruch's stories about Jeremiah's life.[17]

This partial fixity of the tradition does not exclude the development of various collections and tradition-complexes of such sayings. Neither does it exclude an older prophetic saying becoming the starting point for a new one that becomes attached to the old one; and in that way, it would give the older saying a new form and sense. We will deal with this below.

Fixity of wording (at least to a certain degree) was also characteristic at an early stage of the sacral, legal tradition of the priest, even if this does not in any way exclude many and varying collections of such legal judgments and rules. That is seen, for instance, from the many different decalogues (series of ten) and dodecalogues (series of twelve) arising in the course of time,[18] or from the fact that several commandments that have belonged to the firmly fixed *mišpat*-collection in Exod 20:22—23:19 are also found in new combinations in Deuteronomy (D). Of the larger collections of traditions, the collections of laws were apparently the first to obtain a genuinely canonical authority, and presumably first of all D. But it obtained this authority as a written code.

According to Nyberg, the traditions were originally written down as a support to memory, and this occurs in conditions threatening the traditions with wavering or oblivion; Engnell stresses the same thing.[19] That actually means two things. First, the contents of the tradition had obtained a normative authority that made it socially necessary to preserve it. This pressure was initially felt regarding the legal tradition. Second, however, it would also seem to mean that the authority and fixity of the letter has only made itself felt from that point. It is therefore with complete justification that Nyberg has emphasized the primary importance of his approach for *textual criticism*. The text, he believes, has perhaps never been different from the form it has, on the whole, in the Masoretic text. As a result of this, possible errors in or changes to the original that may be proved date largely from the oral stage of transmission. This has only relative validity, as proved by the Masoretic "scribal emendations" (*tiqqunê sopherîm*).[20]

That even a strong oral transmission and the conscious ideal of a word-for-word transmission cannot guarantee an unchanged transmission of particular materials is proved by the Old Testament texts that we have in double form, for example: Psalm 18 and 2 Samuel 22; or Psalms 14 and 53. In Psalm 18 there are few lines or even half-lines that do not have one or more textual variants compared with 2 Samuel 22. It may be admitted that this does not enable us to reconstruct the "original text" of the psalm.[21] But this is not the main point. The primary issue is that neither of the two passages gives us the "original text"; and the existence of the two recensions proves that even an oral transmission (if that is what we have in this case) is subjected to numerous alterations in the details. The very state of the tradition presents us with a problem: Which of the two variants is the superior in each case?

Even if we cannot reach *the* original form in each instance, there are many cases where we may choose between the variants and judge which of them is superior on the basis of the laws of Hebrew poetry, form criticism, parallelism, and even meter.[22] We are obliged to think—or at least have the right to think—that the superior form in such a case is the poet's own. The problem itself exists, and the attempt to solve it exists, even if we may not be able to reach a completely satisfactory solution. In such cases it is by no means certain that the more difficult reading (*lectio difficilior*) should always be the better one; even this principle of textual criticism can be pressed too far.[23] If we have to deal with written texts, a variant due to a mere error of the scribe will very often be the more difficult reading. But in many cases it will be the wrong one, even if it should be possible for exegesis to wring some sort of meaning out of it.

But let us return to the central questions: How did the oral tradition arise and develop and become larger tradition-complexes? How did it obtain its actual form, and what is the literary nature, the genre of the separate traditions (tales, poems, etc.)? What is its historical value? These are the questions for the history of traditions. But Nyberg's contention that the large books have been handed down by oral, word-for-word transmission, is of no importance. Nyberg's approach, valuable in itself, cannot tell us anything of importance about the *real history* of the tradition. But that is precisely what we want to know something about. A traditio-historical approach that cannot tell us anything about these things is not really traditio-historical research and not really a history of tradition. A traditio-historical approach or method must either be an inquiry into the nature, origin, growth, and history of the tradition or nothing at all.

In this way, then, we are again faced with a traditio-*historical* task. There is no point for researchers to be content with "tradition says"—meaning tradition in its present form.[24] We are attempting to understand "tradition" itself—in this case, the formation of tradition. This means its origin, growth, and life throughout the centuries, as well as its final results, when it found its definite form in the written record and in the Masoretic text.

No oral tradition, no matter how firm, ensures an unchanged transmission of the subject matter until that point where the absolute authority and the fundamentalist dogma have appeared, even if the conscious ideal was the "correct" transmission of everything the transmitter has heard and learned. For the opinion of what is "correct" has changed with time. It depends, as I suggested above, on the nature of the material, the milieu in which it is transmitted, and the nature of the interest attached to the act of transmission. I cannot discuss this aspect in detail, but regarding the involuntary and law-directed changes to which an oral tradition is subject, I would refer to the investigation made by Knut Liestøl of a particular Norwegian family tradition.[25] In that case, we are fortunate enough to be able to check the tradition represented by the family tradition in question by means of contemporary legal documents that are independent of the tradition itself. The tradition in this case is not, as a matter of fact, attached to the documents, but to incidents in the family's history that have also partly led to the drawing-up of the documents. Liestøl's general conclusions, based on this family's tradition and on analogous materials, are these. An oral tradition may preserve the memory *that* something happened for some 300 years. But all further particulars—the various "hows," "whys," and words spoken—would become "tales," epic fiction, before that time. After some 300 years there is no longer any guarantee worth mentioning concerning what actually happened.

The ancient Near Eastern and Old Testament oral traditions are dependent upon the same psychological and social laws as all other traditions. In this connection it should be noted that the joining together of the originally independent units of tradition (myths, pseudo-historical tales, legends, historical tales, anecdotes, prophetic sayings, etc.) means a conscious and unconscious work of arrangement, transformation, harmonization, etc. These put their marks on the subject matter, which makes it possible to discover something about the growth and changing fate of the original tradition. The very existence of traditio-historical research rests on this assumption.

The joining together of the separate large tradition complexes (cycles of tales, etc.) means a new composition problem for the transmitters, and must often lead to (for example) one complex being telescoped into another, to a new division into smaller units once again, to be joined together where the transmitter thinks the separate units are most suitable. Furthermore, it must lead to having to retouch and harmonize, adding connecting remarks and interludes, creating a connection between the different topographical statements (for example, letting the hero wander from one place to another and find a plausible basis for these journeys), and interspersing explanatory remarks ("glosses"), etc.

If the transmitter then has to deal with two or more variants of the same story, then there are two main possibilities for this work of composition: He may take them to be two different, though similar, events and quite simply place them side by side. Alternatively, he may introduce them into the tenor of his composition at a shorter or longer interval, which different locales in the two variants may provide him. Compare, for example, the two stories about Saul and David in the cave in 1 Samuel 24 and 26.[26] He may also recognize the two stories as treating the same incident, combining them and including as many of the concrete details from both of them as possible. That means that he has to subdivide them both into smaller units (at least in his mind). And it makes no difference in principle whether these units consist of a single sentence or a long episode. In this connection it must be expressly emphasized that this work takes place and must take place in an oral process of transmission as well as in a written recording of the tradition. The transmitter's conscious work with the material in the oral tradition is also just as necessary a factor as the unconscious work of the psychological milieu that the process of transmission constitutes in itself. Tradition means a constant interaction between these two forces.

Literary/source criticism has been severely blamed in recent years for working with the hypothesis of "interpolations" in the text. It is very probable (no, certain) that it has made too frequent use of this hypothesis.[27] It is also certain, however, that the urging of an oral transmission provides no guarantee against the occurrence of secondary interpolations. On the contrary, we have already mentioned above the explanatory and connecting glosses that are an inevitable consequence of this process, when traditions are joined together in oral tradition. And in a given case, it is very easy to imagine that one of the learned transmitters, who learned a new variant from another "learned man," fit that new material into his "tradition" and later recited it in this new form to his disciples. This might be: (a) a previously unknown saying; (b) an apparently factually correct supplement of a conversation, speech, etc.; or (c) an interpretation and emphasis that seemed to him to be in the nature of the matter, or necessary or desirable in the context. Such a process is even psychologically more easily conceivable than a scribe interpolating a passage into his text.

On the other hand, even the best memory is not proof against forgetfulness. A Chinese proverb states: the weakest ink is stronger than the strongest memory. There is something in that, particularly when that memory has to pass through several persons. Especially in a poetic-lyrical tradition, which is not always supported by a strict logical or epic connection, it is inevitable that a verse, a half-verse, a stanza—or several—may fall out. To take an obvious example, it may be sufficient to recall the fragmentary condition in which the *Draumkvaede*, the grand visionary poem of Norwegian medieval times, had been preserved when it was found by the first collectors of folksongs in the modern era.[28]

When transmission with the psychological and social necessities occurs under such conditions and in the manner outlined here, it is also inevitable that the work of the composer and transmitter must leave marks that can be traced and which traditio-historians must watch closely if they are to elucidate the history of the tradition in question. Oral tradition may also offer problems demanding a kind of "source analysis." To undertake the necessary subdivision of the oral sources that the composer-transmitter has employed is the first step that the traditio-historian must take before attempting to ascertain the original form, nature, setting in life, and possible growth and change of the motif itself. Or more precisely, both of these approaches must cooperate. An explanatory remark or connecting note by the composer is also a gloss and an editorial note, whether the collector (composer, author) has worked orally or in writing.

Nyberg also arrives at the conclusion that in principle the written word has also played an important part in the origin and transmission of the Old Testament literature.[29] I agree with him that earlier discussion of this literature has assumed the material to be too literary and to a great extent has reckoned with written works, even in the ancient Israelite period.[30] It appears as if recording in ancient times was mainly used for certain kinds of literature, such as laws and wisdom. How rare it originally was among the prophets is shown clearly enough by the example of Isaiah and Jeremiah.[31]

What has been stated above is at any rate more than sufficient to show that a traditio-historical consideration of the Old Testament is obliged to reckon with both written and oral tradition, both with the work of the transmitting process and of authors consciously working on the collection, arrangement, and shaping of the tradition.

Tradition Criticism and Literary Criticism

The logical consequence of all that has been said above then is that we are not dealing with an exclusive alternative: *either* oral *or* written. In reality we are dealing with a *both/and*. Oral tradition and written tradition already existed side by side and influenced each other at an early stage.

Finally, however, the written word became predominant. It is a fact that in Judaism the tradition at a certain point, which we do not know, became principally written. "The Law and the Prophets" became scripture. And from that time we also have to take into account many types of scribal and reading errors. We must particularly reckon with omissions owing to *homoioteleuton* (words or phrases dropping out because the scribe's eye jumps to a word with a similar ending); the Books of Samuel offer many indisputable examples of this phenomenon.[32] I would also point out in this connection that no emphasis, be it ever so strong, of the importance of the oral tradition can do away with the necessity of cautious conjectures in textual criticism. In spite of his severe attacks on textual conjectures, Nyberg is also eventually forced to make use of them in some cases.[33]

In textual criticism, however—and consequently in exegesis in general—we are also obliged to reckon with lacunae (missing pieces) in the text to a greater extent than has previously been acknowledged. An apparent textual corruption, a meaningless line, *may* be due to some words having fallen out. This need not be due to carelessness on the part of the scribes or to a lacuna in the memory of the transmitter if one emphasizes the oral tradition, but may quite simply be a consequence of the nature of the writing material. A folded papyrus and ink are not very durable materials in the climate of Palestine. There *must* have arisen many unclear and illegible places in the manuscripts. And the manuscripts on which the Old Testament text is based have not always been good ones. That is proved, for example, by the many instances of *homoioteleuton* in the Books of Samuel. To point out the existence of a lacuna may in many cases be the duty of the exegete.[34] How far one goes then in filling in according to the context and parallelism is a matter of subjective judgment.

This being so, the method of Old Testament research can neither be a purely literary criticism nor have an exclusive emphasis on oral tradition. It must be a working together of literary criticism and traditio-historical analysis and research.

SUMMARY

What is needed in Old Testament research now is continued work with a truly historical approach to the many traditions in the Old Testament *as traditions*. This is in grateful acknowledgment of Nyberg's contribution to the investigations by earlier scholars regarding the history of the tradition and to the understanding of the importance of oral transmission of larger and partly written compositions. It is important to understand the nature of the separate traditions, their origin, growth, development, changes, as well as their collection into larger complexes and how those were joined together into books. Emphasizing the further oral transmission—even of these larger units, and even after they had been recorded—is only one aspect of this historical investigation. Little if anything is gained by using the slogan "traditio-historical approach" as an antithesis to literary criticism and literary critical methods. It is the history of the traditions themselves that is important to grasp.

As a result of the nineteenth century's inquiry into the history of all kinds of popular or more learned traditions, and as a condition for what is to be said in chapters 3–9, I want to state the following theses.

1. In all tradition it is the individual narrative, anecdote, poem, prophetic saying, etc., that is the original unit of tradition and the starting-point for the formation of the tradition. That does not exclude the notion that certain kinds of traditional units may have had a composite character from the beginning. A relatively complex cult ritual, for instance, may very well have been transmitted orally for a long time.

2. All tradition was part of life. Tradition assumes its form, develops, enters into new connections, dissolves, solidifies, etc., according to definite psychological, social, and artistic laws, which are connected with the field of life and the interest to which the tradition in question is attached. The fixed unchangability is, as a rule, the last stage in the life of a tradition.

3. The whole of this complex history leaves certain formal and factual marks on the tradition material, which makes it possible (to a certain extent, at any rate) to analyze and follow the origin, growth, and life of the separate tradition or tradition collection through the changing ages. To grasp, understand, explain, and set forth this history is the real traditio-historical approach.

4. Old Testament and ancient Near Eastern traditions are in no respect exempt from these laws of tradition. One factor among many others in this history of the tradition is the part possibly played by the recording or the influence from written sources and from already recorded tradition. It is undisputed that the form, to a large extent, determines the folktales still told in Norway that they received in their first recording by Asbjørnsen and Moe.[35]

Part II

Tradition History and the Study of the Prophets

3

The Original Units of Tradition

Introduction

The form criticism and tradition criticism of Gunkel and his school have been very important for the study of the prophetic books. Evidence of this is seen, for example, in Gressmann's analysis of the original units of the "book" of Deutero-Isaiah,[1] or *Die Schriften des Alten Testaments* (The Writings of the Old Testament) by Gunkel, Gressmann, and others,[2] when compared with the older commentaries on the prophets.

It is also clear that the interpretation of the traditio-historical method represented by Ivan Engnell has certain important consequences for research on the prophets. Engnell expressly states that the traditio-historical approach implies that one must largely give up—to what extent is still an unsettled question—analyzing and following the history of the tradition. At any rate, this is the consequence when the justification of the attempt to reach the exact words (*ipsissima verba*) of the prophets is rejected at the outset. Engnell also characterizes the attempt to discover and understand strata in a tradition as "wishful thinking" on the part of presumably old-fashioned exegetes. Engnell's idea of traditio-historical method—at least regarding the prophetic literature—consists then of remaining satisfied with the last form of tradition, thus accepting the latter as it is and dropping "history."[3] We shall examine below whether this attitude toward the prophetic literature is justified.

Divisions by Subject and Form

It is well known that the chapters in the MT (including the prophetic books) do not always correspond to the real divisions and pauses. Sometimes a distinctly new subject, partly from another period, starts in the middle of a chapter.

A clear instance is Jeremiah 21–23. Jeremiah 21 starts with an account of a specific historical situation with its own heading: "The word which came to Jeremiah from Yahweh when . . . ." Verse 11 then has its own heading: "And to the house of the king of Judah say . . . ." This second heading begins a collection of brief prophecies about various Judean kings. They were doubtless originally quite independent of each other and spoken at different times. First come some general statements about the royal house ("the house of David"), or at any rate statements without any personal address (21:11b—22:10). In Jer 22:11-30, then, follow some personal ones: to Shallum ben Josiah, Jehoiakim, and Coniah. Then in 23:1-8 follows a prophecy about the kings in general ("the shepherds") and two concerning the future king. Jeremiah 23:9a begins something quite new, a collection of sayings about the prophets, this time under the heading "Concerning the prophets."[4] It is obvious that the natural and correct chapter division would have been at 21:1, 11; and 23:9. Chapter 23 in the MT begins in the middle of a large collection of sayings about the kings.

We are not always fortunate enough to have explicit headings in the text with such clear information as is the case here. There are, however, other occasions where the case is equally obvious. Isaiah 3:16 begins a group of sayings concerning the women of Zion and Judah and the collection extends through 4:1. The famous description of the collapse concludes this section: "And seven women shall take hold of one man in that day" (4:1). But in 4:2a completely new theme begins that has nothing to do with the previous section. In this section, we hear about the messiah and about the remnant and the reconstruction. The form, too, is different: 4:1 is clearly metrical with "thought rhymes" (*parallelismus membrorum*), while 4:2 begins a section of prose.

Isaiah 5:1-7 contains the well-known poetic parable of Israel-Judah as Yahweh's unsuccessful vineyard. In 5:8 a new unit begins that has nothing to do with the preceding verses either in form or content; it is a series of woes over the various sins of the people (5:8-24a). And again in 5:24b-30 we have a completely different unit: a fragment of the same saying whose main part is now found in 9:8-17 [MT 9:7-16].

Isaiah 9:8-17 is something quite new and independent compared to the verses preceding it. Isaiah 9:2-7 [MT 1-6] is a prophecy about the ideal savior-king ("a child is born") and is connected in terms of content (not form and not original) to 9:1 [MT 8:23]. Here it is about the descendant of David on the throne in Jerusalem. Isaiah 9:8-17 concerns Yahweh's numerous judgments upon the kingdom of Israel (Ephraim and Manasseh) and concludes by hinting at the definitive judgment upon the kingdom. The refrain in 9:12b, 17b, and 21b [MT 9:11b, 16b, 20b], which is also found in 5:25b, binds this saying together formally as a single unit. The natural and correct chapter division would have been between 9:7 and 8 [9:6, 7].

Jeremiah 10:1-16 contains a more generally reflective and didactic poem about Yahweh and the idols without any references to or having any characteristics pointing toward a definite situation. In 10:17 begin some sayings about the coming fall of Judah and the capture and exile of the people. That this should have anything to do with the warnings against worship of idols in 10:1-16 is not suggested by a single syllable, directly or indirectly. In the same way, Jer 17:19 begins an exhortation in prose to keep the sabbath. Neither in form nor content does it have the smallest connection with the poetic prophecies against evil that precede it and still less with the personal account between Jeremiah and those who deride him in 17:9-11, 12-18. In these cases, as well as in many others, different topics have been collected within the same chapter.

In other cases the chapters create a wrong separation of things that are intimately connected, not only with regard to subject matter in general, but formally and in terms of setting—"literarily" as the literary critics would say. Some of these cases have already been pointed out above in connection with the instances of incorrect combination of matters within a chapter. We see this, for example, in the chapter division in Isa 4:1, which separates 4:1 from its premises in 3:16-26; and the chapter division in Isa 9:2-7 [MT 9:1-6], which separates 9:2-7 from its (certainly "editorial") introductory formula in 8:23 [MT 9:1].[5] In the same way, the chapter division beginning in Jer 23:1 separates the sayings concerning the royal house of Judah.

A further example is Jer 4:1, where the chapter division separates Yahweh's reply in 4:1-2 from the people's prayer of repentance in 3:21-25. On the other hand, 4:3 starts something quite new, an exhortation to "break fallow ground"; neither the poetic picture of illustration nor the thought has anything to do with what precedes it. And Jer 4:3-4, furthermore, has its own introductory formula. That the general subject matter—warning and threatening against the people's sins—*may* be associated with the preceding passage is of no importance here. Jeremiah 4:3-4 has a connection of this general and indefinite sort with practically all of Jeremiah's sayings.

Furthermore, we may mention the chapter division at Jer 15:1, which separates Yahweh's refusal in 15:1-4 from Jeremiah's intercessory prayer in 14:19-22. The correct division would have been between 15:4 and 5.

Another example is the chapter division at Jer 20:1, which separates the narrative in 20:1-6 (Jeremiah in the stocks) from the pronouncement of the prophecy that caused this punishment in 19:14-15. The appropriate division would have been between 20:6 and 7. The narrative of Jeremiah in the stocks (19:14—20:6) has, in fact, a certain connection of subject matter and catchwords with 19:1-13, the broken earthen flask and the sacrificial burning of children in Tophet (see 19:14). With 20:7, however, a couple of Jeremiah's personal "lamentations" begin: the complaints and appeals to Yahweh regarding the sufferings caused by his prophetic vocation and work. Regarding their association, they have a sensible place after the narrative about the stocks; but he is not referring to the stocks in 20:7-18.

There can probably be no doubt that Hos 5:15 belongs to 6:1-6. Hosea 6:1-3 contains the penitential prayer of the people that states the contents of its "seeking Yahweh in its affliction" (5:15). While 5:12-14 is an unconditional threat of punishment, 5:15 begins a new subject.

A final example is Jeremiah 11–12. Jeremiah 11:18 begins one of the prophet's personal complaints; it has no connection to the words of judgment in the preceding passage, in either content or form. In 12:1-6 there is a poem of the same type as 11:18-23, a complaint on the internal and external problems of the prophetic vocation, with Yahweh's reply at the conclusion.

In terms of content and form, Jer 11:18—12:6 constitutes a connected group of personal complaints by Jeremiah about his enemies, a group that is clearly distinguished from the threats of punishment against the people in both the preceding and following passages. The placement of 12:7-13 after 1-6 is understandable since 12:7 is also a complaint. But vv. 7-13 is an artistic form of the punishment and threat speech. The one crying out is Yahweh, who laments over the country and the people and who ends by threatening complete ruin as punishment.

The Task of Tradition Criticism

In these circumstances, the one who exegetes the prophetic books has the important task of separating the individual units within the total complex of tradition, along with other tasks. Only when one has succeeded in this can one attempt to make a satisfactory reply to the question of why these originally independent units have been placed together in the tradition and what the transmitters may have meant by it—if they meant something beyond collecting the sayings they perceived to have a certain affinity to one another in groups.

The fact is that it is an assured result both of the historical-psychological and form-critical investigation of the prophetic sayings that the prophets did not act as orators with long speeches with a connected development of ideas according to modern rules of logic. This is confirmed by all the examples we have transmitted in the prophetic narratives. They were Yahweh's messengers who stepped forward with concise, spontaneous, topical, brief messages from Yahweh in a concrete situation.[6] From the form-critical point of view it may be said (though it means simplifying matters) that the prophetic saying is an "oracle" clothed in the form of the "messenger-message." Both of these categories of sayings are characterized by their brevity. We will deal below with the prophetic message in the prophetic narrative.

One need not read extensively in the prophetic books to see that here too we are frequently faced with brief messages of the same type. Long passages in the prophetic books consist of just such detached, inherently complete sayings that take no account of each other, either formally or with regard to their more concrete content. The connection that might exist between them is quite general. For example, they are all threats of punishment against Judah or Israel. This connection is seldom if ever suggested; and if it really is there, it is between the lines, so to speak, and must be supplied by the interpreter. It consists as a rule only in the sayings within the group (the sayings complex) dealing with the same general subject: Israel's inappropriate relationship to Yahweh and Yahweh's reaction to Israel. Such a connection, however, exists between all the prophetic sayings, no matter what time period, chapter, or book they are from.

Here, then, the exegete has the same task as that offered by the incorrect chapter divisions. Before it is possible to understand a text fully it is necessary to know what belongs together and what does not. What I have suggested above concerning the prophetic sayings (and to which we will take up again below) entitles us to formulate this exegetical task as discovering the original units within an existing tradition complex.

Should we have to demonstrate that this is a necessary task of research? Interpreting the present collections of prophetic sayings (and the understanding of them as juxtaposed traditions) is of course an important part of understanding the prophetic movement itself. But it is also important to the history of Israel's religion and the history of the Bible. We also seek the deeper understanding that an insight into the concrete situations of the detached saying and into the image of "the prophet in action" may give us. And should it prove possible through such an analysis to distinguish between original units and secondary juxtaposition and the new interpretation that the latter always entails, then it would be a welcome contribution to a more definite and more detailed knowledge of the situation. This would be a contribution to the "accurate observation" that is the primary aim of biblical interpretation. Besides obtaining a full understanding of an intellectual product (in this case the prophetic sayings), which is also poetic in form, we require a knowledge of the typical forms and artistic means that have given these sayings their form and that the prophet felt was the adequate form for their content. Knowledge of the artistic forms of the typical prophetic saying also contributes to a more complete understanding of the matter itself.[7]

4
The Form-Critical Investigation

Form and Content

How can one separate out original units of tradition? It is here that the form-critical investigation introduced by Gunkel (*Gattungsforschung*) enters the picture. It seeks to identify, describe, and explain the elements of style and form that are more or less constant in the typical, detached prophetic saying and that characterize it as a prophetic saying. This leads to understanding how the message is constructed in its typical form.

This is not, however, only a formal investigation; to that extent, the terms "form history" or "form criticism" are misleading. An inherent connection exists between form and content, and both are determined by the setting in life (*Sitz im Leben*) of the intellectual product in question and by the function it exercises in the life of the religious community concerned. On the basis of a series of more preliminary investigations and random inquiries, this research method believes it is possible to state that within the ancient Near Eastern civilizations (that is, within all the ancient states and branches of the international, Near Eastern culture) a strong conservatism prevailed with respect to the cultural forms.[1] Furthermore, life in the different regions was bound within a very firm style. To mention only a single instance, the "thought rhyme" (parallel poetic lines; *parallelismus membrorum*) is characteristic of practically all ancient Near Eastern poetry from every period.

The forms and style of life, and equally the forms and style characteristic of the various intellectual products, were exactly the ones that the period consider adequate for the area of life in question and for what should then be said and written. Just because the form was right and venerable for the content concerned, the coercion of the form was so generally recognized, so conservative, and so enduring. Every typical situation in life had its definite things that should be done and said, which belonged to it, and they should be performed and in exactly *that* definite form. An excellent example is offered by the burial lament and the song of lament (Hebrew *qinah*), in which certain definite formal and content characteristics recur among all ancient Near Eastern peoples, despite the numerous national, local, and time-determined variations.[2]

When "genre research" or "genre criticism" (as we might best render Gunkel's *Gattungsforschung*),[3] then, identifies the formal elements in the psalms of lament, the essential elements of content are also determined, as implied by the terms: the invocation, the appeal, the prayer, the motives for granting a response, the deity's promise (oracle), and the (anticipating) thanksgiving.[4] It is also true, however, that all these content elements had their own definite styles and forms; they might vary in many ways, but they always had a common feature determined by the situation, purpose, and content. This is customary, due to the situation and the nature of religious life.

In the case of the psalms of lament, the task of the interpreter is to describe and explain these forms along with their variations and thus establish the principles for understanding the content exhibited in each case. Is Psalm 139, for example, a meditative reflection on God's omniscience and omnipresence, or is it a specific prayer in a definite situation? That question can only be answered by understanding its elements of form and content and by placing these in a larger framework, comparing them with the place and function they typically have in the Psalms. What is the meaning of the obscure line in Ps 51:6 [MT 51:8], in which we also find a word whose lexical and semantic meaning is very much in dispute: *tuḥoṭ* [RSV: "inward being"]? In order to answer this, we must first see whether the line exhibits formal characteristics recognizable from the psalms of lament mentioned above.

In the case of the prophetic saying, the same holds true: the formal characteristics say something about the content. And because of that, the form-historical investigation and systematizing are needed, not as a compulsory scheme but as a means of understanding. When the usual introductory formula "Thus says Yahweh" has been formally identified as a "messenger formula," we have also recognized something essential about the provenance of the message, the prophet's view of himself (he is a messenger, a herald), his view of the message's authority, the derived authority he claims for himself, and the responsibility he feels regarding the one who entrusted him with the message. A term such as "oracle" (Heb. *maśśa'*) also indicates something about the original setting and connection of the prophetic word and about the character it always preserved.

Form-historical expressions such as promise, threat, admonition, and exhortation are also categories determined by content. In order to understand the relationship between the prophets and their people's sacred traditions (as well as the relationship between Israel's prophets and those of other Near Eastern countries), we need to know if emphasizing history in the threat of punishment—or as a persuading motive in the exhortation—is something typical of the prophets or only an individual element in a few of them.[5] This certainly provides a glimpse into the history of the prophetic saying and consequently into the history of the prophetic movement in relation to the genuinely "Yahwistic" element in Israel's religion. Scholars formerly were inclined to declare the personal sayings in the Book of Jeremiah (the monologues) as nongenuine interpolations *because* they recalled the Psalms so strongly.[6] Form-critical investigation has shown that it is fairly frequent in some of the prophets—in other sayings of Jeremiah, and particularly in Deutero-Isaiah—to employ the style of the Psalms. A certain purpose is apparent in how the saying is clothed in psalmic form.[7] There is no reason to deprive Jeremiah of a saying simply because it looks like "psalmic poetry."[8]

Consequently, the importance of form-historical and style-historical investigation should be clear. And if this investigation can reveal the normal construction of the various kinds of typical prophetic sayings, then something is known about what must belong to such a saying; how it often begins and ends; the relationship between its point, scope, and other elements; and whether it is possibly uniform in content and tone or not. We will then know something about how to recognize what belongs together and what does not.

Starting Points: Outside the Prophetic Books

Where then do we find a fixed starting point for such an investigation, material where there is no doubt about the delimitation of the single prophetic saying? We have such material in the prophetic narratives, where we are confronted with a concrete situation and hear the message that the prophet announced exactly then and there. We may look to the prophetic legends in Samuel, the narratives of Elijah and Elisha in Kings, the Isaiah legends in Kings and in Isaiah 36–39, and Baruch's narratives about Jeremiah in Jeremiah 26–45.[9] We may also consult the Balaam narratives in Numbers 22–24; even though these are imitative, they are basically genuine in form and style. We may also mention "David's last words" (2 Sam 23:1-7), even though this passage is not particularly typical and has been influenced by the *mašal*-style.[10] We must also include the oracles, however, that are sometimes quoted in the Psalms, where the delimitation is also undisputed: Pss 2:7b-9; 12:5; 27:14; 60:6-8; 75:3-4; 81:6-16; 85:10-13; 89:19-37; 91:14-16; 95:7b-11; 108:7-9 [= 60:6-8]; 110:1-3, 4b; 132:11b-12, 14-18.[11]

We meet here the separate, self-contained prophetic message, and it is generally very brief. The only exception within the prophetic narratives is 2 Kgs 19:21b-28 (= Isa 37:22b-29). An analysis of that narrative, however, seems to indicate that we have here a parallel to the more ancient and much briefer one in 2 Kgs 19:32b-34 (= Isa 37:33b-35). Otherwise, the four Balaam sayings are the longest: two of them consist of three stanzas, each of three sections; one has five stanzas and one has four, each with two sections, of which two are spent on the bombastic, self-serving introduction. Of the psalmic oracles, only Ps 81:6-16; 89:19-37; and 132:11b-12, 14-18 are correspondingly long. The very briefest type we have in sayings like 1 Sam 10:1b; 23:2b, 4b, 12b; 30:8b; 2 Sam 2:1 (two oracles of one word each); 5:19b, 23b-24; 1 Kgs 11:31; 17:1, 3-4, 9; 18:1b, 41; 20:13-14, 22, 28, 36a, 42; 21:19; 22:6b, 11b, 12b, 17; 2 Kgs 1:3-4, 16; 3:16-19a; 4:16a; 5:26-27a; and others. The usual introduction is the messenger formula "Thus said Yahweh," sometimes with an added "Say to X" or a corresponding formula of introduction.

Regarding the content, there are two types. The simplest one contains only the message itself, which may be either a prediction of what is to happen.

> "And I will send rain upon the earth." (1 Kgs 18:1b)

> "in the place where the dogs licked the blood of Naboth shall dogs lick your blood, even yours." (1 Kgs 21:19)

> "About this season, according to the time of life, you shall embrace a son." (2 Kgs 4:16)

It can also be an instruction (guidance for correct behavior in the concrete situation), a command, or a task:

> "Go up." (2 Sam 2:1)

> "You are a priest forever after the order of Melchizedek." (Ps 110:4b)

> "With this Yahweh has anointed you to be a captain over his inheritance." (1 Sam 10:1b)[12]

Or it may be a combination of both:

> "Go up, for I will doubtless deliver the Philistines into your hand." (2 Sam 5:19b)

> "Sit at my right hand, until I make your enemies your footstool."
> (Ps 110:1)

> "Go, strengthen yourself, and mark, and see what you do; for at the return of the year the king of Syria will come up against you."
> (1 Kgs 20:22).

The second type contains two elements: the prediction and its motivation. For example, "Thus said Yahweh, 'Because the Syrians have said Yahweh is a god of the hills, but he is not a god of the valleys, therefore I will deliver all this great multitude into your hand; and you shall know that I am Yahweh" (1 Kgs 20:28). The order of the two elements may vary.

An extension of the basic type may occur when both elements are developed further. The prediction may become a broad description of what is to happen or of the situation that is to come; and the motivation may be extended into a long treatment of the sins that have caused the predicted disaster ("punishing speech") or of the piety and virtue that the promise will reward. Each of the elements may be varied in many ways. The prophecy of disaster may be formed as a cry of woe or be transcribed as an anticipatory lament over the disaster. The promise may take the form of a beatitude. The motivation may be extended by reference to aggravating or mitigating circumstances, for example, Yahweh's benefactions or his previous punishments. But ultimately all forms and elements of the prophetic message may be derived from these two basic elements.

We see already from this material that it is the separate "message," determined by the situation, which is the typical prophetic saying. It has always been a rounded, complete statement, introduced, sometimes also concluded, by genre-determined formulas, even if variable within the basic type, and with fixed elements of content in a traditional style.

It might perhaps be objected that in these narratives the prophetic saying, which is only one element in the narrative, may be rendered in an abbreviated form. In the case of the very briefest sayings—which, according to the evidence of the sources, are also the most ancient, like those in the Book of Samuel—this is not true. For here the oracle is merely a transcription, in words determined by the situation, of the reply actually given as a symbolic "yes" or "no" through the casting of lots of the ephod-oracle, in reply to a question of this form: "Shall I go and smite these Philistines?" (1 Sam 23:2b); and "Will the men of Keilah deliver me and my men into the hand of Saul?" (1 Sam 23:12b).[13] In other cases, however, the narrator may have abbreviated; that is seen, among others, by a comparison between the Jeremiah sayings in Baruch's narratives that have parallels in a more explicit form among the transmitted sayings in the collection.[13]

These parallels, however, also show something else, which is also endorsed by the epic traditions and by parallel analogies from the ancient Arabic visionaries, namely, that the real form is poetic and metric.[14] We have several of these within the narratives: 1 Sam 15:22-23, the Balaam oracles in Numbers 23–24, and the oracles in the Psalms. The poetic form of course allows several individual variations, but the basic type is the same.

Applications to the Prophetic Books

It is not my intention here to treat the style and formal elements of the prophetic message in detail. I only want to show the formal basis in sources that such a comparative "form-historical" (form-critical) analysis has and to point out that it is not constructed or obtained by reasoning backwards.

We must apply and develop the results already reached on the basis of this material to the prophetic sayings collected in the prophetic books. It then becomes apparent that we also find there the same characteristics and typical features with regard to form and content. In these books, it is also the individual saying—determined by the situation, the message with or without motivation and further description—which is the original unit. In a majority of cases, the situation is stated and the delimitation of the saying is accordingly provided. In others, it is the typical introductory and concluding formulas that show where one ends and another begins.

The form may vary in many ways, but the basic type is the same. New elements were added, but they too may be understood on the basis of the original types, as "developments" determined partly by the religious interest and the special vocation in special situations that these prophets had, partly by their individual personalities. An example would be Jeremiah's partiality for clothing the message in the garb of the various types of lament psalms.[15]

I must stress as strongly as possible that this investigation of the sayings of the "writing prophets," and the delimitation of the individual units to which it has led, has not started with purely subjective conclusions, which have only afterwards been put to the test. The investigation has been based on the delimitations that we know objectively from the tradition itself in a variety of cases, namely, the traditional introductions and conclusions that generally frame the individual saying and identify it as a separate saying (in the Book of Amos, for example). This approach has been stressed emphatically by both Gunkel and Gressmann.[16] By following the clue of these formulas, one finds twenty-eight to thirty small, independent units in the Book of Amos, which neither presuppose nor demand one another; in fact, there are even more.[17]

The result we obtain is a confirmation of what we know from other traditions, namely, that the prophets were men of the spoken word, who appeared with brief sayings ("messages"), determined by the situation and the moment. Each message was a rounded and complete unit that had its setting in life in and through that definite occasion. The prophets did not write; their "books" are collections of originally independent, orally transmitted, detached sayings. Between the origin of the saying and its recording in the book, there is a long period of tradition, history of tradition, and development of tradition.[18]

It is important, then, to grasp the course and tendency of this history. We can see how tradition—consciously and unconsciously—has arranged the sayings in groups. Sayings have come to form tradition complexes because they share the same catchword, have similar content, have the same addressee, or are from the same period in the prophet's work. These tradition complexes have also been arranged according to different principles.[19]

This is not simply a hypothesis but a conclusion based on objective evidence in the sources. A number of sayings about the kings of Judah (and kings in general) have been collected in Jer 21:11—23:8. That we are dealing with originally independent units is apparent. They have been spoken at different times, over a period of many years, as is evident from the names of the kings mentioned. After the writing of Baruch's Book of Jeremiah,[20] they have been made into a separate tradition complex on the basis of the common theme: "Against the House of Judah." The same is true of the collection of sayings "Against the Prophets" in Jer 23:9-40.

These two collections, however, teach us something else as well. The complex of sayings in Jer 21:11—23:8 includes three sayings that are not addressed to the royal house but to Jerusalem (characterized as "Lebanon"[21]): namely, 21:13-14; 22:6-9, and 20-23. That Jerusalem is the addressee is plainly stated in 22:8-9. Here, however, by means of the connecting note in 22:6a, a kind of connection has been established to the preceding royal prophecy in 22:1-5: "Thus says Yahweh: 'Go down to the house of the king of Judah.'" This connecting note is inexact and accordingly secondary from the point of view of the history of tradition. It does not belong to the prophecy itself but to the collecting work; it creates a connection between two independent sayings that was not there from the beginning.

Jeremiah 22:18a is probably a similar secondary connecting note. The two sayings in Jer 22:13-17 and 18b-19 concerning Jehoiakim must be regarded as originally independent. "Yahweh's words concerning Jehoiakim" would hardly have come to Jeremiah only once. The same holds true regarding the collection "Against the Prophets" in Jer 23:9-40. This also consists of originally independent separate sayings as may be seen, for example, from the intermittent introductory and closing formulas: Jer 23:12b, 15b, 16a, 28b, 32b, and 33b. Here too, however, the collectors (or, in other words, the process of transmission) have sometimes suggested a kind of connection by means of a "therefore": Jer 23:15b, 30. The same is also true in a number of other places where the case is not so clear, as in the collections already discussed, because the limitation in the other cases must partly be undertaken on the basis of the criteria given us by stylistic analysis, whereas in Jer 23:9-40 it can be demonstrated on the basis of such outward facts as those mentioned here.[22] Sometimes, however, the LXX confirms that such a "for" or "therefore" is secondary; that the LXX itself would have omitted the word is very improbable.[23]

We may consequently conclude that the tendency in transmission is toward creating a kind of connection between the originally independent units within a tradition complex by adding such small words and stereotyped formulas. This tendency may in fact be exegetically and form-critically proven in so many cases that it is justified to say that it is a general "law," and that the apparent connections that exist, on closer investigation, prove to be secondary as a rule. This is also a piece of the history of tradition that we have no right to overlook. The tradition historian has the task of attempting to show how the collection process itself has occurred in each separate prophetic passage and how we are to explain the place of the separate pieces and complexes in relation to one another. I have attempted to perform such a piece of traditio-historical work in the introduction to the Book of Micah in *Det Gamle Testamente* as an example of the task and method. I have also explored the principles of collection in Deutero-Isaiah.[24]

When we consider the way in which the separate sayings have been arranged within a tradition complex and how they have been placed in relation to one another, it is not difficult to discover what principle has been followed in the formation of tradition. It is the principle inherent in the matter and in human psychology itself, namely, that the prophecies of disaster and the threats come first, followed by the promises. It is so obvious that no further proofs are needed. Merely by way of example we may point to the following tradition complexes: Isa 1:2-31; 6:1—9:6; 9:7—12:6; 28–32 (resp. 35?); Micah 1–5; 6–7; or the arrangement of the Books of Hosea and Amos in their entirety. It is completely justified to speak of a scheme according to which tradition has arranged the sayings. We may consider it obvious that not all thirty-nine separate sayings contained in the Book of Hosea or the thirty-two (or thirty-three) sayings in the Book of Amos were spoken at one time and that they are not a connected, original composition. It is even more obvious in a case such as the various Isaiah collections, which cover a period of more than thirty years; and the same is true of the sayings in the Book of Jeremiah. We will discuss the compositional scheme of Jeremiah below (see p. 60).

TRANSMISSION OF DETACHED UNITS AND TRADITION COMPLEXES

The form-critical method, like any other, has its limitations and cannot be the only approach to research of the prophetic materials. In evaluating it, however, one must be aware that it does not merely concentrate on form, but that it always looks on the form in relation to a definite content. This form is provided by the tradition and determined by the situation, which the ancients themselves deemed adequate. Theoretically one may believe that its danger is that it may become a "compulsory scheme" applied to the texts, "which are then cut down or rearranged as soon as they cannot be made to fit a given scheme."[25] It is said that this "particularly applies to [the use of the method on] the Psalms." But such a procedure is in no way characteristic of form-critical research. It is incorrect, therefore, to argue quite generally and without specific proof that it "has too often degenerated into such a violation of material." As far as I know, this has seldom been the case.

Hermann Gunkel's commentary on the Psalms, for example, has most consistently treated the Psalms with a form-critical approach.[26] One will not find many places where Gunkel has "cut down" or "rearranged" the text of the psalm to fit the usual scheme of the genre.[27] The danger in Gunkel's interpretation of the Psalms is actually a very different one, not necessarily connected with the form-critical method. He has not sufficiently recognized the connection between the final form of the Psalms and the cult. Accordingly, he has not always realized that the heterogeneous character of many psalms, form-critically speaking, really corresponds to the changing acts of the cultic ritual itself.

Another objection has been made to form-critical research of the prophetic materials that must be discussed since it touches the very essence of this chapter. We are warned against its being made "such an exclusive analysis that the synthesis, the total view, is lost sight of."[28] Stated this generally, the warning is, of course, justified. The question is only what it is specifically aimed at. Of course, the subject and range of view of a particular work of research may have been so narrowly chosen that the investigation is limited to pointing out and analyzing the form-critical elements found in the prophetic book in question without asking about the volume, nature, and purpose of the specific passage in which these elements play a part. None of the form-critical analyses that have appeared so far have been content with this.[29]

Already in Hugo Gressmann's work, the aim of research was to find the original units, which in some cases may well be larger compositions. At times, however, Gressmann also may have been wrong and on the basis of one-sided form-critical criteria may have separated "primary units" that belong together in a saying. To a somewhat greater extent, this is also true of Ludwig Köhler. The reason for this, however, is that the scholarly eye has not always been fixed steadily enough on the real purpose of the prophetic saying: to bring a specific message about God's purpose and plan, or the demands of God's will, or the right relation to God. In that way one sometimes perceives separate units that are only elements of a larger whole and that—regarded in isolation—lack the "prophetic point" of the prophetic saying.[30]

That the representatives of form-critical research have also paid attention to the larger units is seen from the fact that form critics have investigated "prophetic liturgies" and "compositions."[31] The various questions here will always leave room for discussion. But there seems to be no valid reason to complain about the lack of understanding the "synthesis."[32]

When it is demanded in general terms that "synthesis" should be considered (as Engnell does), it is of course correct in itself, but we must ask: which synthesis? If by synthesis one means something other than the more or less accidental accumulations of independent sayings that are one aspect of transmission of a prophet's words by "tradition," then the task is first to show when and where a real "synthesis" exists—an original connection between apparently independent types of genres (*Gattungen*). The secondary syntheses of tradition also, of course, have significance. They show something of how the transmitter has understood the prophetic sayings, and thus they contribute to the picture of the religious shape of Judaism. But with the recognition of this "synthesis," only a very small part of the research on prophetic tradition has been performed. It would, for instance, be of no small interest to learn how the prophets themselves have understood their sayings. It is not at all certain that the original and still recognizable meaning of the detached sayings was the same as the one it eventually received in a secondary "synthesis."

Stressing the general exegetical principle that the interpretation should be determined "according to the context" is obviously correct.[33] No exegete has denied it. But again we have to ask: which context? An unavoidable question is then encountered at once: How far does the context go in the specific case? For instance, in the "connection" to which Engnell refers in the quotation above, the "connection" that the 'Ebed-Yahweh passages are standing in (in Engnell's opinion) comprises the whole of Deutero-Isaiah.[34] The question is this: Is the existing connection between the separate passages (which on the strength of clear form-critical criteria stand out as independent units) relatively original or secondary? Here it is necessary to provide actual evidence that these different passages really refer to and need each other, and that they require the greater connection to provide a clear sense with an unmistakable point, a target that is aimed for with all the different means of logic and style.

Factual means of connection cannot be considered (for example, common catchwords within a tradition complex). Too often it is obvious that the connection established by catchwords is merely the relatively external means of association that the collecting tradition has employed in order to bind independent units together in a bundle.

Let us take another and clearer example, namely, Isaiah 2–5. These chapters form a tradition complex of their own, marked out by the heading in 2:1 and the new opening in 6:1. What is "context" here when one is to interpret, for example, Isa 5:8-24a? No one can really believe that 2:2-5 is definitive for the understanding of 5:8-24a. The context in this case actually comprises only the passage 5:8-24a, which appears as a real synthesis based on clear formal and content characteristics.

Or let us once more turn to the burning question of the interpretation of the 'Ebed-Yahweh poems. The *possibility* that the placement of the poems together with the surrounding passages is secondary (as in many other cases) does of course exist and must be admitted by any non-dogmatic research. This evidently does not mean that they should necessarily have been literarily interpolated in the context, but that the whole collection of the Deutero-Isaian units may be—and are!—traditio-historically secondary in relation to the original preaching. If we are now to let the "context" be the whole of Deutero-Isaiah (or a larger or smaller part of it), it cannot be doubted that "the Servant" was understood to be Israel; then, indeed, he is not parenthetically the messianic king (that is, not in the same psychical act of conception).[35] When now in the poems themselves, however, there are strong signs that "the Servant" is something other than Israel (for example, the suffering king, Messiah, or someone else), what then? How strongly and how far does the supposed context bind us? Would we not neglect one of the tasks of historical interpretation if we refuse to test without bias the *possibility* of the poems having to be (in the first instance) considered separately,[36] and that we may perhaps thereby reach a clearer understanding than by being bound by a context—where signs are strongly opposed and which *may* be secondary—and determine in advance that this context is binding? General statements are notoriously of little research value. It is the specific use and shading of the general statement, with due allowance for all that is characteristic of the specific case, that are of importance.

Criteria for Original Connections

The first task that confronts anyone doing research on the prophets is to disentangle the units, on the basis of the leading approach and the criteria given by the form-critical "genre-research" (*Gattungsforschung*). I will briefly indicate these criteria.

1. The starting-point, as already shown by Gressmann in his analysis of Deutero-Isaiah, remains the fixed and typical prophetic formulas of introduction and conclusion. In addition, there are other typical introductory formulas: a woe, a beatitude, a request to hear or listen, or an imitated hymnic form of introduction (see Isa 42:10; 52:9; 54:1).

2. Then the typical prophetic elements of content must be taken into consideration. When a passage has set forth both the message and the motivation, possibly with some of the extensions and variations that have been mentioned above—the punishing speech, the appeal, and so on—then one may normally expect that the prophet has said what he had to say on that occasion; the saying is then, both formally and as to content, rounded off and has reached its aim; the active force contained by the prophetic word has been set in motion. Then the saying may normally be considered as concluded, if there are no clear signs to show that it is not.

3. This implies that any prophetic saying must have a prophetic point at which it aims, and which is in accordance with the nature and character of the prophetic saying that always and from the beginning has belonged to it and makes it a prophetic saying. That is to say, it must say or hint at what Yahweh now intends to do or what he demands should be done. The prophetic element is always, in one respect or another, concerned with the future, with what is to come, or what ought to be, but is not yet. This is also an aspect of the demand for inner and outward completeness.

4. The typical prophetic saying is always specific. Before the eye of the prophetic imagination there is always a plastic picture, which in itself may equally well (or better) be painted or drawn than expressed in words. This "situation picture" or "intuition picture" or "imaginative apperception" is, as a rule, a unity; otherwise it would not have been concrete and plastic. The verbal art of the prophets aims precisely at making the listeners see in their imagination at least the outlines of the "imaginative picture" that is still clear before their own mental eye. But such a conjuring up of the picture of coming events in the imagination of the listeners would not be possible if the picture itself was confused, kaleidoscopically changing, oscillating. It is in the later traditionary and artificial apocalypses where more and more traditional features are accumulated, that allegories and intuitive pictures within the same "vision" succeed and crowd each other or are combined to chimerical conceptions and abstruse fabrications.

Why is it that several elements that are independent from a purely form-historical point of view, or several smaller units (stylistically complete) may be combined in a larger, actual connection, an imitated "liturgy," a "composition." Several demands in respect to form and content then must also be met. The most important are as follows:

1. A "prophetic liturgy" must have an recognizable pattern, according to which it has been formed. We must exercise caution in the use of foreign patterns as comparisons; we must at any rate be able to show traces of its having also been used in the Israelite cult.

2. The demand of a uniform "imaginative picture" also makes itself felt to some extent in the case of a larger composition. Its uniformity may be implied in the cultic situation of many scenes that served as a pattern. Such uniformity is for instance present in Isaiah 33, where the conceptualities of the enthronement festival were converted into prophecy.[37] The same is the case in Habakkuk's prophecy, even though it is due here in a higher degree to a subsequent arrangement and was not so definitely aimed at in the original sayings. It may also be imagined, however, that the prophet has independently employed a combination of originally independent elements of form and content as an expression of his thought, without relying on any cultic or other pattern. He may, for instance, have used two types of oracles because he desired to approach the subject from several angles.

An example of this phenomenon is evident in Amos 1:3—2:16. With regard to style and content, these oracles, both those against foreign peoples in 1:3—2:3 and the disaster prophecy and punishing speech against Judah in 2:4-5, are each complete units, which may well have existed separately. All the same, however, they have been formed by Amos with the purpose of their forming a unit, which again was the background for the oracle against Israel and was effective by the contrast: disaster for all these neighbors for whom you are desiring disaster, and accordingly, disaster also for Israel! We have such a combination of punishing speech and promise in Isa 48:1-11 and 55:6-13, contrary to the general rule: punishing speech and prophecy of disaster.[38]

Where such a combination is intentional, however, there the "intuition picture" must be uniform, as the pictures of the total composition must belong to the same sphere and succeed each other in a natural way. In Amos 1:3—2:16 the listeners see in imagination one hated neighbor after another emerge and hit by the curse. When the list has thus been exhausted, the thought of Israel itself naturally follows: this means a glorious future for us! Just then, Israel itself is hit by the same curse; the unifying thought and the uniform "intuition picture" is exact: the just punishment of Yahweh over all the enemies surrounding him, Israel included.

In the passages of Deutero-Isaiah already mentioned, the "intuition pictures" are also uniform. In Isa 48:1-11 it is the covenanters, the descendants of Jacob, with both good and bad sides, who stand there listening to Yahweh's judgment. True, they are the covenanters and worship and trust in Yahweh; but all the same they are stubborn and doubting. It is therefore uncertain what judgment such people may receive. Much evil had already befallen them. The effect of the promise of Yahweh's unchangeable mercy and the "new things" that are to happen is, therefore, that much stronger.

Isaiah 55:6-13 is of a similar type. In such compositions the unity of the imaginative picture must not be broken, for example, in the way that would have been the case if Isa 42:18—43:7 and 43:8-13 were to form a unit. In 42:18—43:7 Israel is described as already gathered in front of Yahweh, who will now convince them of his plan and profound meaning in what has happened in history. Isaiah 43:8-13 begins with a request to bring the people forth so that they may be present when foreigners are summoned to the trial before Yahweh.

In the same way, Isa 52:11-12 cannot continue 52:1-10. In 52:1-10 the exiles are described as already on their way home from Babylon. The intuitive picture is the caravan homeward bound in festive procession. The prophet imagines himself in Jerusalem seeing the procession arrive. In 52:11 the intuitive picture is the prophet in front of the prisoners in Babylon, requesting them to start for home.

3. From what has been said so far, a third requirement follows in determining an original composition. The postulated continuation of a form-historical unit must not only be *possible*, on the basis of such connections as may be established on the strength of such formal and notional associations as may always be found between the different sayings of one and the same prophet, and which have made the transmitters place them together in tradition complexes. The real connection must also be *necessary*. The first of two such sayings must—directly or indirectly—point to something unsaid, which must be said in order for it to be fully comprehensible. And the second passage must prove defective and unclear if it had not been preceded by the previous one and is seen in connection with it. Or it must correspond in ideas and expression with that which it is to complete and conclude. For instance, the "prophetic point" is lacking if both passages are not combined.

4. Passages that are intended to belong together, despite their apparent independence, must also have certain stylistic characteristics in common that show their interdependence. One example would be a formal symmetry in construction indicating that the passages have primarily been created with a view to each other. This is the case in Amos

> 1:3—2:16. The five genuine sayings have identical introductions, and only the names of the peoples are different. The construction of the paragraphs is the same, and the wording is the same as far as this is possible: (a) the threat; (b) the motivation (the specific transgression); and (c) the description of the punishment. The length is also the same in each of the prophecies of disaster against the neighboring peoples. In the "woes" of Isa 5:8-24a we meet a corresponding symmetry in the construction of the separate woes, carried through more or less consistently. Each of them might very well have existed separately, but the symmetry shows an intended composition.

These fundamental requirements have not been set up arbitrarily but are empirically deduced from the recognizable, original, prophetic sayings themselves. But if one does not heed them, then one never gets beyond the arbitrary limitations and connections that any exegete with a little diligence and acumen can establish between practically any independent sayings of such a relatively uniform character as the prophetic sayings.

On the basis of the criteria mentioned here it may be proved with a high degree of probability that the prophecies of Habakkuk have been arranged according to a cultic-liturgical scheme, for instance. And they are also probably meant as the connected parts in a cultic festival of humiliation and prayer.[39] It can also be clearly shown, however, that such compositions or original connections between long series of the sayings in Deutero-Isaiah (as Budde and Staerk, for example, believe themselves able to trace) do not exist.

Roughly speaking, we may say that research has reached a consensus regarding the prophetic books. Regarding the delimitation of the original units—the separate, complete, and once independently oral sayings (for example, in Amos, Isaiah, Hosea, Jeremiah)—the various recent commentaries do not differ much from one another in either their principles or practice. Deutero-Isaiah is the prophetic collection that still generates opposing views. The typical contrasts are Karl Budde's interpretations on the one hand,[40] and Hugo Gressmann's subdivision into units on the other, further developed by Ludwig Köhler and myself.[41] Budde reckons with six large passages with a train of thought that is mainly progressive. Stärk counts eight of them, but he admits that there is no original connection between them. The form critics count forty to fifty originally quite independent prophetic sayings. I count exactly fifty, inclusive of the Eded-Yahweh poems. The most recent Isaiah commentary I have seen is by Bentzen, and he is close to the view of Budde regarding larger units.[42] Bentzen, however, does not disagree in principle with the method of form criticism; the difference is more one of degree than of principle. To a greater degree than I, he believes in originally large collections. His method, however, is not quite clear; he has not supported the theory of large compositions that the tracing of a ritual pattern might have facilitated. Nor is it always clear where Bentzen draws the limit between original compositions and the collecting and complex-forming of tradition. Elsewhere I have provided a detailed discussion and testing of Bentzen's positions.[43] And I believe I have shown that Bentzen's view represents an unfounded and unjustified surrender of insights and results that form-history has reached with good reasons.[44]

Conclusion

We will have to be satisfied with the following result: the relatively brief—complete and circumscribed, independent, separate—saying (an oracle) is the original and genuine form of prophetic speech and message.[45] This is also largely the case with the historically known prophets, the "writing prophets" as they are often misleadingly called. These separate sayings were transmitted by oral tradition in the prophetic circles, partly unchanged, partly adapted to and revived in the new situations of later periods. They have a life in tradition and served a religious purpose within the circle of disciples; the tradition was not static.

In the course of the history of tradition, larger tradition complexes and collections developed from these separate sayings, which in their turn have been joined together into final collections of tradition. The latter may also have been handed on orally. Finally, however, they were written down; they became books. This fixity in writing may have started earlier with separate small complexes, and the oral tradition may have continued alongside the written form.

5

Tradition and Writing

Early Evidence of Written Traditions

When did recording of the prophetic tradition begin, and what was its importance in the history of tradition?[1] Isaiah provides the earliest information about a prophet writing something or having something written. In two cases he had a symbolic, enigmatic prediction written on a tablet to prove that he had predicted the coming event (Isa 8:1-8; 30:7-8).[2] The first recording consists of four Hebrew words ("Belonging to Maher-shalal-hash-baz"; Isa 8:1b); and the other consists of two ("Rahab still sits"; Isa 30:7b).

Yahweh also ordered Habakkuk to write the revelatory vision he had on a tablet: "Write the vision; make it plain upon tablets, so he may run who reads it" (Hab 2:2). This time the text comprises two stanzas of four lines.[3]

> Behold, he whose soul is not upright in him shall fail,
> but the righteous shall live by his faith.
> Moreover, wine is treacherous;
> the arrogant man shall not abide.
>
> His greed is as wide as Sheol;
> like death he has never enough.
> He gathers for himself all nations,
> and collects as his own all peoples. (Hab 2:4-5)

We hear that Jeremiah twice used an opportunity to have a letter sent to the exiles in Babylon to impress them with a revelation he had received (Jer 29:1-32; 51:59-64). The first written prophetic book we hear about—and certainly also the first to have existed—is the original form of the Book of Jeremiah. It came into being in the way that Jeremiah dictated to Baruch, the scribe:

> In the fourth year of Jehoiakim the son of Josiah, king of Judah, this word came to Jeremiah from Yahweh: "Take a scroll and write on it all the works that I have spoken to you against Israel and Judah and all the nations, from the day I spoke to you, from the days of Josiah until today." (Jer 36:1-2)

The recording then was to serve as a support to memory, as "the words" on a special occasion were to be recited to the cultic congregation. But Jeremiah himself, due to special circumstances, was prevented, and therefore had to leave it to Baruch. He could obviously not rely on Baruch's memory as he could on his own.[4]

Now we learn explicitly that later on "many similar words were added to them" (Jer 36:32). That undoubtedly means words of judgment and prophecies of disaster; note the characterization of "the words" in v. 2 as "all the evil which I intend to do to them" (v. 3). The final form of Jeremiah shows that in the course of time there have been added not only "similar words" but also narratives of incidents in the life of Jeremiah that had occasioned noteworthy sayings.[5] That these narratives originate from Baruch himself is extremely probable, not to say certain.[6] And here it is worth noting that one of the narratives by Baruch includes the notice about the many similar words added to the book later. Baruch owned the scroll, and it is therefore natural to conclude that it was also Baruch who started adding other words to it: first, Jeremiah's words spoken later than the dictation in the fourth year of Jehoiakim, but then also the narratives about his friend Jeremiah.

Baruch is the literal and spiritual heir to the preaching of Jeremiah: the one who took care of the spiritual remains of the prophet, the founder and transmitter of traditions about Jeremiah, and the author of the Book of Jeremiah. This is confirmed by the fact that the book closes with a word to Baruch himself (Jer 45:1-5). The saying is not placed where it now stands because it belongs there chronologically; the saying is dated and has been made in connection with the origin of the book/scroll in the fourth year of Jehoiakim (Jeremiah 36).[7] It now stands as a conclusion and period, as unmistakable as anyone might look for.[8] At the same time, it is also the indirect presentation of the author to the reader. In its present context, the phrase "all these words" in Jer 45:1 cannot be applied to the actual prophecies that were once dictated, but to everything that precedes: the prophecies and the narratives. No clearer statement than 45:1 could indicate the identity of the book's author. And it is equally plain that the subsequent complex in Jeremiah 46–51 (prophecies against foreigners) was originally a collection, a tradition complex of its own—units that are, on the whole, considerably later than Jeremiah. These later traditions have also been ascribed to Jeremiah and may possibly contain some

Jeremiah elements; but they were only joined to Jeremiah 1–45 at a later time.[9]

In the transmission of Jeremiah's sayings and the tradition about him, therefore, oral and written tradition went hand in hand from the beginning. This is an important recognition.

Parallel Oral and Written Traditions

The Book of Jeremiah, however, also furnishes evidence of how a further developed, "secondary" transmission of the prophets originated and continued beside the literary transmission, even if to some extent formally and thematically transformed. In its turn, it interacted with the book and was eventually worked into it. This is seen in the many long prose speeches with strongly deuteronomistic features of style and ideas.[10] These often have their own headings, sometimes dated, that are now found scattered throughout the Book of Jeremiah in between the poetic sayings and Baruch's narratives. These prose speeches are neither planned, literary, editorial adaptations of an existing book (as held by Duhm), nor a separate literary source, as I previously maintained.[11] Rather, they represent a circle of tradition of their own, within which certain of the sayings by Jeremiah have been transmitted and transformed according to the ideas and style that prevailed in the circle—the deuteronomistic ideas, style, and interests.[12] Indeed it is evident that the core, the "themes," of these speeches are words by Jeremiah also found partly in the literally transmitted metrical sayings, partly in Baruch's narratives, and partly in both places.[13] The abbreviated form and the deviations in content that these parallels in the speeches offer show that they cannot have been taken literarily from Baruch's book; neither is this very likely from a traditio-historical point of view. They represent an independent parallel transmission of the memories about Jeremiah's sayings.[14] The fact that most of them are parallels to sayings transmitted in Baruch's narratives also reveals something about the tradition circle. Baruch was a scribe and belonged to the learned. That the Deuteronomists were also associated with the learned circles of the scribes is obvious. Jeremiah already offers us a piece of evidence that the law—the *torah* tradition and the literary pursuit of it—belongs to the scribes: Jer 8:8.

This deuteronomistic Jeremiah tradition was incorporated at a particular time into Baruch's book. Whether this took place in the further oral transmission of the book or occurred as a literary process—so that the deuteronomistic Jeremiah tradition was recorded simultaneously with its being joined to Baruch's book—may remain an open question for the present. Either alternative is possible. In any case, however, the incorporation has obviously taken place as much as possible in connection with such Jeremiah sayings as were found in Baruch's book. And a parallel was formed with the deuteronomistic

Jeremiah speech in question or with one which the latter was in factual and formal conformity.

It is evident then that the dated prose speech in Jer 3:6-12a, 14-18 forms a factual parallel to the metrically formed sayings in 3:1-5, 12b-13, 19-20. The speech has been inserted into the saying in such a way as to break an original formal and factual connection. The speech about the offering of the innocents at Tophet has been coupled with the prophecy by the Potsherd Gate about the broken earthen jug because these two localities were close to one another (Jeremiah 19). The words "from Tophet, where Yahweh had sent him to prophesy" (19:14) is the connecting note that joins it to Baruch's narrative in 19:14—20:6 about Jeremiah in the stocks. The speech to King Zedekiah in 21:1-10 is naturally placed before the collection "Against the House of the King of Judah" in 21:11—23:8. The speech in Jeremiah 27 concerns the same issues as Jeremiah 28, and they have consequently been juxtaposed. The speech on the occasion of Jeremiah's purchase of a field has been intertwined with Baruch's narrative about the same issue. In the same way, the two speeches in Jeremiah 34 (vv. 1-7, 8-22) include notes from Baruch's narrative, and the same is true in Jeremiah 35. It is clear that the speech to the exiles in Egypt (Jer 44:1-14) breaks the connection of Baruch's narrative, where 44:15-30 is the direct literary or epic continuation of 43:1-7.[15] It is consequently very probable that the speech in Jeremiah 7 or the speech of the covenant in 11:1-14 and others are found in their present positions because a corresponding word by Jeremiah was found in the same place in Baruch's book and has now perhaps been incorporated into the relevant speech.[16]

Interaction between Oral and Written Transmission

How, then, has this incorporation of the speeches into Baruch's book taken place? I suggested two possibilities above. We observe how in Jeremiah 3 and 43–44 connected parts have become separated, and this has resulted in brief retouching notices.[17] It appears, at any rate, to be certain that they have been inserted into the existing Book of Jeremiah by Baruch. It is less certain whether the speech complex was available to the editor in written form or whether he inserted it from memory. The manner in which both the speech and the Baruch text in Jeremiah 3 have been subdivided and combined with each other would seem to suggest they both existed in writing.

The same is also suggested by the introductory dating note in Jer 32:2-5. It hardly belongs to the speech, which has its usual heading in v. 1 and is furthermore erroneous with regard to the date. According to 32:7-15 the action cannot have taken place while Jeremiah was shut up in the palace court of the guard. The note, however, alludes to several different Jeremiah-words from different places in the book, both from Baruch's narratives and from the speech complexes, and is obviously editorial.[18] It also seems to presuppose someone working with a written text. When one adds to this the connection between the Deuteronomists and the scribes mentioned above, it appears most likely to assume that the deuteronomistic Jeremiah tradition was written, as was the Baruch tradition.

This interaction between oral and written transmission is also proved by additional evidence. The Book of Jeremiah contains a second specific example of it as well. The fact is that there can be no doubt whatsoever that Jeremiah 52 was taken directly from 2 Kings 24–25, that is, from the saga book of the Deuteronomistic History, which was doubtless available in written form. A comparison between the two recensions also shows beyond contradiction that in Jeremiah 52 some small additions were made, partly of a complementary nature, but partly also as expressions of a favorite Judean theory: that all real Judeans in Palestine were descended from the exiles. Accordingly, we also see in Jer 52:1-27 the constant tendency to increase the extent of the abductions in 598 and 587 B.C.E.[19] On the other hand, Noth and several other scholars are undoubtedly correct that the source the Deuteronomistic Historian used in 2 Kgs 25:1-26 is Baruch's narratives from Jeremiah 39–41.[20] These chapters in Jeremiah were excerpted so that all the personal information about Jeremiah was systematically removed.

The Book of Isaiah also offers another clear example of literary extension in Isaiah 36–39. As commonly observed, these chapters are also found in a somewhat briefer form in 2 Kgs 18:17—20:19. The Isaiah recension, however, starts with the note in Isa 36:1, which is almost verbatim from 2 Kgs 18:13. But it is also quite certain that 2 Kgs 18:13 is the work of the Deuteronomistic Historian, formed by him in adherence to his annals source.[21] Consequently, Isaiah 36–39 contains not only the Isaiah narratives (the Isaiah complex) of 2 Kings but also an introductory verse written by the Deuteronomistic Historian. The collectors of the Book of Isaiah, therefore, cannot have taken this material from an independently existing Isaiah tradition or from any source of tradition common to the Book of Isaiah and the Book of Kings; they must have taken them over from the saga work of the Deuteronomistic Historian, the Book of Kings. The collectors, or editors, or whatever one chooses to call them, wanted to conclude their Isaiah collection with these traditions that they had from the Book of Kings. This of course does not exclude the possibility that these Isaiah narratives may have also existed in a more or less identical complex in the Isaiah tradition circle. But in this specific instance, the collectors have accordingly not taken these narratives from this assumed tradition but in the form they found them written in the Book of Kings.

In the case of Isaiah 36–39, the material has not remained unaltered. The person who added Isaiah 36–39 to the pre-existing and (relatively) concluded collection of Isaiah traditions (or a later transmitter) has also chosen to include the thanksgiving psalm in Isa 38:9-20. This psalm was not in the Deuteronomistic History.[22] According to a different tradition (or according to a note on the copy of the psalm to which he had access, for example in the temple archives), he knew that King Hezekiah sang this psalm after his illness. To any exegete who is unprejudiced and not too slogan-bound, it is apparent that this psalm existed in writing, and that in a very poor copy. This is clear because of the obvious lacunae and errors found in the text.[23]

From an early period, transmission occurred as an interaction between oral and recorded tradition. The combining of originally independent sayings into tradition complexes of varying lengths is both an oral and a written process. The recording means a further step in the establishment of such secondary connections. And one must also take into account the possibility that whole complexes, such as Jeremiah 30–31 or Isaiah 24–27, for example, may have been inserted into already existing books at a relatively late stage of the recording.

Regarding the prophetic books, moreover, the correct way of posing the problem is not "traditio-historical criticism or literary criticism," with respect to literary history, but *both/and.*

6

The Growth and Development of Tradition

Original Sayings and Later Sayings

In the preceding chapter I have shown that not even the oral tradition offers any guarantee of unaltered transmission of the original content. The orignal content is influenced both by the tendency of combination and leveling that makes itself felt within the oral tradition as well as in the literary activity to which it was also exposed. And in the course of its continued life it is subject to transformation and change, partly imperceptible, partly radical. The Jeremiah tradition offers the best example of this. We have the same sayings partly transmitted in triple form: (a) in the characteristic metrical form of the prophetic saying and prophetic style, which obviously gives the original wording; (b) in brief summary in Baruch's narratives; and (c) extended to fairly long, deuteronomistically shaped speeches.

The incorporation of later prophecies into the tradition about Isaiah or Jeremiah, for example, is something inherent in the tradition process itself. I will show this in a bit more detail.

The transmission of the prophetic sayings and the fixing of the tradition in larger complexes and books are—when viewed as a whole— the work of the Judean congregation as a religious body. It occurred as a result of the practical religious interests attaching to the preservation of the words, and obviously also in constant interaction with the leading religious ideas and thoughts in the prophetic circle and in the congregation.[1] Within the circle, both fresh, living prophecies and inspired interpretation of the older prophecies were constantly produced.[2] The prophets' disciples, as we know, were prophets themselves. The very existence of a circle of Isaiah disciples, to which several of the later prophets may have belonged, is proof of this.[3] Even the later learned transmitters belong to the "wise men," who were heirs of the prophets, and who even reveal a fully lived consciousness of charismatic facility and inspiration, even down to the time of Ben Sira (c. 200 B.C.E.).[4]

It is a matter of course then that prophecies of later disciples within the circle were transmitted together with words of the master and were understood early on as sayings of the master. Specific proof of this is the same saying appearing in both Isa 2:2-5 and Mic 4:1-5. Theoretically, there are three possibilities: the saying was created by (a) Isaiah; (b) Micah; or (c) an unknown prophet in the circle of Isaian disciples, to which Micah belongs.[5] The third possibility is at least as probable as the other two. At any rate, we see that precise knowledge concerning the originator of a prophetic saying might sometimes be lacking.

Growth of the Tradition among Disciples and Transmitters

The connection between tradition and later prophetic sayings may also be proved on a larger scale; indeed, it is simply an essential element of tradition history. The transmission is at the same time a stream of living and topical prophecy. The relationship between the Isaiah circle, Deutero-Isaiah, and the Deutero-Isaiah circle provides a good illustration of the matter. The existence of such circles is proved by the very existence of these tradition complexes.

Within the transmissions of the Isaiah circle of and about Isaiah—such as finally recorded in Isaiah 1–39—we meet (among others) the strongly Deutero-Isaian-sounding sayings in Isaiah 34–35. That the latter do not derive from Isaiah ben Amoz himself is evident and generally acknowledged. Their Deutero-Isaian character is also generally recognized. Indeed, that does not mean that they can be ascribed to the individual personality of Deutero-Isaiah, who is the originator of the sayings in Isaiah 40–55.[6] Chapters 34–35 originate from the Deutero-Isaian circle of disciples; they are Trito-Isaian in spirit, style, and tone.[7] It is not surprising in the least that such a complex is found transmitted within the collections of Isaian traditions as a final passage of the book ascribed to Isaiah ben Amoz.[8] What can be concluded in a traditio-historical vantage point, then, from this relationship? The fact that Isaiah 34–35 have been attributed to Isaiah by the tradition shows that there is a connection between the Isaiah circle and the Deutero-Isaiah circle. Or more specifically, the Isaiah circle, whose existence is proved by the sources, and whose marks can be traced through the post-Isaian prophecy,[9] has continued down to Deutero-Isaiah and his era and posterity. In reality, this means that Deutero-Isaiah sprang from the Isaiah circle and marked it with his spirit for posterity. That also explains the fact that has provoked so many unanswered questions, namely: the sayings of Deutero-Isaiah and his successors (Trito-Isaiah) have been transmitted as an appendix to the Book of Isaiah.

As long as such a circle of prophetic disciples is a living, spiritual, and productive entity—borne by the consciousness of being charismatically inspired prophets themselves and not simply transmitters—the activity of this circle will always be the result of interaction between creative and dominating personalities and a milieu of less distinguished people, who take most of their thoughts and forms of activity from the great one. These leading and creative spirits within the circle are often anonymous to us, in the same way the authors of popular poetry are anonymous; but they are not lesser poets because of that, and they often form "schools." Such a creative personality is just the sort of person behind the prophecies in Isaiah 40–55 and who is known by the label "Deutero-Isaiah": someone who partly releases and brings tendencies already existing in the circle to full bloom, and who partly gives a new look to these tendencies. All these prophecies (with a few exceptions) are so highly marked as belonging to the same spiritual and historical situation—in terms of ideas, temperament, and style—that literary criticism is fully justified in having postulated a single prophetic figure as their originator.[10]

It has long been clear to me that the prophetic milieu from which Deutero-Isaiah sprang was a continuation of the pre-exilic circle of Isaiah's disciples. It explains the place tradition has given his sayings, as a continuation of the Book of Isaiah and his strong connection with important Isaian ideas, such as the remnant, the emphasis on Yahweh as "the Holy One of Israel," etc.[11]

Deutero-Isaiah himself, in his turn, created a school and determined the circle spiritually, thematically, and stylistically. And he probably gave rise to the formation of a new circle, as suggested by the Trito-Isaian sayings in Isaiah 56–66. On all points, the Trito-Isaiah sayings reveal their dependence on Deutero-Isaiah, but to some extent they develop the thoughts further and modify them. On the other hand, Trito-Isaiah does not, like Deutero-Isaiah, demonstrate a uniform view and does not presuppose one and the same historical situation as background. It is fully justified that most scholars have pointed out the differences between the sayings in Isaiah 56–66 and have shown that the various passages date from different times in the late post-exilic period. Even among literary critics, Karl Elliger has not found many supporters for his opinion that "the prophet Trito-Isaiah" was a definite single individual.[12]

The interpretation of the traditio-historical issues as I have outlined them is independent in principle of whether one believes that the three parts of the Book of Isaiah ever constituted separate "books" or not. And the division of the Book of Isaiah into the three main parts (1–39; 40–66, with the subdivisions of 40–55 and 56–66) is not at all founded "entirely on the mechanical book views of literary criticism,"[13] but on observations regarding actual history, the history of ideas, and style.[14] These observations are fully valid whether one imagines a fluctuating circle of transmitters throughout the generations or tradition-collecting and writing editors as producers of the finished collection and book. Since prophetic circles and circles of tradition were connected in the manner indicated above, then it is a matter of course that there are sayings of Deutero-Isaian and Trito-Isaian character found within the Isaiah collection (1–39) and sometimes (even if to a far less extent) words that recall the spirit of the old "judgment prophets" in the later "restoration prophets." The main thing—from a historical, religio-historical, and theological point of view—is that there are actual grounds to distinguish between older and later materials within the transmitted prophetic books. Compared to this, it is really of less importance whether, for example, the post-exilic elements in Isaiah 1–39 are considered later material that has gotten in during the transmission process or as literary interpolations in a written, fixed collection.

The correct, traditio-historical alternative provided here gives a much more vivid and faithful picture of the spiritual life within the circle and the congregation and also makes it easier to understand that these later elements were also inspired prophecy, along with the older ones. This holds true even if the later material should appear as an adaptation, a supplementing of an older prophecy. In the latter case, it is the older prophecy that has been the medium of inspiration for the later prophet. The addition has "come to him," owing to his intense spiritual occupation with the original; and the original has received new life and been actualized in a new situation through the addition.[15]

The older literary critics spoke of "non-genuine interpolations" in such cases. The expression is misleading because it has been formed on the assumption of written books in which the scribes or editors made interpolations. That is not the case. The problem of a real historical analysis of the prophetic books, however, does not disappear because the matter is considered traditio-historically. But one must be fully aware that when one speaks of the authenticity or inauthenticity of a saying, then this might mean several different things from a traditio-historical point of view. It may be a question whether a saying (for example, Isa 2:2-5) is an original part of the tradition complex concerned. That is, through form criticism we can follow the process of origin of this complex. For example, we can tell how it has been created through a system of associated catchwords or the saying concerned may be supposed to have been added later on the basis of recognizing complex-forming motives. Finally, the question may also relate to proving retouching and interpreting extensions as those connected with the literary development of the existing oral or written tradition complexes.[16]

The oldest literary critics, like traditional interpreters of scripture, simply identified the prophet's creation of the saying with its recording on paper. Thus, all these questions coincided, so answering one of them answered them all. From a traditio-historical point of view, however, the matter cannot be viewed in this way. It is very possible, perhaps even probable, that Isa 2:2-5, for example, always belonged to the tradition complex of Isaiah 2–5. Or it could be that from the start the identical Mic 4:1-5 was created in connection with Micah 1–3.[17] But this, however, resolves nothing about the authenticity of this saying in relation to Isaiah or Micah. That there exists a problem here becomes evident in this case from the fact that the same saying has been ascribed to two named prophets. This fact simply increases our curiosity concerning the possibility that this saying may include elements that suggest a later period than either Isaiah or Micah.

This case is really analogous as well to a series of cases where we do not have the circumstantial evidence implied by the double transmission. Amos 9:8-10, for example, may very well have belonged to the collection of Amos sayings from the beginning—from the earliest collection of them. But does that offer any *guarantee* that it belongs to Amos? Of course not. The task of testing the separate sayings transmitted with a view to whether the tradition is correct or not still exists as before. There may be correct tradition a priori, and there may be secondary and incorrect tradition.

7

The Transformation of the Separate Prophetic Sayings

The Problem

The prophetic sayings existed as a living spiritual force in the religious struggle and activity within a circle of transmitters who were themselves prophets and attributed to themselves prophetic inspiration. It is, therefore, evidently possible that the prophetic sayings (as suggested in the previous chapter) during this use in the spiritual conflicts of the time have marched on with time and have become transformed and marked to some extent by new situations and demands. It may be imagined in the way that the new topical and situation-determined inspiration coming to one of these prophetic disciples and transmitters came into contact with one of the older sayings by the master. It lived in the consciousness of the disciple and constituted part of his spiritual property and arsenal. What he has from Yahweh has come to him as a continuation of—or partly a bending of—one of the master's words. Analogously, it would correspond to, for instance, when one of the New Testament authors got his thoughts and formed them in connection with a word from the Old Testament, or when a later Christian author or preacher grasped what to him was a new and clearer truth with the strength of personal experience in association with a biblical quotation—a guidance associated with a text. Have such cases occurred in the prophetic transmission? Yes, without a doubt.[1]

Examples

Earlier I suggested that the sayings of Amos and Hosea come to us in a new Judean actualization.[2] Words that Hosea spoke to the kingdom of Israel have come down as words to Judah by replacing "Joseph," "Israel," or the like with "Judah." It is evidence of the continued life of the prophetic sayings in the religious reality. What Yahweh first said to Israel he now says to Israel and Judah, or to Judah alone. In these cases it is most often simple to demonstrate that such a new edition has taken place. In Hos 5:8-11 both the places mentioned in the introductory request in v. 8, and the fact that the threat of punishment in v. 9 as well as the motivation in v. 9b only speak of Ephraim-Israel show that in reality it must also be Ephraim who is addressed in v. 10, where we now have "the princes of Judah." If not, one must expect a punishment speech against Judah as well.

Hosea 10:11-13 provides another example. The introduction (v. 11a) about Ephraim the heifer shows that it is she who is pictured as a heifer needing instruction in what follows. To comply with the demands of style when employing parallelism (thought rhyme), "Ephraim" is paired with "Jacob" in v. 11b, where they are a parallel pair referring to Israel.[3] This is partly on account of the parallelism and partly on account of completing the image of the plough with two beasts as a team. In this connection, it is evident that "Judah" is nothing more in v. 11b than simply a case of a clumsily placed written gloss.

In other cases, however, the matter is not so obvious. But all the same, one also frequently finds detached sayings in which one is struck by formal and factual incongruities that appear to require an explanation.

The matter is comparatively simple in a saying like Isa 28:1-6. Verses 1-4 undoubtedly form a threat against Ephraim-Samaria, in a genuinely prophetic style and in a metrical form, ending with a clear prophecy of doom. Verse 5 is a promise in prose to "the remnant of his (Yahweh's) people" about a glorious salvation that is to take place "in that day." This transition is not marked by any mediating connecting link. That vv. 5-6 are not a new independent saying but belong to vv. 1-4 is evident from the echo of the image and expression from v. 1—"the proud crown of the drunkards . . . the fading flower of its glorious beauty"—with "a crown of glory and a diadem of beauty." But why should the promise be in prose? Is it a less important or solemn part of the saying since it does not get the traditional form in "the tongue of the gods"? And what does "in that day" mean? According to the context it must be the day when Samaria is destroyed. But that cannot be the meaning; the salvation of the remnant to come *then* was demonstrably not the opinion of either Isaiah or his disciples. The expression actually only becomes understandable when it is interpreted as a conventional technical term. It is a phrase that cannot be demonstrated to appear in any assuredly ancient prophetic saying but which at any rate is very popular among the latest, more or less literary prophetic transmitters.[4] It is evident in v. 6 that we find an extension of the original saying, an extension that wants to add the promise to the threat of punishment.[5]

Hosea 2:2-23 [MT 4-25] is of the same type. The threat of punishment and destruction in vv. 2-13 [MT 4-15] are metrical and the most original, rounded off with a conclusion formula in v. 13 [15]: "sounds the inspired oracle of Yahweh" (*ne'um Yhwh*). To this threat a promise has been attached in prose (vv. 14-23 [MT 16-25]). Why in prose? Was the sight of the glorious future not sufficiently inspiring for the imagination and art of the prophet to be formed in the rhythms of prophetic style? Hosea would have had no psychological or style-historical reason to have formed the promise in the same way as the threat if it constituted an original part of the same saying. To this we must add that vv. 14-23 do not only point back to vv. 2-13, but they also contain allusions to other independent sayings of Hosea (1:2-9). Accordingly, they can really only be understood by those who have other parts of the Hosea tradition in their memory. But there are also allusions to Jeremiah's sayings (compare Hos 2:15 [MT 17] to Jer 2:2-3 and 3:19-20). In Jeremiah we are dealing with a "new formation" of the Hosea saying, where the threat of punishment against Israel (supplementing Ephraim with the future hope of Judah) looks forward to the re-establishment of David's kingdom (see Hos 3:5) and the new exodus of the scattered Judeans through the desert and the "valley of hope" to the promised land. Here it even seems as if one can grasp the spiritual connection between this branch of the tradition and Deutero-Isaiah and Trito-Isaiah circles (see Isa 65:10).

Other passages are less clear but still raise problems of the same sort. Isaiah 31:4 contains an unveiled word of threat against Jerusalem. In the same way as the lion attacks the flock without being frightened by the noise of the shepherds, "Yahweh, the Mighty Warrior[6] shall come down to fight against Mount Zion." Yahweh is compared to the lion. The comparison "As a lion growls . . . so shall Yahweh come down to fight" shows that Yahweh, no more than the lion, will let anyone deprive him of the prey he has selected. The prey is obviously Mount Zion; the fate of Zion will be that of the prey over which the lion is already roaring—no one can save it (see Amos 3:12a). The historical background is probably the same as in Isa 31:1-3: the plans of an uprising against Assyria with help from Egypt.

In itself, Isa 31:4 might well be a completely independent saying. The outcome of that struggle, everyone will understand. Were this beginning to have a continuation, however, then it is clear that in accordance with the picture it had to be to the effect that no one can prevent Yahweh from clutching his prey and destroying it like the lion among the flock. Instead, v. 5 continues—without mediating or explanatory transition—with an equally unconditional promise of Yahweh's protection of the Jerusalem that he attacks in v. 4. "Like birds hovering, so Yahweh, the Mighty Warrior, will protect Jerusalem; he will protect and deliver it, he will spare and rescue it." And to this is attached a promise of Assyria's ruin (31:8a) with "the sword, not of man"—by the hand of a "non-mortal." And v. 5 has obviously been formed to continue v. 4: *ken yared* in v. 4b corresponds to *ken yagen* in v. 5a.

But is it psychologically conceivable that Isaiah would simultaneously announce the threat (v. 4) and the exact opposite (vv. 5-9)? This is problematic in his current situation where he mobilized everything to prevent the alliance with Egypt and the revolt against Assyria,[7] and threatened with Yahweh's inexorable punishment over Judah and Jerusalem—if they were to commit such madness. Is it believable that he would have predicted the ruin of Assyria by Yahweh's sword and also have stressed the insoluble association between Yahweh and Zion (v. 9b)? Is it not more likely that Isaiah's saying in v. 4—in a new situation where the prophet's disciples were anxious to kindle courage and hope in a better future for Zion and to exhort and encourage to conversion—has been actualized once more by another prophet and made the starting point for a new proclamation in the new and different situation, together with the exhortation to believe and to leave the future to "the Non-mortal One"? And is it not more likely that the "struggle *against* (*'al*) Mount Zion" (which v. 4 mentions)[8] has accordingly been re-interpreted as a "struggle *on* (*'al*) Mount Zion," namely as a protection against all conceivable enemies, according to the view and the hope involved by the experiences and promises of the new year and ascension festival, and which find expression in Psalms like 46 and 48?[9] Since the saying in v. 7 also contains an allusion to another Isaiah saying (2:20), this also speaks in favor of 31:5-9 as the work of Isaiah's circle of disciples.

The same reinterpretation of a word of threat into a prophecy according to the scheme of first disaster, then deliverance, is also present in Isa 29:1-7. That "woe" (*hoy*) always introduces a threat or states a disaster (grief), there should never have been any doubt.[10] Ariel shall be "visited by Yahweh Sabaoth with thunder and with earthquake and great noise, with whirlwind and tempest, and the flame of a devouring fire"—that is, the town will be destroyed.[11] That this is the meaning is also confirmed by the fact that a number of interpreters (most recently Bentzen) feel compelled also to understand Isa 29:5 and 7 as words of threat. Here too, however, v. 8 adds (and once more in prose) a promise that all the attackers of Zion shall be disappointed in their hopes. That this promise is not original is apparent from vv. 2 and 6, where "the enemies" are not the attackers, but Yahweh. The same may be said of the prose as in the case of Isa 28:5-6; Hos 2:14-23[16-25]; and other passages. In reality, this secondary reinterpretation of the saying by "tradition" also comprises vv. 5a and 7, which are most naturally understood as threats against "the enemies." Verse 5a brings a completely different "intuition picture" into the clear connection with vv. 2-4+5b.

A final example is Isa 32:9-20. Verses 9-14 comprise a merciless word of threat about the ruin of Jerusalem. Verse 19 also belongs with vv. 9-14, where "the forest" refers to "the house of the Lebanon forest" (compare Isa 10:34;

22:8; Jer 22:6-23). This connection is now broken by the promise of restoration of the people in vv. 15-18+20. It cannot be an independent saying; "until" (*'ad*) in v. 15 expressly attaches it to the preceding passage. In other respects as well it points backward to vv. 9-14—the choice of words and ideas, and the spirit and tone are plainly "Deutero-Isaian."[12] Here too an older Isaiah saying became the starting point for a new supplementary promise of the end of the period of punishment, once "the Spirit is poured upon us from on high" (v. 15) and justice and righteousness settle on the land (v. 16).

Conclusions

These examples show that in all circumstances one is forced to take up the problem of the relation between the tradition and the original saying, also in the case of the transmission of the separate saying and its formation. But the traditio-historical approach also gives us a clearer understanding of the spiritual history of which the process of transmission is part and with which it has interacted.[13]

At the same time, what I have discussed above shows that in practice it is not always possible to draw sharp boundaries between tradition criticism and literary criticism. For instance, no one can decide with certainty whether one or the other appearance of "Judah" in the Hosea tradition has entered at the oral or written stage of the transmission for an original "Joseph" or "Ephraim." The factual arguments the literary critics used to separate presumably "non-genuine" parts of the "text" retain their reality and must also often be employed to distinguish between older and more recent strata of tradition. Or in other words, the literary critics have, in reality, often reasoned and worked tradition-critically when, on the basis of an incorrect opinion of the nature of the fixation of the tradition, they believed that they were performing literary criticism. Often, therefore, the correctness of their results is independent of their incorrect presuppositions.

In this connection, I venture to point to my work on the prophets in *Det Gamle Testamente* vol. 3. Here it should be clear to anyone reading the introductory remarks and the passage about the origin of prophetic literature in the introduction,[14] and conferring with my opinions stated in my 1942 article,[15] that the approach of the analysis in *Det Gamle Testamente* is (to a great extent) traditio-historical rather than literary-critical (in the old sense of the term). The appearance of the letter T in the margins (next to an Isaiah saying, for example) does not intend to suggest a *literary* interpolation in a written text, but a revision that the original saying has experienced in the oral tradition, where it has lived a real life and in new situations has become a starting point and attachment point for new prophecies in addition to the older one. To what degree this has taken place, and exactly how it is possible to prove it in each case, may be subject to disagreement and subjective decisions. But that it has taken place, and that, in principle, one must make a distinction, is beyond any doubt. And this is admitted not least by those who give up discriminating in details. A really critical traditio-*historical* method here gives a richer insight into the life of prophecy.

8

The Trend of Tradition Development

Prophecies of Disaster and Deliverance

The transformation of the tradition in the cases already mentioned means an addition of promises to older prophecies of threat and punishment (prophecies of judgment). The transformation to which the separate sayings have been subjected in the tradition corresponds to the scheme that forms the basis for the arrangement of the details in a larger tradition complex (see p. 45 above).

The result reached by the form-critical analysis of the prophetic sayings with regard to the division of the tradition complex into original units shows, among other things, that in the predominant number of cases a saying is either a pure prophecy of disaster or a pure promise.[1] This is indeed something that is inherent in the saying as a specific, topical, situationally determined saying. The specific situation with the specific people or the specific person as the addressee of the message is generally such that it both psychologically—seen from the point of view of Yahweh—demands and produces a definitely unmistakable response with a message of punishment or deliverance. It is only a small minority of the transmitted, detached sayings that contain both, and then, generally, as in the same scheme according to which the collections are arranged: disaster–deliverance. One must then admit in the name of all reason that this presents a problem and that these exceptions demand an explanation. Whether the explanation can be found at all, and whether it is then to be this or that, is a separate question that must be the result of research. But one cannot deny that research on the prophets is confronted here with a question that may require a traditio-historical solution. That is, the solution may lie in the transforming effect of tradition and in the tendency expressed by the collection scheme. This is shown by the examples discussed in the previous chapters.

The possibility cannot be dismissed, however, that a prophet who actually only proclaimed announcements of judgment, in the tradition process may little by little have come to be an advocate of both the aspects of the future hopes of the Judean congregation: punishment and restoration. Or to express it differently, the image of the prophet may have gradually shifted over time in the tradition.

The problem that arises may be illustrated by means of an example. The main impression obtained by a study of the sayings of Amos goes so definitely in the direction that this public message to Israel was a pure announcement of judgment. Thus it appears more than doubtful whether the saying included among his sayings by tradition and placed as a conclusion of the collection may be ascribed to him personally. One cannot dismiss the possibility that tradition is wrong on this point; on the contrary, it is likely. In fact, Isa 2:2-5//Mic 4:1-5 demonstrates that the tradition was not always certain who originated a particular prophetic saying. If it is the case, then, that the doubt concerning Amos 9:8-10, 11-12, 13-15 may be strengthened by other criteria—for example, stylistic arguments or possible allusions to the historical background of the sayings—then it may approach scientific probability or even relative certainty.

Arrangement of Tradition Complexes and Collections

In this connection, it may be of interest to look once more at the *scheme* forming the basis of the formation of the tradition complexes. This scheme, disaster–salvation, offered no problem to traditional church exegesis. In fact, it corresponds on the whole to the dogmatic view of Israel's history and the history of salvation. Nor does the older theology appear to have conceived it as a consciously employed scheme. Rather, the scheme was conceived as something characteristic of prophecy as such, as something inherent in the matter. This might appear reasonable as long as the prophets were conceived as authors of books and equally when they were conceived as eschatological preachers; for this scheme is exactly that of the eschatological drama. Hugo Gressmann was actually the first scholar to find anything surprising in it.[2] He focussed on the unmediated and inorganic transition from the preaching of disaster to promise that is found in several of the transmitted, detached sayings, which we have discussed above, and did not rest contentedly with the explanation of the radical literary critics that there were "non-genuine interpolations" based on a later eschatology. He believed he had found something governed by "laws"; and since he also conceived the prophets as eschatological preachers, he chose his starting point for the explanation of their eschatological preaching in exactly the remarkable inorganic character of the scheme. Furthermore, he believed that the prophets on this point were dependent on an ancient scheme, the origin of which they did not themselves understand. The unmediated transition from prophecy of disaster to prophecy of deliverance was a tradition from an ancient Near Eastern cosmological and eschatological scheme, which had once contained both these elements in an organic combination but which had reached Israel in a disintegrated form (compare the later "disintegrated patterns"). What was left, therefore, was only the traditional awareness that this was the manner of prophecy, because the drama of future and final times would take place in two such dramatic acts. The difficulty with Gressmann's theory was the essential point that such a cosmological and eschatological scheme and an eschatology of such a content could not be traced at all in the ancient Near East until the later Persian religion. For purely chronological reasons, therefore, the prophets of Israel were not in a position to draw from that religion.

Often lacking better analogies, some scholars have referred to prophecies from Babylon and Egypt, where this scheme was said to prevail.[3] These analogies are neither surprising nor conclusive. We are concerned here with *vaticinia ex eventu* (a prophecy after the event) for the glorification of kings who had once more given their country good conditions after bad times of decay and tyranny.[4] When this was represented in the form of the prophecies of an old wisdom about the new king, it simply could not be avoided that the deliverance was depicted against the background of the dark picture of an earlier era. And when the whole had the form of prophecy, the deliverance–disaster scheme was created automatically. There is no question here of the Israelites adopting this scheme, and still less a possibility of their taking a form that artistically belonged to Egyptian prophetic forms. We are dealing here with a form that was inevitable in a certain form of prophecy, namely in such "literary" *vaticiniae ex eventu* (prophecies after the event) of a king who had really brought happy days after disastrous times. On the other hand, it appears as if such an eschatological scheme really arose in the latest Persian-Hellenistic Egypt. If so, however, we are undoubtedly dealing with an influence from Persian religion, which has its closest analogies in the dualistic eschatology of late Judean apocalyptic.[5]

A more imaginative conception seeks the explanation of the scheme in the cult, where the ritual to commemorate the dead and rising god was accompanied by prophetic words about the disasters, and the blessings that follow these two acts. Within the ritual, the scheme disaster–deliverance is then seen as traditional, and the prophets are then supposed to have felt obliged to follow this stylistic tradition.[6] The existence of such an Israelite cult of the dying and rising god in the person of the king is nothing but sheer hypothesis and cannot be proved by means of "ritual patterns" from Babylon or Ugarit. Such a ritual scheme, moreover, could in no way explain the origin of a stylistic pattern that the prophets were obliged to follow because of existing stylistic pressures. In the cult of the dying and rising god we are concerned with words that accompany occurring actions that are separated from each other by shorter or longer intervals and accordingly have a "situational" independence in relation to each other, like the various acts in a drama. To one situation/act belong words expressing disasters and complaints; to another act belong words that express joy and guaranteed blessing in the coming year.

In the prophetic sayings, on the other hand, one finds a scheme corresponding to its nature, according to which the prophet, forced by the stylistic tradition, should be obliged, in the same historical situation—or even the same saying—to speak both parts in unmediated connection with each other. It is impossible to imagine such a stylistic scheme to have originated from a ritual arrangement like the one assumed above. It must also be noted that words accompanying the grief over the dead god (in the texts that explicitly indicate such a situation) do not have the character of prophecies but of lamentations accompanying and explaining what happened.[7] Rather than prophecies concerning things to come, the announcement of the joyful message of the god's resurrection and the blessings attached to it has more the character of a message about things that now have been experienced and that are given in and by the resurrection.

There is still some truth in drawing the analogy between the scheme of the prophetic transmitters and the cult. Ancient Israel did, in fact, observe a cultic festival dominated by this movement from grief to exaltation. They lived through a state of unhappiness (such as the "death" of nature in the dry season) and moved on to salvation. This exaltation was experienced in the coming of Yahweh, which emerged in and through the New Year Festival—the epiphany and God's ascension to the throne.[8] The cultic-mythological situation included a variety of elements. The congregation was in a state of disaster at the beginning of the festival. The powers of chaos, or all the united peoples, flood the earth, surrounding Israel and threatening their lives. This is all depicted in psalms and rites (see, for example, Psalms 46, 48, 75, 76). But then the temple prophet announced the coming of Yahweh, resulting in the destruction of the enemies and the deliverance of Israel. In the background of the description of the disaster, the psalms paid homage to the God who has already appeared (revealed himself), conquering and bringing deliverance.

In light of this cultic-mythological scheme or pattern of the Enthronement Festival—depicted as Yahweh's victory and universal throne ascension—Deutero-Isaiah already had the coming deliverance in view. According to the same scheme, the transformations of the prophecies of disaster we discussed in chapter 7 have taken place. Moreover, according to this scheme, prophets of the restoration[9] and the latest prophets depict the hope of Israel: Joel, Deutero-Zechariah, and others.[10]

It is quite clear that the prophetic oracle had a fixed place in the Enthronement Festival.[11] It is conceivable that there were also prophecies in which the coming deliverance was described against the background of the disaster that the Israelites had just endured. There is reason to believe that this annually experienced movement from the disaster of chaos to the glorious certainty of deliverance in the Enthronement Festival determined ancient Israel's view of reality and history: a constantly repeated transformation from disaster to deliverance. This pattern in their worldview is indeed, to a certain extent, ancient and common to the whole ancient Near East.[12] It also forms the foundation of the ancient Sumerians view of history, which is expressed in their lists of kings and dynasties, with occasional historical information.[13] This mythological thinking is no doubt connected with the repeated cultic experience. The gods of the Sumerians were also fertility deities who died and rose again.[14] And their festival cult, too, was a real drama, where the resurrection of the world from chaos and death was experienced once more. It is not necessary to conclude that there was any direct influence from this historical pattern of the Sumerians and Babylonians on the Israelites. The analogous cultic experience of disaster to deliverance may have led to analogous views of reality and history in both Mesopotamia and Israel. This was especially true of Israel, which had a strong sense of history in its religion.

The collection and pattern of arrangement of the prophetic transmitters were determined by this cultic-mythological view of reality and by the cultic prophecies expressing it. Obviously that does not mean that there may not occasionally have occurred separate sayings built according to this pattern in the prophets of reform and reaction (or perhaps better, prophets of revolution). As prophets of reaction and judgment, however, it was inherent in their proclamation that this would not have been the rule.[15] Here each separate saying must be investigated on the basis of form-critical criteria and a conclusion reached in each particular case. It is characteristic, primarily in the later prophets of restoration and their predecessors among the younger disciples of Isaiah, that we find clear instances of this pattern within the separate saying.[16]

This ritual pattern from the Enthronement Festival, however, is insufficient to explain the predominating use of the disaster–deliverance scheme in the collections of the prophetic transmitters and in the occasional transformation by tradition of the transmitted sayings (see chap. 7 above). One fails to appreciate the peculiar character of Israelite (or Judean) religion if one does not take into account its close relationship to real history and its experiences. For historical Yahwism—particularly furthered by the proclamation of the prophets—the real history gradually became the locus where the true God reveals himself and acts. No doubt the actual history and spiritual situation in the congregation and the circle of prophetic disciples were more influential than any ritual pattern or disaster–deliverance scheme. The disasters that the older prophets had predicted—the ruin of the state, the destruction of the city and the temple, and so on—had already occurred and the congregation still partly lived in their wake. The restoration in the early part of the Persian period was only a partial restoration and a pale realization of what Deutero-Isaiah (for example) had prophesied. The hope of restoration and the current promises of a new era still lived, however, in the prophetic circle. The disaster–deliverance scheme, then, was proclaimed with factual and psychological necessity as soon as the process of transmission and combination began.

Arrangement of Complexes and the Nature of Prophecy

Nothing may be concluded on the basis of the disaster–deliverance scheme itself regarding the existence or nonexistence of both kinds of prophecies originating with the prophet-master, to whom the tradition traces its origins. It merely demonstrates that in the prophetic circle both existed at a particular time.[17] The mass of tradition contains materials from very different periods (note the Book of Isaiah) and accordingly has received additions and grew in the course of the history of the tradition (as we have articulated in earlier chapters). It is not possible, therefore, from a traditio-historical point of view, to maintain a priori that, for example, the "positive, Messianic sayings originally belonged to the material."[18] This *may* be true; but it also may have happened differently. Anything is possible, and our task is to examine each specific case with all the methods at our disposal.[19] That task can only be evaded if the tradition historians decree that tradition history is not allowed to inquire into the history of tradition. But that was presumably not what was intended.

9

The Prophets and the Tasks of Tradition History

Tradition History as the Critical History of Tradition

The attempt to distinguish between the strata of tradition, between old and new, between the origin of tradition and what it became all belongs to real tradition history. Research can never shirk its duty regarding a critical classification of the prophetic materials as far as this is possible or may lead to probable results. Also part of this critical classification is the question of how much of the material can be connected (with probability) to the prophet under whose name it passes in the tradition.

It is conceivable that the tradition is of such a type that it does not allow us in most cases to penetrate far back into its history. It is also possible that tradition has grown over the original material to such an extent that the latter can only be dimly perceived or determined as larger or smaller "erratic blocks" in the complex tradition and cannot always be sharply distinguished. It is certainly not possible to discriminate cleanly "original" and "editorial" (for example, in the Book of Ezekiel) along the lines of literary criticism, as attempted by Gustav Hölscher and Nils Messel, each in his own way.[1] To that extent one can understand, if not approve of, the fact that one goes to the other extreme and declares the whole book a "Pseudo-Ezekiel," as C. C. Torrey has done.[2]

The fact about tradition is briefly this: tradition assigns the sayings in the Book of Ezekiel to the prophet Ezekiel, who is described as being among those carried away in 598 B.C.E. and who worked among the exiles in Babylonia. This accords with a number of passages, regarding both content and ideology. On the other hand, other and larger parts of the book were addressed to the Judeans in Jerusalem and assume the conditions after the restoration in the early Persian period. The former passages (Babylonian) are everywhere embedded in the latter passages (Jerusalem) without sharp boundaries. Here the most natural explanation seems to be that the sayings of the exiled prophet have been used as starting points for an actualized preaching to the Judean congregation after the restoration. In modern terms, the earlier prophecies became "texts" for sermons by the later prophetic disciples. What was once said to the exiles is later applied to the restored congregation and the bad conditions that prevailed there. In that way the original tradition became subject to such a radical change that it cannot be separated with any complete certainty. As a whole, in its present form, the book is a work by Ezekiel's disciples after the restoration.[3]

Even a fairly uniform tradition such as the Ezekiel tradition, however, may present us with cases where a decision in one or the other direction is not possible. To take another example, it may be true in one sense that we cannot penetrate behind the figure of Jesus represented in the tradition. But that does not mean that we cannot identify more than one saying of Jesus that was not spoken by Jesus in its present form, based on traditio-historical criteria.[4] Similar cases also appear in research on the prophets. Thus there can be no doubt that a saying like that in Jer 23:1-4, which plainly assumes the Diaspora as a fact, cannot date from Jeremiah himself. The same is true about Jeremiah 33, in spite of all the Jeremian phrases and clichés in which the chapter abounds. These show that the chapter was created in a definite circle of tradition as a result of an intense preoccupation with the Jeremiah tradition.[5]

Accordingly, a critical discrimination within the collections of prophetic words representing the tradition is not only a task of research and an ideal but also—in a number of specific cases—a task that can be accomplished to a certain extent. And here real tradition history (with the emphasis on *history*) is a means to the solution. It is important to grasp the interests and the historical forces that have carried on the tradition and the influences that have had a formative and transformative effect on it during the transmission. To resign before this task is like a horse "refusing the fence"; it is a research petition for bankruptcy, even though the work must often be carried on with great caution. And this caution may be much greater than that frequently shown by literary criticism.

If the traditio-historical approach is to be something more than a pretext to refuse the fences, it also must attempt to be real history. That means, however, that it must operate with strata of tradition and with lines (tendencies, or whatever one calls them) in this history. In other words, it cannot avoid working with issues of tradition development and growth of tradition—with primary and secondary tradition. Tradition history is compelled to reckon with different tradition strata: within the historic tradition, the saga tradition, and the prophetic tradition. We sometimes hear from "consistently traditio-historical" quarters about "strata interpretation" in such a way that it seems as if it was believed that the mere use of this fuzzy phrase is sufficient to refute such attempts.[6] A tradition history that does not want to distinguish between "strata" in the tradition is not tradition history. Still less is it a "consistently traditio-historical discussion." It is a word, "a noisy gong or a clanging cymbal."

Development in Prophecy and Tradition

Even a superficial study of the prophetic books in the light of history shows that the prophets whose literary remains we have were predominantly prophets of doom, even down to the period of Jeremiah. It should be readily admitted that some of the older "literary critics" (for example, Karl Marti and Gustav Hölscher) have carried their schematic views too far and imagined the development (viz., the movement in spiritual history) to be too straight and single-stranded. That era, however, is long past.[7] And the constant polemical blows that are aimed at the older school from certain quarters,[8] or the one-sided posing of the issue as being pro or con Wellhausen,[9] often appear to be fighting against windmills or to be cheap rhetorical victories.

We have long known that not all prophets solely preached death and doom.[10] It has always been maintained that Isaiah preached that "a remnant shall return" (*še'ar yašub*; Isa 7:3) and that a new Israel would once again be established on Zion.[11] In a corresponding and increasing degree, similar thoughts appear in several of his disciples before the exile.[12] And it is equally clear that prophecy after the exile was predominantly a prophecy of restoration and deliverance, which gradually became real eschatology.[13] Not all the prophets are alike on this point. No reference to any "prophetic speech scheme" can solve the problems or justify maintaining that all the prophets must have prophesied both doom and deliverance.

Consequently, the various prophets are different from one another, and a clear line in the history of the prophetic movement exists. The instances cited in chapters 6 and 7 have also clearly shown two things. First, the trend of the tradition went in the direction of supplementing the judgment words of the older prophets with corresponding promises of the restoration according to a definite scheme. Undoubtedly later prophecies in that way frequently came to be attached to the name of an older master. Second, this trend also led in several cases to a transformation and a new edition of an older prophetic saying so that it also came to express the hope of restoration in the new situation.

The insight into the history of the tradition we gain from these conclusions sets the tasks for our research. We must attempt to penetrate backwards to the origin of the tradition—the prophet himself. We must try to form a picture of his preaching as it was before the tradition took it over. We must, if possible, try to penetrate behind the tradition.

It is of no benefit to say that it is a regrettable fact that the tradition is all we have. What exists constitutes a problem by its very existence and our task must consequently be to attempt to reach a genetic understanding of what exists. Birkeland is correct, of course, that it is vain and wrong in principle to search for "genuine" Jeremiah words in the deuteronomistic speeches in the Book of Jeremiah and to attempt to separate them by operations based on literary criticism.[14] This is so even if there are still scholars who seem to consider this a kind of meritorious "conservative" work.[15] For in these speeches there are no literarily extended Jeremiah passages, but remelted Jeremiah tradition—that is, Jeremiah recast into a deuteronomistic figure. Even here, however, one may sometimes suspect the existence of metrically formed proto-cells (such as in Jeremiah 7), which have still preserved something of their original form and content during the remelting.[16]

But the conditions are not always like those in these Jeremiah speeches. We have also seen examples where the transformation in the tradition has left such clear marks in the form and construction of the saying that it is possible to make a traditio-historical investigation here as well.

Ipsissima Verba

In the face of such circumstances, it is not correct to state as a necessary consequence of the traditio-historical approach and as a principle of scientific dogmatism that it is of no avail to desire to get behind the tradition circle that has been the intermediary in bringing the matter to us, and to say that it is "erroneous in principle" to try to reach the *ipsissima verba* (exact words) of the prophets.[17] With such a dogma, tradition history becomes a "Do Not Enter" sign, a prohibition against the very exercise of tradition history.

Research, however, cannot submit to a "Do Not Enter" sign. But by its very nature, it adopts the same attitude to such orders as our own "illegal" struggle did to the thousands of "prohibitions." And in this case as well there is no reason for research to respect the prohibitions. Behind the tradition, after all, loom the powerful figures of the prophets, who have created that very tradition. And in a number of cases their own words speak to us so clearly that we cannot miss them. We are not going to allow anyone to deprive us of the right to attempt to let them speak as clearly as possible. In many cases we may have to give up. Sometimes the voice of the prophet sounds like a powerful leading melody, at other times like a deep undertone in the chorus of the tradition, and at others more subdued, flooded by the multi-stringed accompaniment of tradition. We will attempt to ascertain their words, get hold of the original sayings, approximately as they once sounded in the streets and marketplaces of Jerusalem and by the gates of the temple. We will attempt to find them by all means within our power—through form criticism, tradition history, and literary criticism.

Part III

The Prophetic Experience

10

The Spirit and the Word in the Prophets

Yahweh's Spirit

The pre-exilic reforming prophets never really expressed a consciousness that their prophetic endowment and powers were due to possession by or any action of the spirit of Yahweh (*ruaḥ Yhwh*). After studying the spirit of Yahweh in the Old Testament, I was surprised to come to this conclusion. On the other hand, the whole of their consciousness and prophetic message rested on another fundamental religious conception: the word of Yahweh (*dabar Yhwh*). My object here is to examine this insight in greater detail.

One must assume that the idea of a possessing, immanent spirit of Yahweh as the cause of the prophet's special qualities and powers was fundamental in the older, primitive "nebi'ism." Considerations of space preclude me from pursuing this point. And it should further be observed, as important for the understanding of what follows, that the idea of Yahweh's spirit in the older nebi'ism refers almost exclusively to the ecstatic behavior and activities of the *nabi'*. His possession by the spirit was what made him ecstatic; it was precisely this that explained to the ancient Israelites the strange, irrational, "frenzied" character of the *nabi'*, as well as his conduct and work. The spirit made him lose control of himself and behave differently from normal people.

Very seldom, on the other hand, is the prophet's utterance ascribed to the spirit, as the spirit's words. The only occasion when this occurs seems to be in the story of Micaiah ben Imla, where the spirit becomes "a lying spirit in the mouth of all his [Ahab's] prophets" (1 Kgs 22:22), so that the *nabi'*s words are withdrawn from his conscious, rational control.

What actually led me to investigate the attitude of the reforming prophets toward the idea of the spirit was the discovery that if one wanted to give an account of the content of this idea in prophecy—the idea, that is, of the spirit of Yahweh in the prophets—only two directions practically afford sources for such a study and in which the idea of Yahweh's ecstasy-producing spirit (*ruaḥ*) in the prophet is conspicuous. One was the occasional references to the original, primitive form of nebi'ism. The other was the group of popular, prophetic legends: the Elijah and Elisha legends. Otherwise the spirit idea largely recedes into the background in the "literary prophets" as a whole, even in the form in which their books have come down to us. A detailed study proves that in most of the reforming prophets the idea is not only absent but actually rejected: they regarded possession by the spirit as something undesirable and attributed their own consciousness of a vocation to a different cause.[1]

The prophets Amos, Zephaniah, Nahum, Habakkuk, and Jeremiah make no mention of Yahweh's spirit—whether it is his "subjective" spirit in the sense of his mind and mode of action, or the "objective" spirit of Yahweh as an actuating principle in the world or an endowment of his servants. That their own prophetic vocation and their possession of Yahweh's wondrous word come of their having Yahweh's spirit in them is never suggested by so much as a syllable, although their consciousness of their vocation is in some ways stronger than it is in the ordinary *nabi'*. Hosea makes a single allusion to the prophetic spirit (Hos 9:7); but, as we shall see, he emphatically disclaims all the practices of the "spirit man."[2] In Micah there is a single passage where he seems to lay claim to the spirit of Yahweh himself, but here the words *eth-ruaḥ Yhwh* are a gloss (Mic 3:8).[3] Isaiah shares the usual ideas of spirit (*ruaḥ*) as the living numinous force that is especially characteristic of a deity as compared with a weak, mortal "creature of the flesh" (Isa 31:3); of Yahweh's ability to intervene actively and change the *ruaḥ* of humans, giving them a fatal "spirit of drowsiness" to punish their sins (Isa 29:10);[4] and of Yahweh's "subjective" spirit—his mind, thought, will, and plan—which the people disregard in their political actions (Isa 29:10).[5] But he never speaks of Yahweh's spirit either as the source of prophetic inspiration (his own or another's), or as a force producing religious and moral renewal.[6] Not even Haggai and Zechariah, who in other respects have so little in common with the old reforming prophets, refer to the spirit of Yahweh as a source of inspiration.[7] And the same is true of Malachi.

Not until Ezekiel do we find a certain change in this respect. Here the spirit of Yahweh is mentioned once as the medium of prophetic inspiration (Ezek 11:5). But as a rule it is purely a motive principle, closely akin to the "wind," and the word is used to explain the ecstatic sensation of being transported from one place to another (Ezek 1:12, 20, 21; 2:2; 3:12, 14, 24; 8:3; 11:1, 24; 37:1; 43:5).[8] It is never explicitly stated that this is Yahweh's *ruaḥ*. The passages in which *ruaḥ* denotes the new law-abiding disposition that Yahweh will give to the people, or Yahweh's spirit that will produce this disposition (Ezek 11:19; 36:26-27; 39:29; compare 18:31), are not Ezekiel's but additions made by the post-exilic editors of the book.[9]

Deutero-Isaiah refers several times to Yahweh's spirit; on the whole his conception of it follows the traditional lines;[10] nothing prophetic, at any rate, is implied.[11] And it never stands for his own prophetic endowment.[12] In Trito-Isaiah, however, it does. Here prophetic inspiration is one of the activities attributed to Yahweh's spirit (Isa 61:1-4).[13] The same is true of the author of the Servant Songs or ʻEbed-Yahweh poems (see Isa 42:1-4),[14] in which the work of the prophet is held to be religious and moral: the proclamation and explanation of Yahweh's demands and plan of salvation. The later, purely literary "prophets" have no special significance in this connection.[15]

We find, however, that whereas the older reforming prophets and several of the later prophets say nothing whatsoever about a personal relation to Yahweh's spirit, the consciousness of this relation reappears in Ezekiel and several of the later—chiefly literary—post-exilic prophets.

When, however, we come to the older reforming prophets we must go a step further. Several of them expressly reject the idea of inspiration in the form of possession by the spirit of Yahweh. They speak in a controversial tone of the *nebi'im* who are thus possessed and contrast their own differently conceived endowment with the spirit-endowment. It is very significant that the only passage in which Hosea speaks of the inspiring *ruaḥ* of the *nabi'* he does so in connection with a bitterly scornful repudiation of the common *nabi'* and all his works:

> The prophet is a fool,
> the man of the spirit is mad,
> because of your great iniquity
> and great hatred. (Hos 9:7b)[16]

The *nabi'* and man of spirit (*'iš ha-ruaḥ*) is "a fool [without morality]" (*'ewil*), and "mad" or "wild with folly" (*mešugga'*). Micah expressly emphasizes the difference between the *nebi'im* "who go about and utter wind and lies" (Mic 2:11a)[17] and himself, a man who is really "filled with power, justice, and might" (Mic 3:8). Is it a mere coincidence that, in describing the inanity—the "windiness"—of the ways and words of the *nebi'im* he employs just this word *ruaḥ* here in association with lying (*šeqer*) and deceit (*kazab*)? Does it not suggest that he is intentionally pointing out that Yahweh's *ruaḥ*, which the *nebi'im* boast of having within them, is really nothing but "wind" and illusion? The true prophet does not have spirit (*ruaḥ*) but power, justice, and might. Compare Isaiah's scornful caricature of the ecstatic glossolalia of the *nebi'im* (Isa 28:10).[18]

A similar scornful allusion to the *ruaḥ*-possession of the *nebi'im* may be found in Jeremiah; these ecstatic individuals, who have not got "the word" in them as Jeremiah has, will turn "into wind" (*l^e^ruaḥ*), that is, into nothingness (Jer 5:13; see note 33 below). If we ask why Jeremiah should choose the word *ruaḥ* to express this idea, although Hebrew has many other words meaning wind and nothingness, the answer is that he does so on purpose to suggest that the "spirit-men" will become what in fact they have always been: wind-men, nothing-men.

This attitude is, no doubt, closely connected with the repudiation of popular *nebi'ism* in general by the reforming prophets.[19] In the eyes of the reforming prophet the common *nabi'* is usually a deceiver and a cheat, at best a self-deceiver (1 Kgs 22:19-23), and always a person of low moral character (Amos 7:10-17; Hos 9:7-9; Mic 2:11; 3:5-8, 11; Isa 3:2-3; 28:7-10; Zeph 3:4; Jer 2:30; 5:13; 6:13; 14:18; 18:18; 23:9-22; Ezek 13:1-16; see also Lam 2:14). This disapproval is primarily founded on considerations of morality, as will be shown below. But it is certainly also connected with a dislike of their character and behavior generally (Hos 9:7; Amos 7:14;), evidently including in particular the wild orgiastic ecstasy that is ridiculed already in the Elijah legend with reference, of course, to the prophets of Baal (1 Kgs 18:26-29). But similar excesses on the part of Yahweh's prophets would doubtless have met with the same disapproval. The very frenzy or madness of the *nabi'*, in other words the ecstatic behavior that he and the common people accepted as proof of union with the deity, is regarded by Hosea as synonymous with "foolishness"—intellectual, moral, and religious abnormality and worthlessness. It is this that he attacks. This ecstatic frenzy, the senseless self-torture to which the body of the *nabi'* bears witness, moreover, is what the author of Zechariah 13 especially refers to when he declares that "the spirit of prophecy" is synonymous with a "spirit of uncleanness." That the *nabi'* was a *ruaḥ*-man, and that all the later professional *nebi'im* in early Jewish times, of whose behavior we get some idea from Nehemiah's ironic mention of them (Neh 6:7, 10-14), still claimed to possess Yahweh's spirit and to be actuated thereby, is evident even in Deutero-Zechariah (Zech 9:14). But this manifestation of *ruaḥ* in the *nabi'* is the very thing that makes him "unclean."

When, therefore, we find the reforming prophets either disregarding or expressing disapproval of the idea of Yahweh's spirit in the prophets, the explanation must be on the one hand that the *ruaḥ* idea was so palpably associated with extreme ecstatic manifestations of nebi'ism, and on the other that this ecstatic element in its primitive and exaggerated forms is very much toned down in the reforming prophets, whose own spiritual temper and attitude would, if anything, cause them to see such excesses in an unsympathetic light. In them the ecstatic substratum (viz., the mental concentration upon a single idea, a single passion) has assumed more tranquil forms. On the whole, little remains of the ecstatic element, apart from that which is the sound psychological substratum and core of religious ecstasy: the all-dominating, all-exclusive consciousness of having been called by Yahweh to deliver a religious and moral message. All external stimuli, such as dancing and music, have been abandoned. True, the state in which they deliver that message is "elevated," but it is also characterized by spiritual clarity and reasoned judgment. Their utterances are given in a finished artistic form; to the solemn words of judgment they generally add a clear, reasoned, moral and religious exposition; and their words do not come to them as a wild stammering glossolalia—as involuntary, unconscious words accompanied by unconscious reflex actions—but as moral and religious apprehensions of inexorable facts, apprehensions that "rise up" in them from the depths of the subconscious to attain lucidity, merging into their moral and religious personality. Apart from the occasional visions and auditions to which they allude, there is nothing about the reforming prophets suggestive of any markedly ecstatic experiences in the old "frenzied" form. Isaiah mentions once that he felt himself "seized" and pressed by "Yahweh's hand" (Isa 8:11). But when Micah apparently applies the distinctively ecstatic expression *hiṭṭîph* to himself and his fellow prophets, literally "to speak ecstatic words so that one froths at the mouth" (Mic 2:6), he is quoting a current phrase, but not one that he considers appropriate to his own behavior. Nor is the ecstatic element more in evidence in Deutero-Isaiah's lyrical enthusiasm and imagination than in the reforming prophets' proclamation of judgment.[20] Clear logical argument plays an important part in his utterances, particularly in the "disputations," where he sets himself to demonstrate that Yahweh is the only real God acting in all nature and history, who therefore has sent Cyrus and will not direct the course of history with a view to the restoration of Israel. Zechariah appears chiefly in the "seer's" role, using the old "vision of the night" form of prophecy.[21] And in the case of Haggai, Malachi, and Trito-Isaiah, not to mention the essentially literary Joel, there is no sign of ecstasy in its old extreme form. The latest literary prophets are, indeed, true literary prophets: men of letters in the full sense.[22] In them the old forms are a purely traditional mannerism. Altogether, it is chiefly in the visions of the prophets that the ecstatic element makes its appearance as an outward, visible phenomenon.[23]

This is connected with another point that deserves mention. The reforming prophets—to whom the inferior type of nebi'ism was so distasteful—evidently preferred to associate themselves in their forms of expression with the old seers,[24] who like themselves showed no tendency to pour out their words incoherently in a state of ecstatic excitement, but had them "whispered" to them by a divine being,[25] or saw them in "visions of the night." Accordingly the messenger formula, "Thus says Yahweh" (*koh 'amar Yhwh*),[26] or the old seer (*kahin*) formula, "the whisper of Yahweh" (*ne'um Yhwh*)[27] is the usual introductory or concluding formula of their utterances.[28] Ezekiel, on the other hand, being a true ecstatic of the older type, naturally ascribes his experiences to Yahweh's *ruaḥ*.[29]

It must not be inferred from what has been said above that the experiences of the literary prophets lacked that fundamental ecstatic character that would emerge when their whole consciousness, the sum of their emotions and will, centered upon a single idea and aim, to the exclusion of all side issues and restraints. In them, however, the ecstatic element is manifested not in convulsions, delirious frenzy, and glossolalia, but in tranquil visions and trances and in the consciousness that they have been given thoughts, words, and impulses that do not emanate from themselves.[30]

What is significant and important, however, is the circumstance that they use other expressions than those employed by the old *nebi'im* to describe their experiences (for example, "the spirit of Yahweh came upon me"). Instead, they say, "Yahweh showed me" (Amos 7:1, 4, 7; 8:1; 9:1; Jer 24:1), "I saw Yahweh sitting on a high throne" and "I heard Yahweh's voice" (Isa 6:1, 8), "the word of Yahweh came to me" (Jer 1:4, 11, 13; 16:1; 19:1; see also 29:12; 36:1, 27; 42:7; 43:8), and "Yahweh said to me" (Amos 7:14; Isa 8:1, 3, 5, 11; Jer 11:21; 15:1, 19). Or when something unexpected happens, we find "then I understood that it was the word of Yahweh" (Jer 32:8). In speaking of his ecstatic experiences Isaiah does not use the expression "Yahweh's spirit" but "the hand (of Yahweh) held me fast" (Isa 8:11), which is the characteristic term for the tranquil "merged" (apathic) form of ecstasy. In Jeremiah "Yahweh's hand" expresses the compelling, imperative nature of the prophetic call:

> I did not sit in the company of merry makers,
> nor did I rejoice;
> I sat alone, because your hand was upon me,
> for you had filled me with indignation. (Jer 15:17)

Their rejection of ordinary nebi'ism, again, does not mean that they had not at least as clear a conviction of their true prophetic call as the *nebi'im*. In the same breath that Amos repels the suggestion that he belongs to the guild of *nebi'im* he adds, "And Yahweh said to me, 'Go, prophesy (*hinnabe*') to my people Israel" (Amos 7:15b). And he considers the *nebi'im*, as such, to be valuable: "And I raised up some your sons for prophets" (Amos 2:11a). Jeremiah was a member of the organized temple *nebi'im* (Jer 20:1-2; 29:26-27), as Isaiah was as well (Isa 8:3).[31]

But this is not the decisive consideration, which is that they know they have received a special and express call from Yahweh to preach his word and predict the things to come (Isaiah 6; Jeremiah 1). They know that they have been "sanctified" (Jer 1:5), taken out of the ranks of the people to be servants of the deity, having their mouths consecrated for the words they are to speak (Isa 6:5-7; Jer 1:9). This prophetic call is not merely felt to be *certainty*, it is a *compelling force* upon them and in them from which they cannot escape: "The LORD Yahweh has spoken; who can but prophesy?" (Amos 3:8b). When Jeremiah tries to refuse his call: "If I say, 'I will not mention him, or speak any more in his name,' there is in my heart as it were a burning fire shut up in my bones, and I am weary with holding it in, and I cannot" (Jer 20:9). Woe to him if he fails to preach the word.[32]

Despite this, they never attest, to themselves or others, the genuineness of their call, nor explain the special nature of their experiences, by reference to "Yahweh's spirit." Such utterances as Amos's reply to Amaziah the priest show at once that he is conscious of a sharp distinction between himself and the ordinary *nebi'im*, "the mad spirit-men," as Hosea calls them. Compare also Micah's insistence upon the distinction between himself and the "windy" *nabi'* (Mic 3:8).

The reforming prophets use different words than the *nebi'im* to express their consciousness of their call. They also appeal to other criteria of the certainty of their call and of the genuineness and reality of that immediate contact with Yahweh himself that made them into prophets of a different and higher order than the "spirit-men."

YAHWEH'S WORD

If we consider the terms used by the prophets themselves, as mentioned above, and the stock formula used by the collectors of their utterances to indicate their prophetic inspiration, that is "Yahweh's word came to so-and-so," there can be no doubt that the basic reality that made the reforming prophets so certain of their call was *the word of Yahweh* (*debar Yhwh*). They feel that they are in possession of Yahweh's word (Isa 6:5-13; Jer 1:9; 5:14; 15:19; 20:9; 1 Kgs 17:24), unlike the common *nebi'im* who "will become wind; the word is not in them" (Jer 5:13a)[33] on account of their false predictions of prosperity. Jeremiah again uses the word *ruaḥ* for the "nothingness" that these *nebi'im* will become, almost certainly with intentional allusion to the spirit-men. It is true, of course, that the older *nebi'im* spoke of having the "word" in them; compare the obviously colloquial saying in Jer 18:18: "the law (*torah*) shall not perish from the priest, nor counsel (*'eṣah*) from the wise, nor the word (*dabar*) from the prophet." But this idea only acquired paramount importance in the reforming prophets.

What, then, is the prophets' conception of Yahweh's word?[34] In the first place a "word" in general did not mean to the ancient Israelite what we understand by a "mere word." The word is active, and it is filled with the speaker's "mental content"; his feelings, thoughts, and will issue in a word, which is also an act. One thinks "words" and does "words."[35] Yahweh's word is also an action. It is a real active force, a potency that Yahweh can "send forth" and that can "descend upon" a people with devastating effect (Isa 9:7).

> For as the rain and the snow come down from heaven,
> and return not thither but water the earth,
> making it bring forth and sprout,
> giving seed to the sower and bread to the eater,
> so shall my word be that goes forth from my mouth;
> it shall not return to me empty,
> but it shall accomplish that which I purpose,
> and prosper in the thing for which I sent it. (Isa 55:10-11)

The word is "like fire . . . and like a hammer which breaks rock in pieces" (Jer 23:29). The prophet feels it within himself "like fire in his bones" and must necessarily give utterance to it (Jer 20:9). Its hammer-like force crushes all resistance on the part of the prophet, also his natural feelings and proclivities.[36] But Yahweh's word is also a command.[37] It is given audibly, sometimes by a messenger, and must be obeyed. The word has an urgency that does not derive from the authority of the servant who brings it, but from that of the sender. The prophet can discuss it with Yahweh and be aware that it is quite different from what he wishes himself.

It follows that there is a difference between Yahweh's word and the prophet's own words, ideas, feelings, and so on. Whereas all the words spoken by the ecstatic spirit-possessed *nabi'* in his ecstasy were supposed to be divine words, the prophets see a distinction even in the *form,* and this distinction gradually becomes clearer, being clearest of all in Jeremiah.[38] Not everything they know and desire is Yahweh's word. When it comes it *may* confirm "what is in their own heart" (Amos 7:1-3, 4-6). But it may, on the other hand, refute and repudiate this (Amos 8:2; Isa 6:5-13; Jer 1:6-10; 12:1-5; 14:11; 15:1-2, 10-21; 16:1-13; 17:16; 28:6, 12-16). The prophet must wait till the word comes (Jer 28:6-9; 42:1-7; also Hab 2:1; Isa 21:6-10).

But how can the prophets distinguish? How can they know that what "comes to them" is Yahweh's word? This question is bound up with another: How did the word come to them?

We need to consider the more popular, factual, and—for the prophet's consciousness of vocation—altogether irrelevant criterion that the word proves itself to be Yahweh's word by being fulfilled (Jer 28:9; see also 12:1-5; 17:15). The prophets frequently saw that their words were not fulfilled, and yet they probably continued to believe that they were speaking Yahweh's word (Isa 5:19; Jer 17:15; see also Isa 8:16-18; Mic 7:1-7). It was just one of the problems of their faith.

Unquestionably the psychological form of their experience had a certain significance.[39] We know that the great reforming prophets had experiences of an ecstatic nature. Things they saw and heard Yahweh say in their visions, things that reached their ears externally as voices in their auditions, would be Yahweh's word.[40] But actual visions and auditions appear to have been comparatively rare.[41] A traditional stock formula like "Thus says Yahweh" does not justify the inference that genuine "external" auditions are referred to.[42] On the other hand, it is quite clear that the prophets speak and act in a state of mental high tension, their whole mind so completely concentrated upon a single feeling, idea, and impulse that every other form of external or internal influence that is not connected with the dominating idea and feeling fades and disappears—is uncoupled, as it were—while every inhibition is removed.[43] This is precisely the condition that is the essential characteristic of ecstasy.

Ecstasy in the medical sense only means those extreme cases of this mental condition in which the external phenomena become very conspicuous. In the above-mentioned state of heightened mental concentration and tension, the ideas, thoughts, impulses, etc., that in one way or another have been created in a person will rise above the threshold of consciousness, and in a flash attain sudden clarity. This often occurs both in artistic and scientific work. In this state, moreover, impressions, thoughts, etc., may be concentrated into visual and auditory hallucinations and illusions—into visions and auditions that seem to come from without and impinge upon the outer senses. Psychologically, the visions and auditions of the prophets are of this sort; in reality all their experiences are inner experiences. And they are aware of this themselves. When they employ the vague expression "Yahweh's word came to me" instead of the rarer "I saw," "Yahweh showed me," or "I heard," "Yahweh revealed himself in my ear," and the like, they do so precisely in order to express this inner perception of the coming of Yahweh's word, without, of course, having given a thought to psychological explanations.

It is obviously strong evidence that the word has been given to them when the word suddenly comes to them in this way—when, in a flash, the idea and image are there and involuntarily (Jer 17:16)[44] become rhythmic words, "God-given speech"[45]—on their lips. They do not speak from their own spirit or their own heart. To this extent, then, the ecstatic element is a criterion, even if the prophets do not connect it with Yahweh's *ruaḥ*. On the contrary, they stress that the word comes directly from Yahweh himself.

Here, however, the formal criterion is combined with another—an inner content. Jeremiah speaks, as we have seen, of Yahweh's word that comes like fire and the stroke of a hammer. This certainly refers to the irresistible manner in which the prophet felt the "word" surge up from the depth of his soul. But there is also a suggestion of something in the content of the word that breaks the resistance within him. It is something torturing—a fire that is unbearable unless it can find an outlet (Jer 20:9). It is a power, but a strange, unfamiliar power.[46] In short, not only that which comes suddenly and mightily, but that which comes unexpectedly, surprisingly, contrary to reasonable expectation—"the irrational"—is Yahweh's word. The prophet sits by the cauldron until it boils over, and he is struck by the fact that it boils over *from the north.* This becomes a symbol, a vision from Yahweh meaning that evil is blowing over the land from the north (Jer 1:13-14). He meditates on the almond tree—the "watching tree," as the Israelites called it. Why does it blossom without leaves, unlike all the other trees? And the tree becomes a symbol, a vision, a word of Yahweh meaning "I am watching over my word to perform it" (Jer 1:12). Jerusalem is besieged; the prophet has long been sure that the end is near, that the city will be taken and destroyed, the surrounding country pillaged and the inhabitants carried away into captivity. One day Jeremiah's kinsman comes and asks him to buy a piece of land in Anathoth of which Jeremiah has the first right of redemption. What need has he of this land? Is this a time to add to one's property? In a city, too, which is already taken by the Chaldeans, sacked and laid waste? Senseless folly! And yet, how strange that his kinsman should be the one to come with such an offer at such a time. "Then I knew that this was the word of Yahweh" (Jer 32:8b).[47]

Certainly this cannot be taken as an infallible test. Doubt may even be entertained as to whether the prophets themselves were clear on the subject. And we find no unmistakable signs in the case of the older reforming prophets. To them the main thing would be the element of sudden emergence, filling their whole being with a fierce zeal that drives out everything else. Thus the wrath of Amos, when he is sent away from Bethel, turns at once into Yahweh's wrath; in the prophet's consciousness it assumes the form of another terrible prediction of evil awaiting Amaziah (Amos 7:16-17). And the same thing happens in Isaiah's case when King Ahaz refuses his offer of a sign (Isa 7:10-17). Yet even for these prophets there is a certain element of authenticating "strangeness" in their visions and the rhythmical form their words assume. To Jeremiah, on the other hand, in whom the appreciation of this "strangeness" is, consciously or unconsciously, more evident, the fearful intensity of the overpowering zeal surging up in him is proof that Yahweh's indignation has filled him and that it is finding a vent in Yahweh's operative word (Jer 6:9-11; 43:8-13; 44:15-19, 24-30). The more sudden, unexpected, improbable in content, strange, and unreasonable a word of this nature appears, the more surely is it the word of Yahweh. The "lying prophet" speaks the things he and the people desire (Jer 23:16-22). The true prophet predicts things that cause himself and his audience to become apprehensive; for it is not the *nabi'*—called to secure good fortune and victory for the people by his efficacious words—who is the true prophet but the prophet of disaster (Jer 28:8-9).

Is a word of this kind necessarily Yahweh's word? Cannot a prophet "prophesy by" (be inspired by) Baal or some other demon (Jer 2:8; 23:13)? What guarantee does he have that the spirit has not turned into a lying spirit within him (1 Kgs 22:22)? Here we find that the reforming prophets quite consciously adopt as their criterion not merely the dimly realized standard of irrationality, but (what in reality stands on a higher plane) the clear purport, the moral and religious content of the word. This is not only a formal but a factual mark of genuineness.

Before going further, however, we must inquire into what this single idea is, which engrosses the whole mind of the prophets and underlies their ecstatic states and experiences. There can be no doubt that it is the zeal or passion (*qin'ah*) for Yahweh Sabaoth—found in its classic form as a program in the Elijah legend (1 Kgs 19:10)—for his honor and might, for his recognition as being what he is: the one who alone works and acts. But this, it should be observed, does not mean Yahweh as the exclusive God of the covenant and the nation, but as the Being who is at once holy, terrible, jealous, and morally just. The flipside is also relevant: Israel's terrible sinfulness—religious and moral—which is a flagrant insult in the sight of the holy and righteous God. This idea is, moreover, the prophets' chief criterion of Yahweh's word.

The prophets maintain that they—in contrast to the people and their priests and *nebi'im*—"know Yahweh" (Hos 4:1, 6; 5:4; 6:3, 6; Jer 2:8; 5:3; 8:7; 9:2, 5; 22:16; see also Isa 11:2, 9; Hos 2:22; 8:2; 10:12 [LXX]). They expect the people to have this "knowledge," and the fact that the Israelites lack it is the cause of their sins; for in Hebrew "knowing" includes the ability to act in conformity with the knowledge. When the prophets speak of knowing Yahweh they mean that they have an intimate union, a kind of mutual confidential relation.[48] Acquaintance, "friend," and "kinsman" are synonymous conceptions in the Hebrew language, opposed to the "stranger" who is outside the tribe and therefore, as a rule, an "enemy." The statement that Yahweh has "known" the prophet from his mother's womb means that he has chosen him to be his trusted ambassador, spokesman, and representative (Jer 1:5).[49] A parallel expression is the statement that Yahweh has "sanctified" him so that he is no longer an ordinary man. The prophet has really stood in Yahweh's "confidential council" (*sôd*; Jer 23:18, 21; 1 Kgs 22:19-23), and knows what his plans and wishes are.

If a being is to be "known," an obvious prerequisite is the possession of certain constant attributes and reactions—constant essential characteristics of feeling, will, and action. This rules out from the conception of Yahweh the wholly arbitrary, incalculable, capricious, "demonic" qualities so often associated with Yahweh in earlier times.[50] The "irrational" mystery of the deity no longer dominates the conception of him; a "rational" quality has been introduced.[51] "In himself" Yahweh cannot be comprehended by the human mind (Ps 139:6, 17-18; Isa 55:8). And no mortal eye can bear to see the glory of his countenance (Exod 33:20). But in his dealings with humanity there is a changelessness that conforms to a law of his own being; and this obedience to law, which is known to himself (Jer 29:11), can also be "known" by those to whom he has revealed himself.[52] To say that a prophet knows Yahweh means that he knows this element of law inherent in Yahweh's nature; that he knows the feelings Yahweh entertains toward people and how he reacts when they oppose his will; that he knows the demands Yahweh makes and his plan for the people, whether they obey or disobey his demands.

To give a summary definition of the qualities that, in the prophets' view, distinguish the nature of Yahweh in relation to humanity is comparatively easy. Yahweh is the holy one (Isa 5:16; 6:5; 8:12-15; 30:15), who reacts with terrible might against the outrage that is committed when people fail to do what he demands of them (Hos 11:8-9; Isa 1:18-20; 2:10-22). And he is the righteous one (Isa 5:7) whose reactions to the violation of his holiness consist precisely in doing "judgment" (*mišpaṭ*) and being "exalted in justice" (Isa 5:16).[53] Over against humans, his nature is determined by what he demands of them: it is justice (*mišpaṭ*), righteousness (*ṣedaqah*), good will (*ḥesed*), and faithfulness (*'emunah*), all of which express action in the moral and social sphere. Just as humans maintain justice in the covenant by keeping everyone in the place they deserve and for which they have the spiritual qualifications, with all the rights and the mutual responsibility inherent in the covenant—the oppressed receiving justice (being "justified") and the oppressor restrained and punished—so also is Yahweh's nature seen to be governed by a righteous will and mode of action. He keeps a vigilant watch to see that the proper state of things is maintained, intervening whenever it is disturbed. And if this intervention mainly and almost entirely takes the form of meting out just punishment to the unjust leaders of the people, it should be remembered that this accords with the prophets' view of the actual condition of Israel and of their own vocation as prophets of judgment.

To "know Yahweh," then, means to know him as a God whose nature and mode of action is governed by these moral norms. When Hosea defines what is demanded (viz., the essence of religion on the part of humans) as tantamount to "knowledge of God" and "good will" (*ḥesed*; Hos 6:6), he does not think of human conduct in relation to God, taking the first, for instance, as a more intellectual and theoretical and the second as a more emotional relation to God. On the contrary, these expressions serve jointly to describe the way in which people should behave toward one another. *Ḥesed* does not mean "love" but the mutual relation of the people within the covenant.[54] The knowledge of God is an intellectual *activity* that, though God is its primary object, is here thought of as the necessary condition for the proper exercise of *ḥesed*. Thus the two terms combine to form a single conception: the active spirit of fraternity toward one's fellow humans that springs from a knowledge of Yahweh's nature and demands. Religion is knowledge of God converted into right-minded activity; religion = doing what Yahweh demands = morality.[55] In modern language (which the prophets did not use), this simply means that Yahweh's essential nature is morality and justice (*mišpaṭ*).[56]

In light of this conception of religion and of the nature of Yahweh, the prophets are able to determine whether the word that comes to them is Yahweh's word. It must accord with what they "know" of Yahweh himself.

This entails in the first place the formal requirement that the word should not be something purely arbitrary and incomprehensible: it must have a clear, rational content and purpose. To the word of Yahweh that the prophets possess and proclaim they often give the name *torah* (Isa 1:10; 8:16; 30:9; see also 42:4, 31).[57] *Torah* is literally the priest's "instruction," which originally meant an oracle, and afterwards came to mean a cult-ritual, legal and moral direction—sometimes in reply to a definite inquiry; from this it acquired the sense of a precept, a law. When the prophets adopt this word, the first implication is that the word they preach is a clearly conceived word of unmistakable purport, indicating the proper line of conduct. It is no mysterious, ambiguous oracle or ecstatic glossolalia, as the word of the *nebi'im* so often was (Isa 28:10). A direction or "guide" must be clear, rational, and easy to understand.

Further, however, the content of the word must be factually up to the standard and able to pass the test of the prophet's insight into the moral nature of Yahweh. That is the second point implied by the use of *torah*, "(divine) instruction." The prophetic word is not regarded primarily as a prediction (*nebûah*) or an oracle (*maśśa'*)—words that rarely occur in the reforming prophets—but as a "guide" to the right action that accords with Yahweh's nature and demands.[58] The true prophet and the true word of Yahweh must call good "good" and evil "evil" (Isa 5:20).[59] The prophet who can say "Peace, peace" to such a sinful people as Israel is a lying prophet (Jer 6:14). Just as the value of the *nabi'* must be judged by his moral character (such things as harlotry, drunkenness, avarice, and deception will obviously stamp him as a lying *nabi'* (Jer 23:14; Mic 2:11; 3:5), so also must his prophecies be judged by their relation to the moral law. A *nabi'* whose prophecies of good fortune "strengthen the hands of evildoers" does not have the word in him, but on the contrary "despises the word of Yahweh" (Jer 23:14, 17).

On moral as well as "numinous" grounds, therefore, Jeremiah maintains that the prophet of disaster is the normal prophet who needs no further credentials. So in opposition to the later literary editors and modern "positive" theologians, he declares with absolute conviction that all the earlier genuine prophets were prophets of disaster (Jer 28:8). Unquestionably he has in mind such men as Amos, Hosea, Isaiah, Micah, and Zephaniah. The reason Jeremiah's burning indignation seems to him to be Yahweh's indignation (which he is expressly bidden to pour out upon great and small, young and old, in the form of fierce, portentous, threatening words) is that his own indignation is moral, provoked by the dishonesty and deceitfulness of the people (Jer 6:9-14).

This moral criterion of Yahweh's word is already expressed in the plainest language by Micah. Contrasting himself with the *nebi'im* and their *ruaḥ*, "which leads Yahweh's people astray" and suits the prediction to a tee, he says:

> But as for me, I am filled with power,
>   and with justice and might,
> to declare to Jacob his transgression
>   and to Israel his sin. (Mic 3:8)

The true prophet and the true word of Yahweh call sin "sin" and transgression "transgression."[60] To do this, Micah is endowed by Yahweh with "power" and "heroic might." The old prophets believed that they had a similar endowment. But in their case the power was first and foremost the magic, wonder-working power—extolled, for instance, by the Elisha legends (2 Kgs 2:19-25; 4:1—8:15; 13:14-21)—while in Micah's case it is the power to wield the scourge of chastisement and bear the attacks that this action would inevitably provoke. And what is significant, Micah here uses the word "power" instead of "the spirit," which in the view of the older *nebi'im* was the vehicle and instrument of the power (Isa 11:2-9).[61] Indeed, it is doubly significant in the light of a passage like Zech 4:6, where in the earlier manner Yahweh's wondrous spirit is contrasted with (human) power. Micah is also endowed with "judgment" (*mišpaṭ*): the faculty of judging, acting rightly. The word connotes, as do all the corresponding synonyms, both the faculty of knowing what is right—a sense of right or moral judgment, as we would say—and the will and ability to bring it to bear, to uphold the fundamental law of the covenant, giving to everyone what justice dictates: rewards and redress to the good, and punishment to the evil.[62] The ability to keep the community faithful to the right social, moral, and religious customs, which in earlier days was ascribed to and expected of the chief or king,[63] is here claimed by the prophet, who exercises it by proclaiming Yahweh's judgments with divine, effectual words that will soon cause judgment to be executed so thoroughly that Israel will lie dead. It is precisely on account of the inability shown by the ordinary nebi'ism—under the ecstatic influence of the Spirit—to "discern spirits" (1 Kgs 22:22; see Prov 16:2), that is to test the words they are driven to speak by a rational and objective criterion, that the prophets dissociate themselves from the idea of the Spirit.

This view of the real criteria of Yahweh's word is fully in conformity with the prophets' attitude to *Yahweh's law*. In the eyes of their contemporaries, Yahweh's laws (*toroth*) were the accepted rights, usages, and customs, as well as the special priestly tradition of cult ritual, canon law, and civil law. Whether it was written or unwritten mattered not at all. As custom and usage, it was more deeply rooted in people's minds than any written law could implant it; as priestly tradition it possessed all the sanctity that the cult ritual and sacrificial ordinances owned for the people of those days.

The reforming prophets also regard it as a sin that the people scorn Yahweh's law (Isa 5:24; 30:9; Jer 6:19; Hos 8:1-12; Hab 1:4). It is an important part of their vocation to utter warnings and threats against such conduct. But the decision as to whether a sacred traditional custom or rule is Yahweh's law does not depend upon such formal criteria as the fact of its belonging to the legal or sacrificial tradition of the priests or being found in some venerable book such as, for example, the Yahwist Sinai narrative. To begin with, the prophets' rejection of the sacrificial cult is a departure from what was then supposed to be the sacred law of Yahweh (Amos 2:6-8; 5:21-24; Hos 6:6; Isa 1:10-17; Mic 6:1-8; Jer 6:20; 7:8-15; 11:15). And the fact that they expressly mention justice (*mišpaṭ*), righteousness (*ṣedaqah*), good will (*ḥesed*), and walking humbly before God as the proper substitute for the cult shows that they recognize Yahweh's law by the criterion of its content—the test of its correspondence with their religious and moral consciousness and their apprehension of Yahweh as a moral God, who exacts true piety of heart. When in Jeremiah's time the people of Judah find a new Book of Yahweh's law, and having carried out a religious reform and cast out all foreign cults believe that they are assured Yahweh's favor, Jeremiah still asserts that they despise and have no "knowledge" of Yahweh's law, laying stress once more on the *moral* sins (Jer 5:1-17; 6:19; 7:28; 8:5-7, 9; 9:2-9; 12:8; 13:23-27; 17:1-4). When the people also pride themselves on the law and say, "We are wise" (that is, we have all needful understanding and "knowledge of God"), "and the law of Yahweh is with us," the prophet argues clearly and trenchantly that a law that does not place the moral commandments first cannot be Yahweh's law. "But, behold, the false pen of the scribes has made it into a lie" (Jer 8:8).

CONCLUSION

The result of this survey, then, is that the reforming prophets emphatically stress the fact that they have received Yahweh's word and are furnished with religious, rational, and moral criteria for knowing what really is his word. But they do not derive their power from or authenticate their prophetic call by the conception of Yahweh's spirit (*ruaḥ*)—which, in fact, they have rejected—but by their own consciousness of possessing his word. To them this means a word that is authenticated by expressing Yahweh's moral nature and demands, and the prophet's own knowledge of God and moral sense. Yahweh's word resembles Yahweh's law in being recognizable by its content rather than by its form. The test is religious and moral, an "apprehension" or "knowledge" of God—not the ecstatic *ruaḥ* and mystical union of divine possession.

Here then we are confronted with the peculiar trait that something of the same dread of Yahweh's "holy" person that induced the old *nebi'im* to substitute the divine spirit (*ruaḥ*) for the deity itself also prompts the later prophets of the moral reformation to avoid the *ruaḥ* idea and appeal to Yahweh's word instead. The difference is that for the latter, holiness is associated with justice (Isa 5:16), and morality is placed before everything. They do not see any holiness in the unusual, wild, and ecstatic. Yahweh's nature is clearly and definitely moral, and his gift to the prophet is the clear, intelligible, moral word that speaks of justice, uprightness, fraternity, and humility before God.

It is clear, moreover, from all that has been said here, that the Spirit is used in Ezekiel as the obvious expression for the ecstatic motive power that, in visions and the like, lifts him up and transports him from one place to another. And when in connection with this idea the prophet, again as a matter of course, traces the impulse and ability to speak the word of prophecy back to the Spirit of Yahweh that comes upon him, the explanation is that Ezekiel (unlike the older reforming prophets) is a true ecstatic of the ancient type, even though he shares the reforming prophets' moral and religious ideas.

In the later prophets the Spirit reappears, as we have seen. This is connected with their ideological "throw back" to the older nebi'ism of the national religious type. In relation to the reforming prophets they are merely epigonic and were probably not aware of the gulf between the reformers and the old *nebi'im*. Still, there is a distinction between these prophet-epigoni and the older nebi'ism. In the former the Spirit is no longer an ecstatically experienced power but a traditional formula. The main thing is their consciousness of a call and of the special endowment received with it. This is described in traditional language. The assertion that they have Yahweh's spirit is a comprehensive expression meaning that they have to deliver a moral and religious message from Yahweh (Isa 61:1-4; also 42:1).

The fact that late Jewish rabbinic and subsequent Christian theological theory have made "the Holy Spirit" into the medium or source of prophetic and scriptural inspiration is due (like so much that goes by the name of theology) not to lending an attentive ear to the pulse of life and the witness of living prophets but to theoretical, speculative preoccupation with "sacred" literary documents. It is also due to a heightening and systematizing (not without rationalizing and loss of content) of precisely the comparatively primitive elements of prophecy. In a rationalized form, these are employed to explain the essentials of the whole movement.

But the connecting link here is the purely conventional and diluted sense of the word "spirit," even in the latest prophets and still more in the deuteronomistic, canonical conception of prophecy. According to these, the prophets and the spirit are no longer living realities (Zech 1:5-6) but blessings once enjoyed in classical history, which will only be accorded again to humanity in the eschatological epoch (Joel 3).

11

The Prophets and the Temple Cult

Introduction

If the prophetic elements in the Psalter presuppose a cultic reality, this is an indication that the communication of the divine replies must have had a firm place in the cult. That will strike us initially as a bit unusual. We find it natural, to be sure, that the cult—and thus also the cult liturgy—must have contained a sacramental moment. But the idea that we ordinarily connect with the word "prophecy" apparently does not correspond to the idea we have of cult. After all, we are accustomed to finding in the "prophetic" the antithesis of the "cultic." And at first glance there appears to us to be an unbridgeable gulf between the fixed forms and formulas of the cult and the free inspiration of prophecy.

In fact, a connection does exist between them. In Israel it appears in that the priest is often at the same time the one who reveals God (see below). The priest can mediate revelation through technical means; thus it was the priest who used the Urim and Thummim (Num 27:21; 1 Sam 28:6; Ezra 2:63). But as an officeholder the priest can also be the one who enjoys a special inspiration that adheres to the officeholder and that is transmitted by succession or initiation into an office: to whom God gives the office, he also gives understanding, in this case inspiration, the prophetic gift. Thus, according to late Judean belief, the high priest has the gift of prophecy (John 11:51).

We have already indicated that we are not using the word "prophetic" in the usual sense of the word in Old Testament history of religion. In itself, the concept "prophetic" is a formal concept. But in theological discourse it has usually received a very precise content. And the very fact that a formal concept usually, but not always, is used with a precise content has contributed, I think, to the squabbling over what is and what is not "prophetic" in Israelite religion.[1] Many scholars use the word in an imprecise manner and are themselves unclear about which meaning they are employing.

In this context I do not, as apparently is usually the case, understand by "prophetic" those trends, persons, and thoughts in Old Testament religion that are also represented, among others, by the so-called "literary prophets," who emphasize the ethical and the anti-cultic, and in part certainly also the personal side of religion. I am taking the word here precisely in the original, formal sense. I understand the "prophet" here as one who, by appointment of society as well as by the deity, provides the community with necessary information concerning religious things directly from a divine source by virtue of an extraordinary supply of power. The prophet is one who definitely knows about divine things, either through inspiration, through the capability to receive revelations, or through access to technical means allowing the mediation of divine will and instructions in order to convey answers to questions or prayers originating from the community. In this sense of the word, the prophet is not altogether a private person who coincidentally appears but an employee of the society, an institutional link between the two members of the covenant—the community and the deity. In this sense the Babylonian-Assyrian religions had their prophets, as did the Greek religions and those of Syria and Asia Minor, and in this sense the primitive religions generally had their prophets, whether called priests, shamans, medicine men, or whatever term might be used.

It is obvious, however, that with this word alone nothing is said about the value or lack of value in the different sorts of these manifestations. Rather, this question is everywhere dependent on the sort of religious and moral content that the various forms have held. In many places the institution of the prophet did nothing to bring the development of the religion to higher levels. In Israel, by contrast, for reasons that do not interest us here, it became the basis of one of the most significant influences in religious and moral development.

Every cult, as far as its contents are concerned, consists of two elements: the sacrificial and the sacramental, as Christian scholars of liturgics have often expressed it. In place of these terms, however, we might also say the human and the prophetic. We should not understand this in such a way that the two elements are apportioned purely externally to congregation and to liturgist; the liturgist, the priest, can appear as the one who conveys the sacramental, as well as the sacrificial. Sacrificial elements are actions and words that come from the community—from the people—and addressed to the deity, such as offerings, prayers, and complaints. Sacramental elements are actions and words in which the deity speaks to the people and deals with them through benedictions, answers to prayer, consecrations, sacraments in the strict sense of the word, and so on.

Since the cult is composed of both these elements and consists of speech and response, action and counteraction, it takes on dramatic characteristics and becomes a drama. And since it is directed toward something and produces something—and this it always does—this drama is a creative act, a real, creative drama.[2]

In some form the sacramental, the prophetic, exists in every cult. And because it appears in the form of words, we must speak about prophetic words in the cult. Since almost every cult, except perhaps those from certain extreme Protestant movements, begins with the presumption that the transmission of such prophetic words cannot come from just anyone, but rather that certain personal qualifications are necessary, the cult almost always has certain functionaries whose task and privilege it is to be bearers of the cultic word of the prophet. That is, the cult has special cult prophets. It need not always be the case that the cult prophet is a different person from one of the actual liturgists; liturgist and cult prophet can be combined in one person. In other cases, however, the cult under consideration has certain officials who function exclusively or primarily as cult prophets. Then we distinguish between liturgist, that is, the priest in the actual sense, and the cult prophet. In Israel, as we shall see, both cases appear.

The personal qualifications associated with the office of cult prophets consist of special equipment, a special gift of power or inspiration that makes them bearers of the prophetic word. This gift of power distinguishes them from the laity. And where the cult prophet is different from the priest, occasionally the gift of power is also different from that of the priest. Thus in Israel, where the priest emphasizes a serious calling, the cult prophet, as do prophets generally, emphasizes a free inspiration by the spirit.

When the prophetic word appears as part of the cult, we can think of two cases and see them demonstrated. The liturgically fixed elements—for every cult insists on fixed forms of an "agenda" and sees in them a guarantee of its holiness and effectiveness—need only be the matrix of the prophetic appearance; the form and content of the words are left more or less to the genuine momentary inspiration of the individual prophet who appears. Or else the content of the words is also fixed in the agenda; only the style and form of the words that are proclaimed there in the name of the deity are the product of a free, momentary inspiration. The transition between these two forms is fluid insofar as it frequently may also be true that in the first case the content is also prescribed for the particular prophet delivering the divine announcement; he has to prophesy as the authorities wish (1 Kgs 22:5-13). Only the more precise poetic formulation of the words is then left to the prophet.

If the Psalms are really cultic psalms, and if therefore we are examining psalms that are cultic prophecies, it is thus probable from the very outset that we are dealing with words of God of the second of the two different types mentioned above. For these pronouncements in Yahweh's name through the mouth of a prophet are usually to be considered elements in the agenda of a fixed, frequently repeated liturgy whose content as well as form are prescribed for official reasons. The divine answer is then not "inspired" anew each time but rather prescribed by the "agenda." Then all that remains for free inspiration in the worship service is the prophetic form.

But here an intermediate form is also conceivable and probable. This or that prophetic psalm may originally have come into existence as the product of a momentary, subjective, genuine inspiration at a time when it was left to the prophet's free inspiration to produce the formulation and in part perhaps also the content of the words. Precisely this kind of oracle was regarded as exemplary and therefore later became associated in the agenda with a certain cultic celebration. This is almost certainly the case with the oracle in Psalm 60 (see below). I also have the impression that this is the way it happened with most of the royal oracles.

Here the pious reader of the Bible may object to this notion that the production of inspired prophecies, yet with prescribed contents, was a responsibility of the cult prophets—and consider it a profanation of the psalms. It would certainly almost lead to a conscious hypocrisy of the authors involved; something like that should not be ascribed to the holy men of the holy scriptures. But the profanation of the psalms is not nearly as great as the orthodox profanation that lies in suddenly regarding such a burning, fervent cry from the depths as Psalm 22 or Psalm 69 not as real prayers but as "prophecies" of Christ. How the pious could tolerate and endure this mockery of prayer life for centuries is something I simply cannot comprehend.

But if we think about this a bit more carefully, we shall realize that the interpretation mentioned above concerning the "prophetic" psalms in question is not a disparagement of them at all.

First, if we are correct that people with prophetic gifts and inspiration had their place and calling in the fixed order of the cult, the fact remains that these prophetic psalms—that unquestionably come from the circles of cultic functionaries—were certainly composed by prophetically gifted people. The initial origin of the psalm may then be an "inspiration"; nevertheless, they were written by people who were filled with the consciousness of their calling and their gift of being able to proclaim the will of God. Whether we share this conviction depends precisely on the impression of personal genuineness that the individual psalms can awaken. Let me note that, in my opinion, the prophetic psalms of the Psalter enjoy a pre-eminent position. I sense more of what is genuine and personally experienced in Psalms 73, 122, 123, 126, 130, and 131.

Second, we have to say that we must distinguish between spiritual origin and practical use. The subsequent practical use cannot degrade the origin. On the contrary, the noble origin justifies the subsequent practical use. Thus the

Christian pastoral minister—whether priest or lay—has an unshakable right to apply to any Christian seeking help the "revelations" of Jesus that promise forgiveness of sins to very specific individuals in his time and thus to claim that in these words God is speaking through me to you. In so doing the minister will be neither a hypocrite nor a deceiver, and the words of the Lord will not be dragged into the dirt.

THE SEER AND THE PRIEST

As already indicated, cultic prophecies presuppose a firm connection between prophets and holiness, or, if one prefers, between the priestly and prophetic calling and person. That the priest gave divine replies to certain questions, that is, oracles, is sufficiently known. These oracles are the so-called *tôrôt* (sing. *tôrah*), the same word that later became the all-encompassing designation of the divine law. The priestly *tôrôt* have their own style.[3] But now it is noteworthy that it is not this priestly torah-style, but the "nabiistic" oracle-style that we encounter in the Psalter. In Israel the *nabi'* (pl. *nebi'im*) is the real bearer of the divine revelations (see Deut 18:9-22).

Older than the *nabi'*, however, is the seer (*rô'eh* or *ḥôzeh;* see 1 Sam 9:9), who, however, in the course of time merged with the *nabi'*. The seer's forms of revelation—vision, nocturnal apparition, dream—were taken over by the *nabi*.[4] The *nabi'* is demonstrably of non-Israelite origin, as is already indicated by the foreign word *nabi',* whose root appears nowhere else in Hebrew, although it does occur in Assyrian;[5] "nabi'ism" is a common Canaanite manifestation. But in all probability "seerism" is genuinely Israelite. The type of the seer is Samuel, and a form of this type is Moses; not until the later tradition are both of them turned into *nebi'im* to correspond to the changed situation at the time.

But it is true that the ancient Israelite seer is a priest at the same time. As we said, his type is Samuel. The redactional note in 1 Sam 3:21, which calls him a *nabi'*, is not part of the original content of the tradition. This Samuel belonged to the temple in Shiloh ever since birth. He is a disciple and apprentice of the priest Eli and is his assistant in performing his priestly office: he cares for Yahweh's lamps in the sanctuary. The account of the first revelation to Samuel is now abbreviated for the sake of the later legends that make him into a judge over all Israel. It is really arranged in order to correspond with the account of Samuel's assumption of the priesthood after the death of the old teacher and the collapse of his godless house.

Samuel's priestly position is also presupposed in the account in 1 Samuel 9. It is closely related to the altar (*bamah*): no sacrificial meal takes place without him. He first must have blessed the sacrificial meal. The cultic blessing, however, is a priestly calling. Even the later accounts of 1 Sam 13:7b-15a and 15:1-35 know Samuel's relationship to the sacrificial worship.

Like Samuel, Moses is also a priest and seer. Numbers 12:6-8 places him high above a *nabi'*. Samuel too stands higher than the *nebi'im* who are subject and obedient to him (1 Sam 19:20). The passages in Deut 18:15; 34:10; and Hos 12:13, which make him into a *nabi'* are deuteronomistic.

Like Samuel, Moses entered into training for the priesthood, with his father-in-law Jethro (Exod 18:14-27). He is the priestly mediator at the establishment of the covenant between Yahweh and Israel (Exod 24:8). He is the custodian of the holy tent of revelation, the portable sanctuary, and he presents before Yahweh the affairs of the people and of individuals (Exod 33:7-11). As a priest he is at the same time a revealer to whom Yahweh conveys his will. In Yahweh's name he makes decisions of legal and cultic nature. And finally, his descendants become priests after him (Judg 18:30).

That the priests as such were still mediators of revelation in a later period of history is something we can see elsewhere. They are the bearers of the ephod and, as such, they deliver oracle replies (1 Sam 14:3, 18-19, 37, 41-42; 22:18).

We also find that seers were people who were officially appointed. David had his own seers at court (2 Sam 24:11). But someone officially appointed as a seer has little to do with free inspiration; his activity is of a priestly sort.

In reality, this connection between priestly and prophetic is of great antiquity, and, as we have said, very widely attested. We also find other traces of it in the soil of the Semitic world. In Assyria there was a special class of priests that was called *barû*, that is, seers. It has long been noted that there is a hint of an original connection in the Arabic equivalent (*kahin*) of the Hebrew *kohen*, which also means seer.

The connection, or better, the identity, of the two offices rests upon the fact that the seer-priest was originally the one gifted with extraordinary power (*mana*), who because of this also had the discernment to associate with the deity. The gift of "seeing," prophesying, and performing wonders, moreover, are interrelated. Moses the priest is a great wonder worker, who with his miraculous staff performed the most remarkable feats (Exod 4:1-5; 7:14-24; 8:16-19);[6] so were the *nebi'im* (1 Kgs 17:7-24; 2 Kgs 1:9-16; 2:8, 14, 19-25; 3:16-20; 4:1—8:6). That the priest is the one who has the power under certain circumstances also to function as seer and soothsayer is indicated by the common Semitic word for priest, *kômer, kûmrah*, etc., whose basic meaning is "the fervent one," that is, the one with power.[7]

The ancient Semitic type of priest is who we meet in the unity of the sanctifier. This one, in certain circumstances, is the priest offering sacrifices and the soothsayer (seer, prophet).

In the Israelite evaluation of the monarchy we find the same presupposition that it is the gift of power that equips one to fill the priestly office as well as to soothsay and to prophesy. The king, the chief, was originally the one who had more power than others in the community—a concept that was replaced in historical Israel with the parallel concept of being possessed by Yahweh's spirit. As such he is priest (1 Sam 13:9-10; 2 Sam 6:12-15; 7:18; 1 Kgs 8:5, 14-64; Ps 110:4b) as well as revealer, one who is prophetically gifted (2 Sam 23:1-7), as was Moses, the chief.

Whether in pre-Canaanite times there existed already this division of the original unity into actual priests (who were more cultic functionaries and manipulators of the technical means of revelation) and the seers (who had a special ecstatic aptitude and whose primary or exclusive calling was that of the mantic)—or in other words, whether at that time there was already a conscious distinction between the general gift of power, knowledge, and skill on the one hand and the specifically ecstatic-visionary ability on the other—is something we do not know.

It is possible that ancient Israel already distinguished between priest and seer; in actuality the label *rô'eh* already speaks in favor of this possibility: a word whose fundamental meaning is perhaps not originally a description of a person whose chief calling was a cultic one. The Arabic *kahin* first took on this meaning in the course of development. Yet we can also say that the original cultural level of the cult in its specific sense is no everyday occurrence. In everyday life people needed the one with the gift of power (the shaman, for example) more than they needed magicians and people with mantic abilities; they needed them more as "seers" than as leaders of the cult. The cultic functionary in the particular sense often developed from the "seer." To this extent it is quite possible that the term *rô'eh* in Israel was an original name for the "seer-priest." At any rate, the sagas of Moses and Samuel show that it was quite well known at that time that *rô'eh* stood in a precise relationship with the place of the cult.

The original unity of priest and seer had twofold consequences in Israel. First, in certain cases the priest—in the later specific sense of the word, that is, the cult priest—always remained the revealer of the deity. Second, the heirs of the seer, the *nebi'im*, took over many elements from the original connection between cult and priesthood. Thus in later times we also often find priest and *nabi'* united in one person (Jeremiah, Ezekiel).

THE PRIEST AS MEDIATOR OF REVELATION

That the priest performed prophetic functions is frequently attested. Serious and difficult situations were laid before them, and to these they were to give a divine answer. Here we can distinguish cultic questions, juridical questions, and questions that relate to the future.

A cultic question was once presented to the priests by Haggai: If one carries holy flesh in the skirt of his garment and the garment accidentally touches something edible, does the food then become holy? The priests answered "No" (Hag 2:10-12). In Haggai's era this question had probably become traditional; but in similar situations a direct divine answer would once have had to be obtained.

When it says in Exod 18:26 that the elders rendered judgment in simple matters while all difficult cases were presented to Moses, the presupposition is that Moses laid the questions before Yahweh and obtained his decision. This priestly pronouncement of oracles in juridical cases ("God's judgments," ordeals) is something we may suppose happened frequently. This is especially so when it was a matter of revealing a concealed perpetrator of a crime. Compare this to the narrative in 1 Sam 14:36-42. Who had provoked Yahweh's anger, a member of the king's house or one of the people? Through the Urim and Thummim, administered by the priest, the culpable one was discovered.

Saul also attempted to use the same means to obtain an authoritative reply to the practical question: Shall I go after the Philistines or not? (1 Sam 14:36-37; 28:3-6). The same is true of David (1 Sam 23:2-5; 30:7-8; 2 Sam 5:19a). These are questions that really pertain to the future: "What will happen when?" is their content. Thus one inquires what the outcome will be before going to war or engaging in battle. David asks, "Is it true, Yahweh, that Saul will come?" Yahweh answers through the one bearing the ephod (the priest), "Yes." "Will the men of Keilah surrender me and my men into Saul's hand?" Answer, "Yes" (1 Sam 23:9-14). Or "Shall I pursue after this band? Shall I overtake them?" Answer by the priest, "Pursue; for you shall surely overtake them" (1 Sam 30:7-8; 2 Sam 5:19b).

If we observe the form of these questions we see that they are so formulated that a simple Yes or No suffices as an answer. The answers given also correspond to them. Things are no different in 1 Sam 30:7-8 either. Verse 8b is nothing but a simple Yes to the elaboration in the question.

This agrees with what we know about the priestly means of oracles. Where the revealer is an officially appointed servant of the authorities or of society, then the means of revelation must be purely of a technical sort. The priest must have means in his hands by which he can call forth an answer whenever one is desired. The answers mentioned above were given by the priest bearing the ephod. But the ephod—even in ancient times—is not an idol or image of God, but a container or a garment of some sort used in connection with the safekeeping or use of the Urim and Thummim (1 Sam 14:41-42; and 28:6 LXX). But Urim and Thummim in all these passages are holy lots that are used in delivering oracles. When casting the oracle lots the question can be put in the form of alternatives; the lot will then give the briefest reply possible.

But the example of 1 Sam 30:7-8 shows that the priest who proclaims the answer is not satisfied with giving a simple Yes or No. He formulates each reply in the style of the question, giving it a richer form. Very probably we have an instructive example of this sort in 2 Sam 5:23-24:

> And when David inquired of Yahweh, he said, "You shall not go up; go around to their rear, and come upon them opposite the balsam trees. And when you hear the sound of marching in the tops of the balsam trees, then bestir yourself; for then Yahweh has gone out before you to smite the army of the Philistines."

Here, too, analogous to the other uses of oracles, David inquires of Yahweh using the lots, and the answer, looked at carefully, contains nothing more than what the priest can discern by the lots. The question was, in effect: Shall I go after the Philistines or shall I attack from the rear? The lots gave the answer: You should attack from the rear. But now the appropriate time for initiating an attack on the rear is at the end of the night, in the morning twilight. But the morning twilight will be signaled by a freshening of the wind before sunrise. The noise of the wind in the treetops will be regarded as the steps of God striding over the heights of the earth. The priest accompanying the troops knew this well. Instead of the simple "You shall attack them from the rear," the answer gives a richer, more mythological form by providing at the same time the consequences and the self-evident reasons of the divine answer.

THE *Nabi'* AS CULTIC FUNCTIONARY

The ancient Semitic office of the seer and the priest was repressed on Palestinian soil by Syrian-Canaanite "nabi'ism." Nabi'ism is not of genuine Israelite origin, if we understand by "Israelite" that which stems from the pre-Canaanite period. This fact is not generally acknowledged, to be sure; but it should not be doubted. The office of the enthusiastic-orgiastic prophet—which is the core of the old nabi'ism—is a common occurrence in Canaan, Syria, and Asia Minor, while we find nothing of the sort in purely Semitic contexts.[8] The arguments that have been given for an inner-Israelite origin of nabi'ism are futile. It is claimed that it must have originated as a reaction against what was specifically Canaanite, since the *nabi'* wears the clothing of the wilderness period. But the camelhair coat, as such, as well as the ascetic lifestyle, may not be derived from life in the wilderness and the nomadic ideal. The "magic" coat of the *nabi'* would more likely indicate an orgiastic cult and the initiatory sacrifice associated with it.[9]

That the nabi'ism in Amos 2:11 is regarded as a gift of Yahweh naturally does not serve as proof.[10] When the amalgamation of Israelite and Canaanite elements had become a fact, everything of value naturally became regarded as Yahweh's gift and institution. Neither does the cooperation of the *nebi'im* with Jehonadab the son of Rechab (2 Kgs 10:15-17), which Stade also emphasizes, speak in its favor, nor does the general zeal of the *nebi'im* for Yahweh. For whom should the Yahweh *nebi'im* be zealous if not for the God who inspired them? The most zealous adherents of Islam are not the Arabs but the southern Sudanese dervishes. As those possessed by Yahweh, the *nebi'im* naturally were fanatical devotees of Yahweh. People then seek the same thing in any activity inspired by the same fanaticism. But from this we cannot conclude anything about a common origin.

The Yahweh cult of the period of the monarchy, just as the people of Israel during the monarchy, arose as a mixture of Israelite and Canaanite elements; nevertheless, the people always felt themselves a unit. The attitude of the later prophets, of whom not a few were really *nebi'im* (Amos 7:14), against Canaanite cultic elements is naturally not proof for its source and original nature; these prophets do not at all represent the genuine and actual nabi'ism. But they are mostly rejected by the *nebi'im* of their time and thus are involved in continual polemics against them (1 Kings 22; Jeremiah 27–28).[11] The common appearance of the *nebi'im* with Jehonadab the son of Rechab thus does not mean that they are reacting to the Canaanite elements as such, but rather that as Yahweh *nebi'im* they are defending themselves against the competition of the Baal *nebi'im*, and that as Yahweh's fervent devotees they are combating the cult of Baal. At that time one could no longer distinguish the Canaanite from the genuine Israelite because at that time both elements had already inseparably amalgamated and had formed the unit of historical Israel.

We also see, therefore, that everything that was valuable was uncritically represented as Mosaic, even something with such an indubitably Canaanite origin as the ordinances (*mišpaṭim*) of the "Book of the Covenant" (Exod 20:22—23:33) and the culture that they presuppose. As representatives of the state religion, the *nebi'im* are self-evidently always "nationalistic" in orientation, and in particular circumstances they represent what was considered the ancient legacy of the ancestors, as did Samuel against Agag (1 Sam 15:32-33). But that state and state religion were the Canaanite-Israelite mixed state and mixed religion. After the mixture had taken place and was no longer recognized as such by those who were alive, its old customs and sanctuaries, from wherever they had come, were venerated and defended with equal zeal by all the elements that had combined in the mixture. The antithesis between Saul and Samuel in 1 Samuel 15 is that between practical, political reason and blind, religious fanaticism, not between Canaanite and Israelite.[12] Thus it is undoubtedly no coincidence that we first hear of *nebi'im* under Saul. Their origin has no connection with the uprising against foreign domination.

In the course of time this nabi'ism that was taken over from the Canaanites now assumed the nature and functions of the seers. This was especially true of its connection with the temple and cult. We can state it in this way: the old temple "prophetism" always took its character more from the *nebi'im*.

From the very beginning the *nebi'im* were not priests; the Old Testament always distinguishes between priests and prophets. As the priest is the one who bears the *torah*—which first of all is connected with the cult—so the *nabi'* is the mediator of the divine word (*dabar*)—which is principally regarded as free inspiration (Jer 18:18). According to the Priestly Code, the *nebi'im* were to have no access to the actual temple building; this mirrors the old fact that from the beginning they were not cultic functionaries (*mešaretim*) in the narrow and specific sense of the word. And thus it is also true, as we shall see below, that not all *nebi'im*, who have entered into a firm institutional connection with the cult, stand among the old *ro'im* and *ḥozim*. Those *nebi'im* of a later period who are active as institutional cult prophets are at the same time viewed as Levites (singers), and perhaps also in most cases they have emerged from their ranks.

Since the nature of nabi'ism is always one of orgiastic behavior,[13] it may be assumed that the *nebi'im* were originally representatives of the community that was captivated by the ecstasy of the orgiastic frenzy of the cultic festival and were filled by divine power to the point of madness, as the entire community ideally and theoretically really should have been. They, along with the priest-seers, were the real religious specialists (*religiosii*) of the community who had come forth from the laity.

And yet—or precisely because—they have a close connection with the sanctuaries; in this respect their position is analogous to the *galli* in Hierapolis.[14] The *nebi'im* are active at festivals in cultic actions (1 Kgs 18:16-40; Jeremiah 26, 28, 36). The first *nabi'* band we meet comes from the high place (1 Sam 10:5). The *nabi'* organizations are based at the cultic sites: Ramah (1 Sam 19:19), Bethel (2 Kgs 2:3), Jericho (2 Kgs 2:5), and Gilgal (2 Kgs 4:38). Balaam must first build an altar and offer sacrifices before he can prophesy (Num 23:1-4, 14-15, 29-30). The *nebi'im* are often mentioned together with the priests (Isa 28:7; Jer 4:9; 6:13; 14:18; 18:18; Mic 3:11; Zech 7:3).

According to Jer 29:26 they are under the supervision of one of the priests of the temple. Jeremiah was a priest and a *nabi'* (Jer 1:1), and so was Ezekiel (Ezek 1:3). We shall not err if we suppose that perhaps most of the later temple prophets came from the circle of the lesser cultic personnel (2 Chron 20:14).

This close connection with the priests and the temple rests partially upon the fact that the old cult prophets were replaced by the *nebi'im* or were transformed to accord with that image. The connection of the *nebi'im* with the temple thus became an institutional one.

In Jer 29:26 we are unquestionably dealing with an institution of temple prophets. That there was such an organized institution of temple prophets is proved to us also by the passage in the Chronicler, which is either understood incorrectly—or worse, not understood at all (1 Chron 15:22, 27). The verses speak about Chenaniah the Levite, identifying him as the *śar hammaśśa'* (reading with the LXX, rather than the MT *ysr bmś'*).[15] The sense of the words is quite clear. The chapter deals with the preparation for the festival of bringing in the ark, which was celebrated each year with a great procession.[16] Along with sacrifices, singing, and music, the prophetic voices also belong to this festival.[17] As Psalms 81 and 132 show, this prophesying is fixed in both content and form (see below). First Chronicles 15:22, 27 is to be interpreted in this context. *Maśśa'* here does not mean burden, but oracle. Chenaniah was "the leader of the oracle (affairs)."

This passage in Chronicles shows us that there were also some among the temple functionaries whose calling it was to give divine utterances (*maśśe'ot*). They were organized like the other temple functionaries; at their head was a leader (*śar*) who "understood" the art of proclaiming oracles (15:22b). These temple prophets belonged to the Levites, and according to the context and v. 27b, to the singers (2 Chron 20:14). All of this is very natural. Prophetic ecstasy is nurtured by music (1 Sam 10:5; 2 Kgs 3:15); revelations were occasionally accompanied by music (Ps 49:1-2); and, as we shall see, we have cultic oracles in the form of psalms. Thus we find it completely normal to seek cult prophets and also authors of prophetic psalms employed among the temple singers. This accords with the circumstances in Babylon. Here a class of priests were called *barû* ("seers"). The (raving) prophets (*muḫḫū*) were also officially organized here.[18]

What we see of such temple prophets at a somewhat later time does not have the character of the old seers but that of nabi'ism. Or, more precisely, in the main it has the peculiar characteristics of nabi'ism, but it has been influenced by certain distinctive characteristics of seerism. This accords with the general course of the development of things in Israel: the old Israelite seerism was absorbed and replaced by Canaanite nabi'ism. Ever since ancient times the seer-priests' most important means of oracles had probably been visions and dreams on the one hand and the purely technical means (oracles, lots, and so on) on the other hand, which we have already seen practiced. The ability of these people—according to primitive thought—rested on the possession of special power: they were clairvoyants, visionaries, and performers of miracles. For example, they had the necessary "soul power" to bless. At that time, the vision or dream was probably also stylistically the actual form for revelations.

Later nabi'ism set the tone. This development is revealed in the following way. In place of the more indefinite gift of power there is inspiration by the divine spirit, the *ruaḥ Yahweh*. This means, however, that the enthusiastic form of the prophetic office has supplanted the visionary-ecstatic one. The visionary, the ecstatic person, is "outside himself." His soul, his "heart," sometimes departs from him, seeks faraway places, and sees secret things (2 Kgs 5:26). He is whisked away and his alter ego looks on tranquilly in the heavenly councils (for example, Zechariah's night visions), or his soul wanders to some distant place (Ezek 8:1-3; 11:1-4, 24-25). Meanwhile the seer's body lies absorbed and as if dead in its usual place (Num 24:4). While Ezekiel's soul is in ecstasy in Jerusalem, his seemingly lifeless body lies in Chaldea "before the elders of Judah" (Ezek 3:12-15).

In contrast, an alien power has entered the one possessed by the spirit, has taken control of him; he has been "divinized"; the spirit of Yahweh speaks through his mouth. The *nabi'* also performs miracles; this he does because the spirit is in him. Because the spirit, who knows everything, is the divine word "in him," he utters true prophecies. The form of revelation that is characteristic of the *nabi'* is therefore the word spoken rhythmically by the spirit or by Yahweh, the word in which Yahweh speaks in the first person. Here, therefore, the purely technical means of revelation, such as oracle lots and the like, recede; the *nabi'* always appears as one observing the form of free, momentary inspiration, even when, upon request or as his duty, he is proclaiming the word expected and required of him. Such things appear as indirect means of revelation which, according to experience, encourage the enthusiastic-orgiastic situations: music and dance (1 Sam 10:5-6, 10-13; 2 Kgs 3:15), loud, repeated shouts, self-inflicted wounds (1 Kgs 18:26-29), hand clapping, and wild movements (Ezek 6:11; 21:19, 22), etc. While the seer by the nature of his gifts and his priestly office was usually, if not always, a man who stood by himself, the first *nebi'im* always appear in bands and communally seek even greater excesses of orgiastic ecstasy (1 Sam 10:5; 19:20; 1 Kings 18; 22:6; 2 Kings 2; 6:1-7). The phrase "sons of the prophets" (*benê nebi'im*) refers to organization and communal life (1 Kgs 20:25; 2 Kgs 2:3; 4:1, 38; 5:22; 6:1; Amos 7:14). The term *newayôt* ("dwelling") probably goes back to a communal dwelling, a type of cenobium or monastery (1 Sam 19:18-24). Thus in later times the term *rô'eh* also disappeared; from now on someone who conveys divine revelations is instead always called a *nabi'*, even when he does not belong to the *nebi'im* (Amos 7:14).

This does not mean that the older forms of revelation have disappeared. It is well known that visions and revelations in dreams were forms that the *nebi'im* also favored highly. In reality there is no psychological distinction between ecstasy and enthusiasm; in large measure the actual psychic concerns of the seer and the *nabi'* were the same. In ancient Israel, too, the conceptual demarcations were fluid. Thus Ezekiel says that his transferal in a vision from Chaldea to Jerusalem was done by Yahweh's spirit (Ezek 3:12, 14;

8:3; 11:1, 24). This spirit is depicted in part as a being that grasps him externally (Ezek 8:2-3), and in part it is thought of as a spirit that has entered into the prophet (Ezek 2:2; 3:24).

Alongside what in theory is the free inspiration of the *nabi'*, certain of the purely technical means of revelation also remained in existence, the sacred lots, for example. But it appears that in later times these were restricted to those who were priests in the strict sense of the word; this was the case, at any rate, with the Urim and Thummim. But the revelations of the *nebi'im*, insofar as they are subjectively genuine, are always psychologically transmitted. The *nabi'* is viewed as someone permanently endowed with the spirit. As such, when speaking professionally, he always speaks at Yahweh's commission. This explains the cult prophet's authenticity and inspired manner of speech, both when speaking in the line of duty and to some degree when speaking the precisely prescribed words of the cultic liturgy. In many cases this consciousness would have evoked certain psychic conditions in him that he would have interpreted as being possessed by the spirit and that would have allowed him to appear as authentic.

That these temple prophets were obligated at certain cultic ceremonies to give an oracle with a content appropriate for the ceremony and one that agreed with the faith and expectations of the majority of the community or its authorities is something that we can conclude from numerous accounts. For example, the four hundred prophets of Ahab came together on a day of prayer before the military campaign in order to deliver a prophecy about the outcome; naturally they prophesy in the same way as most clergy in warring states now preach. In this regard the Old Testament prophets are no better and no more perfect than Catholic, Lutheran, Anglican, or Methodist priests and pastors; they even expected a favorable oracle from Micaiah and declared it treason when he did not give one (1 Kings 22).

The same thing is found in Jeremiah 28. Here, too, all the people have assembled to pray in the temple. The event is the planned revolt against Nebuchadnezzar. Will it succeed or not? Give us good fortune, O Yahweh; let it succeed, O Yahweh! Then Hananiah the son of Azzur, the prophet from Gibeon, steps forward; he knows his "state-churchly" duty and responsibility. "Thus says Yahweh Sabaoth, the God of Israel: I have broken the yoke of the king of Babylon" (28:2).

The account in 2 Chronicles 20 is typical. The enemies of Judah are about to attack. King Jehoshaphat appoints a great day of repentance and celebration, and the whole community comes together in the temple. The king as the priest and the people's intercessor calls upon Yahweh for help. It is obvious that this is not something without form, but that it is taking place according to a fixed ritual. And, in accordance with the analogies above, it is also part of the ritual, the "agenda," that the Levite (a singer), Jahaziel the son of Zechariah, falls into an ecstatic rapture. As we learn in 1 Kgs 18:28; 2 Kgs 3:15; and 1 Sam 10:5, the *nebi'im* knew of technical means that could induce rapture. Its form is naturally a free, unsought, momentary inspiration. Therefore, the Chronicler also says: "The spirit of Yahweh came upon Jahaziel" (2 Chron 20:14). The enthusiastic singer now promises in Yahweh's name the complete destruction of the enemy. Thereupon all in the community fall upon their faces to honor Yahweh; the festival concludes with an song of (anticipated) thanksgiving.

Both in this account as in the above mentioned passage in 1 Chron 15:22, 27, the cult prophets involved were numbered among the Levites, more specifically among the singers. Indeed, we certainly must conclude from the latter passage that if the leader of the oracle-givers belonged to the singers, the same must have been true for the entire organization of institutional cult prophets. This accords with the view of the later, post-exilic period that permitted no non-Levite among the temple officials. Even the Gibeonite woodcutters and water carriers are made into Levites in P and the Chronicler's Work. Nevertheless, we must conclude that the post-exilic period had taken the cult prophets into the ranks of the Levites (singers) in order thereby to legitimate them. From then on they are primarily singers, secondarily prophetically gifted men. To the same degree that the cultic prophecies they presented were bound to the agenda and yet came to be regarded in line with the other cultic psalms, the distinction between cult prophets and ordinary singers was obscured, until finally the sense that the cultic giving of oracles had once been a special cultic task of a special order was lost. Thus to the Chronicler the above mentioned Jahaziel the son of Zechariah is scarcely more than an ordinary singer-Levite who was grasped by the spirit in a coincidental way at this special occasion and who thus could proclaim Yahweh's answer. Perhaps the Chronicler thought this was a special display of Yahweh's grace toward the pious King Jehoshaphat.

Thus the institution of cultic prophecy gradually died out. It was slowly and almost imperceptibly replaced by a precentor singing certain, long-fixed prophetic psalms. The entire music of the temple became more or less the work of a very pallid divine inspiration indeed (1 Chron 25:1-3), within which the choral presentation of oracle psalms was nothing out of the ordinary.

How early or late this happened is something we cannot say. The old institution of cultic prophecy, whose nature and form were free, was surely alive until the exile; this is shown by Jeremiah: "Yahweh has made you [Zephaniah son of Maaseiah] priest instead of Jehoiada the priest, to have charge in the house of Yahweh over every madman who prophesies to put him in the stocks and collar" (Jer 29:26; see also Jer 20:1-2). This is also indicated by the circumstance that at that time so many of the completely free *nebi'im* came from the ranks of the priests (Jeremiah and Ezekiel).

But even after the exile we meet prophets who are totally temple prophets: primarily Haggai and Zechariah. Especially with Zechariah it is apparent that virtually his entire imagery and general worldview come from the cult: the candelabra, the temple oil, the cultic cursing, the purification rites—symbolically expelling the impurity by swinging birds (see birds of purification in Lev 14:6-7), the days of fasting, and so on. It was his chief aim to see the temple completed and the cult re-established. Besides that, he is extremely interested in reconciling the two rival temple authorities: the governor and the high priest. Zechariah, too, is very probably of priestly descent.[19]

Joel is most likely also a cult prophet (see below). And even under Nehemiah we meet *nebi'im* who reside in the temple and appear in the religious and political controversies as supporters of the concerns of the priestly party, and who are subject to the authority of the priests, as are the temple *nebi'im* in Jeremiah's time (Neh 6:10-14). It is very natural to assume that these temple *nebi'im* were also active in some way in the official cult.

At the time of the Maccabees, in contrast, there apparently was no institutional cultic prophecy, just as there no longer was institutional prophecy at all (1 Macc 4:45-46; 14:41)—unless Psalm 110 is regarded as "Maccabean." But I reject this claim because, among other reasons, it cannot be reconciled with the aforementioned passages.

The Form and Technique of the Cultic Oracle

At any rate, the means by which the priest or prophet learned the deity's answer to a question or request originally presented to him were certainly also of a technical nature.[20] This is clearly seen in the obtaining of oracles by using the Urim and Thummim, the sacred lots, and the ephod mentioned above. Other legitimate means of oracles also appear to have been known. Thus it is possible that the superscription "on the lilies of revelation" (*'al šošannim*; *'al šošan 'edûth*) in the Psalms refers to a particular method of obtaining cultic oracles (Pss 45:1; 60:1; 69:1).[21]

Many analogies support the assumption that obtaining oracles in Israel was somehow related to sacrifices; compare the Babylonian-Assyrian inspection of livers (extispicy) and the Etruscan-Roman reading of omens (*augurium*) and reading of animal entrails (*haruspicium*).[22] Balaam's sacrifice (Num 23:1-3, 14-15, 29-30) points to a relationship between sacrificing and prophesying. Compare the account of King Zakar-Baal's sacrificial festival in Byblos:

> Now while he [Zakar-Baal, Prince of Byblos] was making offering to his gods, the god seized one of his youths and made him possessed. And he [the youth] said to him [Zakar-

> Baal]: "Bring up the god! Bring the messenger who is carrying him!"[23]

The sacrificial auguries consisted of taking certain characteristics of the entrails (for example, the liver) of the animals sacrificed, or the circumstances surrounding the sacrificial acts, such as the rising of the smoke or the like, and regarding these as "signs" and interpreting them as the deity's will. Genesis indicates that such auguries were also practiced in Israel:

> In the course of time, Cain brought to Yahweh an offering of the fruit of the ground, and Abel brought firstlings of his flock and their fat portions. And Yahweh had regard for Abel and his offering, but for Cain and his offering he had no regard. So Cain was very angry, and his countenance fell. (Gen 4:3-5)

There are many of these signs, to be sure, and not all of them need be interpreted in the context of auguries. In Ps 74:9 the people complain that they no longer "see our signs," that is, oracles that are favorable to them (the expression used in Assyrian); on the contrary, they say, the prophets are silent. When Ps 86:17—a typical complaint psalm dealing with illness[24]—says "Show me a sign of your favor," it is certainly to be interpreted in the light of the petitions that frequently appear in the Babylonian-Assyrian psalms: "Give me a favorable sign." And it is very probably a reference to the sign of an augury.[25] Finally, mantic signs could have been part of the prophet's everyday experience.[26]

Dreams must also be considered as sources of cultic oracles and signs. It is well known that the dream is a means frequently used by the *nabi'*.[27] "Give me a good dream (viz., one that promises well-being)," appears frequently in the Babylonian-Assyrian psalms.[28]

A special sort of dream oracle that must have been employed by the cult prophets is incubation. We see in 1 Sam 28:6, 15 and 1 Kgs 3:3-15 that this form was known in Israel:

> And when Saul inquired of Yahweh, Yahweh did not answer him, either by dreams, or by Urim, or by prophets.
> (1 Sam 28:6)

> At Gibeon Yahweh appeared to Solomon in a dream by night; and God said, "Ask what I shall give you." (1 Kgs 3:5)

The complaint psalms may also refer to incubation a few times.[29]

The account in 2 Chron 20:14-17, as well as the prophetic psalm of

Habakkuk 3, show, however, that in the course of time the cult prophets adopted the forms and expressions of nabi'ism, which were free and based on inspiration of the spirit.

> I hear, and my body trembles,
>   my lips quiver at the sound;
> rottenness enters into my bones,
>   my steps totter beneath me. (Hab 3:16a)

The difference between the technical and the more psychologically based revelations of the *nebi'im* is not a sharp one; technical means can evoke psychic effects that the one involved regards as signs of divine inspiration. This happens, for example, when ecstasy is evoked by external means such as music and dance; the ecstasy then produces mysterious situations of the soul in which faces are seen and voices heard, and the prophet's normal or subconscious experiences of consciousness are objectified as divine inspirations. Hence the oracle forms merge together; everything is derived from the "spirit." Thus the claim will be made that even the professional priest-prophets are possessed by the spirit and therefore they receive the gift of prophecy as part of their office. We have seen above that this belief was still alive in the first century C.E. (John 11:51).

Cultic Prophecy and the Writing of Psalms

The examples that we have mentioned above deal mostly with public days of fasting and repentance and with cultic inquiry about wars and battles. In addition, the cultic oracle appears at a great political-religious festival (1 Chronicles 15). The prophetic psalms must now be set in this context.

We may regard it as already proved that on certain occasions the direct divine speech by the mouth of an official and authorized mediator of revelation had a place within the liturgy for prescribed days in the ancient Israelite cult. That the liturgy, at least in part, must have had poetic and musical forms is something we know from the many cultic psalms. In fact, many psalms are cultic liturgies. And from the very beginning the word of divine revelation in Israel had a poetic, rhythmical-metrical form. The same thing must have applied to the words of revelation in the liturgies.

A cultic liturgy in which different voices (such as complaint songs, songs of trust, and communal prayers) echo with the cultic prophet's answer given in the name of the deity, and which concludes with a hymnic psalm of thanksgiving—that is, a psalm in both the broad sense and in the Old Testament sense of the word. Truly, the psalms in the Psalter are not always unified creations in the sense that they speak with but one voice and one sentiment.

Many of them are cultic liturgical compositions that express several voices and sentiments.

From this point of view we must now examine the traditional psalms that also contain prophetic voices. It will be our task to identify cultic oracle psalms among the traditional "prophetic psalms" and in certain cases to demonstrate that they are such.

Here a few words may also be said about the author of the psalm. It is in the nature of the case that the responsibility of composing cultic psalms should fall to the cultic officials. They also would be the ones with an interest in having many such psalms available. In addition, the activity of so doing would undoubtedly cause many of the temple officials to have a desire and aptitude for such work.

Among the cultic officials there is one order that we may assume had a special interest in the writing of psalms: the order of temple singers. They were responsible for the temple music, and we know that at that time singing and instrumental music always belonged together. At any rate, the songs that were sung in the name of the congregation, the people, were undoubtedly sung by the official singers. And we shall hardly err in assuming that the cultic songs of an individual, such as the songs of complaint to be sung at the rites of purification, were not sung by the sick person but by the singers. There certainly were not many of the common people who understood the artistically correct way of rendering the psalms that accorded with the tradition and all of the ritual details. All analogies indicate that the songs were not sung from "the printed page" but from memory. And that could not have been expected of the laity. Every ancient cult put great store in correctly performing all the prescribed details with precision. But we also shall not err in assuming that most, if not all, of the ancient cultic songs were composed by men who belonged to the order of temple singers. For that was the order that had to deal with cultic songs.

Moreover we now know from the ancient Near East that writing at that time derived from special inspiration. The writer was a divinely inspired man who had received a "supernatural" gift. We know from many indications that ancient Israel also shared this belief. At that time the writer and the prophet were very closely related. The *nabi'* is always a writer at the same time; in ancient time his oracles always have the rhythmical-metrical form (compare the words of Balaam and the benedictions of Jacob and Moses). The ancient hymn of victory of Judges 5 was ascribed to the prophetess Deborah. Only someone gifted with prophecy—so they thought—could have composed such a song. Just as the prophet "whose eye is closed" can see even distant and future things (Num 24:3) so that his closed eye is in reality the only truly "uncovered" one (Num 24:4), and just as with his open ears he can hear the secret divine and heavenly voices (1 Sam 9:15; Isa 22:14), so does the writer of Ps 19:1-4a receive the hymn of heaven "that cannot be heard (by human ears) without speech and without word."

Just as the prophet is transported by music into the state of inspiration, so also is the writer (Ps 49:1-4). His ear becomes sensitive so that he can receive the secret wisdom that comes from the deity (*ḥokmah, mašal, hidôt*) and transmit it to humankind. At the sound of the lyre he shares his secret tidings; it is precisely the prophetic consciousness that speaks in the introductory words of this psalm. A *maśkil* is a cultic song, originating from such an extraordinary giftedness, ability, and knowledge, which also explains its real efficacy.[30] This is how we also understand it when the Chronicler uses the word *nibba'* (1 Chron 25:1-3) to describe the cultic functions of the singer, or even calls the singers *nebi'im:* the singers are prophetically gifted and exercise their art in the strength of prophetic inspiration.

If this is so, we must also suppose that the liturgies—which evidence a prophetic consciousness in the specific sense of the word and in which direct divine relevations are imparted—originated among the temple singers. But this means, to turn things around, that it was also exceptional singers who appeared in the cult as inspired cult prophets, or perhaps more correctly, whose duty it was to appear as such at certain occasions. For as such they had the gift of singing and writing, that is, the gift of inspiration, of being possessed by the spirit, of prophecy. This was just as obvious to ancient Israel as it was to Mohammed: anyone who can write is inspired, and can, if need be, also prophesy.

Our hypothesis is also confirmed in the sources. The cult prophet Jahaziel the son of Zechariah mentioned above is, according to 2 Chron 20:14, a descendant of Asaph; that is, he belongs to the temple singers. And even the fact that we have so many prophetic psalms among the temple songs confirms the close connection that existed between writing psalms and temple prophecy.

In addition, we have another source that confirms the connection between prophecy and temple singers and psalm writers, namely the Book of Habakkuk.[31] Here we place less weight upon the fact that Habakkuk apparently is a man well acquainted with the cultic writing of psalms and their form. I note that the first two chapters of his book not only adopt individual motifs of psalm composition, but that they take precisely the form of a liturgy for a day of complaint and prayer, with a complaint ("O Yahweh, how long?" 1:2), a description of need (1:3-4), the praise motif (1:12-13), the conviction that one is heard (2:5-20), and a divine answer (2:1-4). One might consequently be tempted to say that the two chapters are to be regarded not so much as a prophecy with complaint motifs, but, on the contrary, as a liturgy for a day of prayer that is strongly influenced by the prophetic style and conceptual world and written by one prophet. It is more important in the context, however, that chap. 3 is a genuine psalm, so strongly influenced by the prophetic nature, that it was certainly written by a *nabi'* (see 3:16). And that this psalm was employed in the cult, and also that it was probably written for cultic use, is shown in the cultic-liturgical notes in 3:1 and 19b (see also vv. 3, 9, 13).

The genre of Habakkuk 3 should be regarded as a mixture of prophecy and a psalm of trust. It begins as a psalm of trust (v. 2); the author's trust rests as much on Yahweh's earlier great deeds (v. 2b) as on the fact that he has received a revelation (v. 16). The content of this revelation is transmitted in vv. 3-15. From this we also conclude that the psalm does not intend to be a psalm of trust in general; the ascription of trust is based on a special circumstance of need in which the people and the king, the whole "congregation," find themselves (vv. 12-14). That the plea for help is being delivered from the need is clearly discernible in the confidence expressed, for the psalm intends to be a petition offered in trust, a prayer (*tefillah*; v. 1). Here the revelation received is not conveyed directly to the congregation as a response to its petition, but instead the author expresses his grateful "assurance of being heard" in the form of describing Yahweh's coming. The description begins with Yahweh speaking in the third person, and then it changes in v. 8 to the second person, thus increasing the impression that the description is intended to function as an "assurance of being heard." All Yahweh's great deeds of deliverance in ancient times and in the present, and those yet to be expected, merge here into a single one, so that one really dare not pose the question of whether here the prophet is describing past or future events. The author wants to say: You who always do such things will also deliver your people and your anointed this time.

Here Yahweh's intervention is depicted in terms of the enthronement myth: appearance in order to do battle, battle of the primeval sea, new creation (the present time of need is a time of chaos, *tohû wabohû*, v. 17), the "war of the peoples" myth, deliverance from need.[32] The psalm ends with an explicit statement of the assurance of being heard and with the anticipated thanksgiving (vv. 18-19), as the complaint psalms and liturgies of the days of prayer often do (for example, Psalm 60).

The author of this psalm is identified as the *nabi'* Habakkuk, the same man whose prophecies in chaps. 1–2 were so strongly influenced by the style of the Psalms, and there is absolutely no reason to doubt the accuracy of this ascription. The psalm must be pre-exilic at any rate, for it presupposes an anointed one, a king of Israel (3:13).

The plight the author contemplates is the foreign rule of the Assyrians. And in the advancing Chaldeans he sees the signs of the approaching great day of Yahweh,[33] the day of judgment and of the enthronement of the God of Israel.

We must assume that the people, the "righteous"—Habakkuk is a partisan prophet of deliverance, certainly standing in the line of the deuteronomic school of thought—who were encouraged by the signs of the time, took some opportunity to organize a day of prayer to plead for an end to the Assyrian foreign rule that had become especially hated after King Josiah's reform (621 B.C.E.). There may have also been special political reasons for it. On this occasion the temple prophet and psalmist Habakkuk, who perhaps was one of the singers, composed the psalms (or one of them) that were to be sung and in them promised Yahweh's help to his people. The psalm was sung at one of the cultic rites as a psalm of petition with the intention of "getting Yahweh to be gracious" (*lmnṣḥ*, literally "to make [Yahweh's countenance] shine").[34]

And if there is anyone who wishes to dispute the accuracy of the tradition in v. 1, it will have to be said that the verse is still evidence in support of our main thesis. It shows at any rate that it was considered quite natural to look for the author of a prophetic cultic psalm among the *nebi'im*. This would hardly be the case, however, if such a thing did not in reality occur frequently. The Book of Joel also points in this direction; it manifests the same mixture of psalm style and prophetic style. Gunkel is certainly correct that the first two chapters of Joel contain "a liturgy depicting a great plague of locusts."[35]

Notes

1. Form, Tradition, and Literary Criticisms

[1.] Jean Astruc, *Conjectures sur la Genèse,* Classiques de L'Histoire des Religions (Paris: Noêsis, 1999), reprint of 1756 edition with new notes and introduction.

2. See, e.g., Julius Wellhausen, *Israelitisch-jüdische Geschichte,* 9th ed. (Berlin: de Gruyter, 1958) 166–76. Compare also Carl Steuernagel, *Lehrbuch der Einleitung in das Alte Testament* (Tübingen: Mohr/Siebeck, 1912) 237; Carl Heinrich Cornill, *Introduction to the Canonical Books of the Old Testament,* trans. G. H. Box (London: Williams & Norgate, 1907); 6th German ed. 1913, pp. 65–66. Otherwise it is obvious that a fundamental error made by Wellhausen is his inclination to identify "literarily secondary" with "literarily late" and "materially late." [Ed.] For a recent discussion of the problems in dating the priestly materials, see Jacob Milgrom, *Leviticus 1–16,* AB 3 (New York: Doubleday, 1991) 3–35.

3. Rudolf Kittel, *Geschichte des Volkes Israel,* 3rd ed., Handbücher der alten Geschichte (Gotha: Perthes, 1916) 1.328–56.

[4.] For a translation of the Amarna letters see William L. Moran, *The Amarna Letters* (Baltimore: Johns Hopkins Univ. Press, 1992). Regarding Israelite and ancient Near Eastern archaeology, see, for example: Amihai Mazar, *Archaeology of the Land of the Bible, 10,000–586* B.C.E., ABRL (New York: Doubleday, 1990); Eric M. Meyers, editor, *The Oxford Encyclopedia of Archaeology in the Near East,* 5 vols. (New York: Oxford Univ. Press, 1997); Ephraim Stern, *Archaeology of the Land of the Bible,* Vol. 2: *The Assyrian, Babylonian, and Persian Periods, 732–332* B.C.E., ABRL (New York: Doubleday, 2001); William G. Dever, *What Did the Biblical Writers Know, and When Did They Know It? What Archaeology Can Tell Us about the Reality of Ancient Israel* (Grand Rapids: Eerdmans, 2001); Israel Finkelstein and Neil Asher Silberman, *The Bible Unearthed: Archaeology's New Vision of Ancient Israel and the Origin of Its Sacred Texts* (New York: Free Press, 2001).

[5.] For collections of English translations of ancient Near Eastern documents see: James B. Pritchard, editor, *Ancient Near Eastern Texts relating to the Old Testament,* 3rd ed. (Princeton: Princeton Univ. Press, 1969); Benjamin R. Foster, *Before the Muses: An Anthology of Akkadian Literature,* 2 vols. (Baltimore: CDL, 1993); William W. Hallo and K. Lawson Younger, editors, *The Context of Scripture,* 3 vols. (Leiden: Brill, 1997–); and Victor H. Matthews and Don C. Benjamin, editors, *Old Testament Parallels: Laws and Stories from the Ancient Near East,* rev. ed. (New York: Paulist, 1997).

6. Hermann Gunkel, *Genesis*, trans. M. E. Biddle, MLBS (Macon, Ga.: Mercer Univ. Press, 1997); 1st German ed. 1901; 3rd ed. 1910.

7. Hugo Gressmann, *Mose und seine Zeit: Ein Kommentar zu den Mose-Sagen*, FRLANT 18 (Göttingen: Vandenhoeck & Ruprecht, 1913).

8. Hermann Gunkel, *Schöpfung und Chaos in Urzeit und Endzeit: Eine religionsgeschichtliche Untersuchung über Gen 1 und Ap Joh 12* (Göttingen: Vandenhoeck & Ruprecht, 1895). [Ed.] The introduction of this work (pp. 3–120) is translated as "The Influence of Babylonian Mythology upon the Biblical Creation Story," in *Creation in the Old Testament*, ed. Bernhard W. Anderson, IRT 6 (Philadelphia: Fortress Press, 1984) 25–52.

9. Hermann Gunkel, "Israelite Literary History," in *Water for a Thirsty Land: Israelite Literature and Religion*, ed. K. C. Hanson, FCBS (Minneapolis: Fortress Press, 2001) 31–41 (German article 1906).

10. Hedwig Jahnow, *Das hebräische Leichenlied im Rahmen der Völkerdichtung*, BZAW 36 (Giessen: Töpelmann, 1923).

11. For the style and setting in life of this and the other types of psalms see Hermann Gunkel, *Introduction to the Psalms: The Genres of the Religious Lyric of Israel*, completed by Joachim Begrich, trans. J. D. Nogalski, MLBS (Macon, Ga.: Mercer Univ. Press, 1998); German ed. 1933. This work, however, does not sufficiently give the cult its due. See also Mowinckel, *Psalmenstudien*, SNVAO, 6 vols. (Oslo: Kristiana, 1921–24); and Mowinckel, *The Psalms in Israel's Worship*, trans. D. R. Ap-Thomas, 2 vols. (Nashville: Abingdon, 1962).

12. As is well known, the apparent shifts between the divine names of Yahweh and Elohim formed the starting point for source analysis in Genesis and later in the Pentateuch and Hexateuch. One can find information on this in any standard Old Testament introduction. [Ed.] See, e.g., Norman K. Gottwald, *The Hebrew Bible: A Socio-Literary Introduction* (Philadelphia: Fortress Press, 1985) 11–15, 137–62, 180–89.

13. Rudolf Kittel, *Geschichte des Volkes Israel*, Handbücher der alten Geschichte (Gotha: Perthes, 1909) 2.25ff. This is handled somewhat differently in Emil Kautzsch and Alfred Bertholet, *Die heilige Schrift des Alten Testament*, 2 vols. (Tübingen: Mohr/Siebeck, 1922).

14. Compare, for example, the lists in Heinrich Holzinger, *Einleitung in den Hexateuch mit Tabellen über die Quellenscheidung* (Freiburg: Mohr/Siebeck, 1893) 93ff., 181ff., 283ff., 339ff., 411ff. This is still true with Gustav Hölscher, "Das Buch der Könige, seine Quellen und seine Redaktion," in *Eucharistarion: Studien zur Religion und Literatur des Alten und Neuen Testaments. Hermann Gunkel zum 60. Geburtstage, dem 23. Mai 1922*, ed. Hans Schmidt, 2 vols., FRLANT 36 (Göttingen: Vandenhoeck & Ruprecht, 1923) 1.194–95 n1.

15. Leonhard Rost, *The Succession to the Throne of David*, trans. M. D. Rutter and D. M. Gunn, HTIBS 1 (Sheffield: Almond, 1982); German ed. 1926.

16. Ludwig Köhler, *Deuterojesaja (Jesaja 40–55) stilkritisch untersucht*, BZAW 37 (Giessen: Töpelmann, 1923). [Ed.] See now, Klaus Baltzer, *Deutero-Isaiah*, trans. M. Kohl, Hermeneia (Minneapolis: Fortress Press, 2001).

17. Gunkel, *Genesis*; Otto Procksch, *Die Genesis*, KAT 1 (Leipzig: Deichert, 1924). [Ed.] On the final form of Genesis, see Brevard S. Childs, *Introduction to the Old Testament as Scripture* (Philadelphia: Fortress Press, 1979) 145–58; and Walter Brueggemann, *Genesis*, IBC (Atlanta: John Knox, 1982).

18. Already Bruno Baentsch, *Das Bundesbuch Ex. XX 22—XXIII 33* (Halle: Niemeyer, 1892). Compare also his commentary, *Exodus-Leviticus-Numeri*, HKAT 2 (Göttingen:

Vandenhoeck & Ruprecht, 1903). He is aware that the "Book of the Covenant" consists of separate law complexes. And Ernst Sellin interprets the codes as "earlier material for the Pentateuch" in *Introduction to the Old Testament*, trans. W. Montgomery (London: Hodder & Stoughton, 1923). Johannes Pedersen's critical remark about the doubtful foundation of the distribution of the legal material on the various sources is in itself justified; but it does not apply to the actual opinions of many "literary critics" in more recent times: *Israel: Its Life and Culture* (London: Chapman, 1940) 4.725–27.

19. See Hugo Gressmann, *Die Schriften des Alten Testaments* (Göttingen: Vandenhoeck & Ruprecht, 1910) 2/1.229–32; 2nd ed. (1921) 2/1.227–30.

20. Albrecht Alt, "The Origins of Israelite Law," in *Essays on Old Testament History and Religion*, trans. R. A. Wilson (Oxford: Blackwell, 1966) 79–132; German orig. 1934.

21. Mowinckel, *Psalmenstudien* 5.97–116; idem, *Le Décalogue*, EHPR 16 (Paris: Alcan, 1927) 114ff.

22. Axel Olrik, "Epic Laws of Folk Narrative," in *The Study of Folklore*, ed. Alan Dundes (Englewood Cliffs, N.J.: Prentice-Hall, 1965) 129–41; German orig. 1909. [Ed.] See also Hermann Gunkel, *The Folktale in the Old Testament*, trans. M. D. Rutter, HTIBS 6 (Sheffield: Sheffield Academic, 1987); German ed. 1917; Stith Thompson, *The Folktale* (New York: Holt, Rinehart, and Winston, 1946; reprinted Berkeley: Univ. of California Press, 1977); Vladimir Propp, *Morphology of the Folktale*, 2nd ed., trans. L. Scott (Austin: Univ. of Texas Press, 1968); Susan Niditch, *Underdogs and Tricksters: A Prelude to Biblical Folklore* (San Francisco: Harper & Row, 1987); and idem, *Folklore and the Hebrew Bible*, GBS (Minneapolis: Fortress Press, 1993).

23. See Hugo Gressmann, *A. Eichhorn und die religionsgeschichtliche Schule* (Göttingen: Vandenhoeck & Ruprecht, 1914); and Martin Rade, "Religionsgeschichte und religionsgeschichtliche Schule," in *RGG*² 4.2381ff.

24. Hugo Gressmann, *Altorientalische Texte und Bilder zum Alten Testament*, 2nd ed. (Tübingen: Mohr/Siebeck, 1926–27). Anton Jirku, *Alterorientalischer Kommentar zum Alten Testament* (Leipzig: Deichert, 1923). [Ed.] See Kurt Rudolph, "Religionsgeschichtliche Schule," in *Encyclopedia of Religion*, ed. Mircea Eliade (New York: Macmillan, 1987) 12.293–96; and Hendrikus Boers, "Religionsgeschichtliche Schule," in *DBI* 2.383–87.

25. Hermann Gunkel, *Schöpfung und Chaos in Urzeit und Endzeit.*

26. Most clearly in Hermann Gunkel, "The Religio-Historical Interpretation of the New Testament," *Monist* 3 (1903) 398–455 (German ed. 1903). But this article aims only at laying out a program.

27. See Hermann Gunkel, *Die Psalmen*, HAT (Göttingen: Vandenhoeck & Ruprecht, 1929); and idem, *The Psalms: A Form-Critical Introduction*, trans. T. M. Horner, FBBS 19 (Philadelphia: Fortress Press, 1967). [Ed.] See also Gunkel, "The Religion of the Psalms," in *Water for a Thirsty Land: Israelite Literature and Religion*, ed. K. C. Hanson, FCBS (Minneapolis: Fortress Press, 2001) 134–67; orig. German article 1922.

28. The Anglo-American "Myth and Ritual School" and its emphasis on the relationship of myth and a cultic pattern does not, therefore, herald a research principle new to me. I defined myth as statements in a more or less developed epic form concerning what happens and is experienced in the cult and is visibly expressed in its rites; see Mowinckel, *Psalmenstudien* 2.24–25. Examples of the Myth and Ritual School appear in S. H. Hooke, editor, *Myth and Ritual: Essays on the Myth and Ritual of the Hebrews in Relation to the Culture Pattern of the Ancient East* (London: Oxford Univ. Press, 1933);

idem, *The Labyrinth: Further Studies in the Relation between Myth and Ritual in the Ancient World* (London: SPCK, 1935). [Ed.] Note also: Mowinckel, *The Psalms in Israel's Worship,* 1.106–92; S. H. Hooke, editor, *Myth, Ritual, and Kingship: Essays on the Theory and Practice of Kingship in the Ancient Near East and in Israel* (Oxford: Clarendon, 1958); Theodor H. Gaster, *Thespis: Ritual, Myth and Drama in the Ancient Near East,* rev. ed. (New York: Doubleday, 1961); W. G. Lambert, "Myth and Ritual as Conceived by the Babylonians," *JSS* 13 (1968) 104–12; Thorkild Jacobsen, "Religious Drama in Ancient Mesopotamia," in *Unity and Diversity: Essays in the History, Literature, and Religion of the Ancient Near East,* ed. Hans Goedicke and J. J. M. Roberts, JHNES (Baltimore: Johns Hopkins Univ. Press, 1975) 65–97; John Gray, *The Biblical Doctrine of the Reign of God* (Edinburgh: T. & T. Clark, 1979); Jacob Klein, "Akitu," in *ABD* 1.138–40; and J. R. Porter, "Myth and Ritual School," in *DBI* 2.187–88.

29. For example, it is represented by the American School of Oriental Research in its publications *AASOR* and *BASOR*. More popular, comprehensive works are: W. F. Albright, *From the Stone Age to Christianity: Monotheism and the Historical Process* (Baltimore: Johns Hopkins Univ. Press, 1940; 2nd ed. 1957); idem, *Archaeology and the Religion of Israel* (Baltimore: Johns Hopkins Univ. Press, 1942); Stanley A. Cook, *The Religion of Ancient Palestine in the Light of Archaeology* (London: Oxford Univ. Press, 1930); Kurt Galling, editor, *Biblisches Reallexikon,* HAT 1 (Tübingen: Mohr/Siebeck, 1934–37). Evidence of a productive coordination of archaeological-topographical and historical investigations is the work of Albrecht Alt and Martin Noth in *PJB* and *ZDPV.* And one must not overlook the works in *PSBA* and the publications of the PEF.

30. See above, note 24.

31. A traditio-historical work that still contains significant residue of literary criticism is Ivar Hylander, *Der literarische Saul-Samuel-Komplex (1. Sam. 1–15): Traditionsgeschichtlich Untersucht* (Uppsala: Almqvist & Wiksell, 1932).

32. See, for example, Gressmann's analysis of the origin of the Joseph story: "Ursprung und Entwicklung der Joseph-Sage," in *Eucharistarion: Studien zur Religion und Literatur des Alten und Neuen Testaments. Hermann Gunkel zum 66. Geburtstage,* ed. Hans Schmidt, 2 vols., FRLANT 36 (Göttingen: Vandenhoeck & Ruprecht, 1923) 1.1–55; see particularly his methodological introduction (2–3). I may also point to my article, Mowinckel, "Der Ursprung der Bileam-Sage," *ZAW* 48 (1930) 233–71.

33. In light of this, it is peculiar for Ivan Engnell to speak of the oral tradition as "dispatched as pre-literary material," in *Gamla Testamentet: En Traditionshistorisk Inledning* (Stockholm: Svenska Kyrkans Diakonistyrelses Bokförlag) 1.39–40.

34. See, for example, Gunkel's "The Prophets: Oral and Written," in *Water for a Thirsty Land,* 88–93; orig. German article 1923.

35. Mowinckel, *Statholderen Nehemia* (Kristiania: Norlis, 1916) 116–17.

36. Hugo Gressmann, "Die literarische Analyse Deuterojesajas," *ZAW* 34 (1914) 254–97.

37. Compare also Joseph Coppens, *Histoire critique des livres de l'Ancien Testament,* 3rd ed. (Paris: Desclée, 1942) 140ff.

38. Adolphe Lods, "La role de la tradition orale dans la formation des recits de l'Ancien Testament," *RHR* 88 (1923) 51ff.; and Willy Staerk, "Zur alttestamentlichen Literarkritik," *ZAW* 42 (1924) 34ff.

39. Antonin Causse, *Le plus vieux chants de la Bible,* EHPR 4 (Paris: Alcan, 1926) 25–26.

40. Mowinckel, *Hvordan det Gamle Testament er blitt til: Israelittisk-jødisk litteraturhistorie* (Oslo: Universitetsforlaget, 1934) 8, 10ff.

41. H. M. Chadwick and Nora K. Chadwick, "Early Hebrew Literature," in *The Growth of Literature,* 3 vols. (Cambridge: Cambridge Univ. Press, 1932–36) 2.629–777.

42. Frederick C. Grant, "Form Criticism Farther Afield," *ATR* 19 (1937) 181–86; this is a review of the Chadwicks' work.

43. Otto Eissfeldt, *The Old Testament: An Introduction,* trans. P. R. Ackroyd (New York: Harper & Row, 1965).

44. Gunnar Hylmö, *Gamla testamentets litteraturhistoria* (Lund: Gleerup, 1938) 2, 6ff.

45. Aage Bentzen, *Introduction to the Old Testament,* 2 vols. (Copenhagen: Gad, 1948) 1.102–8.

46. H. S. Nyberg, *Studien zum Hoseabuche,* UUÅ (Uppsala: Lundequistska, 1935) 1–20; and idem, "Das textkritische Problem des Alten Testaments am Hoseabuch demonstriert," *ZAW* 52 (1934) 241–54.

47. See Johannes Pedersen, *The Arabic Book,* trans. G. French, ed. with an introduction by Robert Hillenbrand, MCNES (Princeton: Princeton Univ. Press, 1984); Danish ed. 1946.

48. See Ismar Elbogen, *Der jüdische Gottesdienst in seiner geschichtlichen Entwicklung,* 3rd ed. (Leipzig: Fock, 1931) 167.

[49.] Emanuel Tov, *The Textual Criticism of the Hebrew Bible,* 2nd ed. (Minneapolis: Fortress Press, 2001) 58–67.

50. Harris Birkeland, *Zum hebräischen Traditionswesen: Die Komposition der prophetischen Bücher des Alten Testaments,* ANVAO (Oslo: Dybwad, 1938). See Birkeland's review of Nyberg's book in *NTT* 38 (1937) 302ff.

51. We may probably consider Bernhard Duhm to be the founder of the modern view of the prophets, based on his commentary: *Das Buch Jesaia,* 4th ed., HAT (Göttingen: Vandenhoeck & Ruprecht, 1922); 1st ed. 1892. The full weight of this research, however, appears in Gustav Hölscher, *Die Propheten: Untersuchungen zur Religionsgeschichte Israels* (Leipzig: Hinrichs, 1914). See also Johannes Lindblom, *Prophecy in Ancient Israel* (Philadelphia: Fortress Press, 1973); Swedish ed. 1934. We may also note: Nathaniel Micklem, *Prophecy and Eschatology* (London: Allen & Unwin, 1926); Alfred Guillaume, *Prophecy and Divination among the Hebrews and Other Semites* (New York: Harper, 1938); and H. H. Rowley, "The Nature of Prophecy in the Light of Recent Study," *HTR* 38 (1945) 1–38.

52. Mowinckel, "Oppkomsten av profetlitteraturen," *NTT* 43 (1942) 65–111; idem, *Det Gamle Testamente* (Oslo: Aschehoug/Nygaard, 1929–55) 3.33ff.; and my review of Birkeland's book in *NTT* 39 (1938) 318ff.

53. Mowinckel, "Komposisjon av Jesajaboken kap. 1–39," *NTT* 44 (1943) 159–71; idem, *Gamle Testamente* 3.668ff.

54. Engnell, *Gamla Testamentet.*

55. See, for example, his statement of the problem that the tradition regarding the relationship between Ezra and Nehemiah would seem to offer to the historian; Engnell, *Gamla Testamentet* 1.258 n 2.

2. TRADITION CRITICISM AND LITERARY CRITICISM

[1.] For a discussion of Tatian's relevance to Old Testament source criticism, as well as other ancient parallels, see the essays in Jeffrey H. Tigay, editor, *Empirical Models for Biblical Criticism* (Philadelphia: Univ. of Pennsylvania Press, 1985). Tigay's volume also includes discussions of source criticism relative to a variety of other parallels, including: the Epic of Gilgamesh, the Samaritan Pentateuch, and the LXX.

2. See, for example, Ivan Engnell, *Gamla Testamentet: En Traditionshistorisk Inledning* (Stockholm: Svenska Kykrans Diakonistyrelses Bokförlag, 1945) 1.208–9.

[3.] For a classic treatment of the Chronicler's work, see Martin Noth, *The Chronicler's History,* JSOTSup 50 (Sheffield: JSOT Press, 1987); see also Steven L. McKenzie, *The Chronicler's Use of the Deuteronomistic History,* HSM 33 (Atlanta: Scholars, 1985); Ralph W. Klein, "Chronicles, Book of 1–2," in *ABD* 1.992–1002; and M. Patrick Graham and Steven L. McKenzie, editors, *The Chronicler as Author: Studies in Text and Texture,* JSOTSup 263 (Sheffield: JSOT Press, 1999).

4. See Mowinckel, *Statholderen Nehemia* (Kristiania/Oslo: Norlis, 1916) 14ff. [Ed.] See also Joseph Blenkinsopp, *Ezra-Nehemiah: A Commentary,* OTL (Louisville: Westminster John Knox, 1988); Mark A. Throntveit, *Ezra-Nehemiah,* IBC (Louisville: John Knox, 1992); and Lester L. Grabbe, *Ezra-Nehemiah,* OTR (London: Routledge, 1998).

5. See Mowinckel, *Zur Komposition des Buches Jeremia,* SNVAO (Kristiania/Oslo: Dybwad, 1914) 5–14, 31–45. I no longer maintain that we are necessarily dealing with written sources here, and I also have different views of many of the passages that I then assigned to Source C. [Ed.] See Jack R. Lundbom, "Baruch, Seraiah, and the Expanded Colophons in the Book of Jeremiah," *JSOT* 36 (1986) 89–114.

6. Arvid S. Kapelrud, *The Question of Authorship in the Ezra-Narrative,* SNVAO (Oslo: 1944) 95ff.

7. Mowinckel, *Ezra den skriftlaerde* (Kristiania/Oslo: Dybwad, 1916) 49ff.

8. Regarding this remark about Gunkel's view of the Psalms, I refer primarily to my *Psalmenstudien* 2, where I have shown this problem in his method. I have also shown in practice how much further one can get in the interpretation of the Psalms through an equal valuation of form and content; both demonstrate the cultic setting in life. In his reply in *Introduction to the Psalms* (69–81), Gunkel maintains his purely formal definition of the Enthronement Psalms and wants to determine the notional contents and rites of the festival merely on the basis of the limited material obtained in that way. The result is that he can doubt both the importance and the existence of the festival—according to the principle: First, I have not borrowed any kettle; and second, it had a hole in it when I borrowed it! Gunkel's skepticism has been completely refuted by the Ugaritic discoveries in Ras Shamra, Syria, which show the importance the ideology of the ascension of the deity had among Israel's neighbors long before the immigration of Israel into Canaan. It would have been more than a miracle if Israel's cult had not been influenced by these ideas. See Arvid S. Kapelrud, "Jahves tronstigningsfest og funnene i Ras-sjamra," *NTT* 41 (1940) 38ff. [Ed.] See also John Gray, *The Biblical Doctrine of the Reign of God* (Edinburgh: T. & T. Clark, 1979) 7–71.

9. See Mowinckel, *Det Gamle Testamente* (Oslo: Aschehoug, 1944) 2.30. It is just such a determination of the nature of the separate tradition that is so often missing in the archaeologically schooled investigators of the Old Testament. It has also been easy for them to be tempted to find the historicity of a tradition, proven only because archaeological results have shown it to be *possible!* This is made possible if one is first willing to rationalize it a little. That is, for example, when one puts an earthquake instead of the trumpets at Jericho, as John Garstang did (*The Heritage of Solomon: An Historical Introduction to the Sociology of Ancient Palestine* [London: Williams, 1934] 305); or if one makes Mt. Sinai into a volcano, as Charles T. Beke did (*The Late Dr. Charles Beke's Dis-*

coveries of Sinai in Arabia and of Midian [London: Trubner, 1878]), who was followed by Hermann Gunkel, "Notiz über die Lage des Sinai," *DLZ* 24/50 (1903) 3058–59, and by Hugo Gressmann, *Mose und seine Zeit: Ein Kommentar zu den Mose-Sagen,* FRLANT 18 (Göttingen: Vandenhoeck & Ruprecht, 1913) 112. A question like the one discussed above can never be decided through archaeological research, except if we imagine that one found the bones of the five kings inside the Makkedah cave (Josh 10:16-27), or excavated the remains of the fallen outside of Gibeon (10:10)! A question like the above must obviously be answered first, before one starts confronting tradition with archaeology. It is this necessary advance determination of the nature of the tradition itself, of what one can except to find in it and what cannot be demanded from it, which is also lacking in the eminent archaeologist, linguist, and historian, W. F. Albright, in his discussion with Martin Noth on the Joshua traditions and archaeology in the article "The Israelite Conquest of Canaan in the Light of Archaeology," *BASOR* 74 (1939) 11–22. In this article, Albright does not go deeply enough into the form-critical side of the traditio-historical problem and does not, therefore, reach far beyond a more subjective protest against Noth's determination of this or that tradition as an aetiology. In principle, Noth must here be said to be right, not Albright, even if the present author often disagrees with Noth about his individual results.

10. Ivan Engnell's judgment about Gunkel is this: "To Gunkel, and still more to his successors, it was, in spite of a distinct recognition of the oral tradition, almost exclusively a question of written literature, which was analyzed and torn to pieces on exclusively form-critical bases and to which the whole arsenal of literary criticism was applied, while the oral tradition was dismissed as 'pre-literary material'" (*Gamla Testamentet* 1.39; Mowinckel's translation). It is not characteristic of Gunkel that he builds on literary source criticism and partly develops it, but all that he contributes beyond and independently of source criticism. By this I mean his whole form-historical and traditio-historical analysis and interpretation. I have myself heard Gunkel in technical discussions with us who were then young express himself with skepticism and ridicule about the value of the supposed source analysis in P between P^G, P^S, P^X, etc. Neither is it characteristic of Gunkel that he sometimes, particularly in his Psalms commentary, makes form criticism too one-sided. Rather, it is phenomenal that he has discovered form criticism's importance to the understanding of the individual traditions and the setting in life—resulting then in the history of tradition. I have on several issues carried investigations further than Gunkel himself. And I have seen more clearly than he the connection of many texts with the cult and its "ritual pattern"—even though this phrase had not yet been used! But I would be deeply ungrateful if I were to deny the debt we all owe to his pioneering work, and must acknowledge that my own results have often been reached in connection with his ideas.

11. Mowinckel, *Det Gamle Testamente.*

12. This is the case with Engnell, if we are to take him at his word.

13. See P. A. H. de Boer on the harmonization and stabilization of growing tradition: "Only when the story has become tradition and the idea of the 'holy writ' is ripening, the mind for harmonization arises, whereby can be referred to the corresponding phenomenon with the Muslim theologians with the *hadith,* while the immutability, the stabilization into one form is coming on," in *NedTT* 1 (1899) 152. See further on p. 153: "In the evolution of the stories, e.g., in the Midrash, we just see the details increase" (italics mine). Every student of the real history of tradition knows that it is so.

14. This expression is from Edvard Lehmann; see his *Stedet og Vejea: Et religionshistorisk Perspektiv* (Copenhagen: Jespersen og Pios, 1918) 75ff.

15. Some examples are: Gen 12:10-20; 20:1-18; and 26:7-11. [Ed.] See Klaus Koch, *The Growth of the Biblical Tradition: The Form-Critical Method,* trans. S. M. Cupitt (New York: Scribners, 1969) 111–32.

16. See, for example, the "gloss" of 1 Sam 9:9 or the explanatory remark in Judg 17:6, to mention only two out of many.

17. Regarding Jeremiah, the evidence is quite clear in the numerous cases where the full wording of the saying has been transmitted elsewhere in the book whereas the narrative only offers a summary. See Mowinckel, *Zur Komposition des Buches Jeremia,* 24ff.

18. See Mowinckel, *Le Décalogue,* EHPR 16 (Paris: Alcan, 1927) 133ff.; and idem, "Zur Geschichte der Dekaloge," *ZAW* 53 (1937) 218–34. [Ed.] See also Eduard Nielsen, *The Ten Commandments in New Perspective,* trans. D. J. Bourke, SBT 2/7 (Naperville: Allenson, 1968); Hans Jochen Boecker, *Law and the Administration of Justice in the Old Testament and Ancient East,* trans. J. Moiser (Minneapolis: Augsburg, 1980); Walter J. Harrelson, *The Ten Commandments and Human Rights,* OBT (Philadelphia: Fortress Press, 1980); and Calum M. Carmichael, *The Origins of Biblical Law: The Decalogues and the Book of the Covenant* (Ithaca, N.Y.: Cornell Univ. Press, 1992).

19. Engnell, *Gamla Testamentet* 1.42–43.

[20.] See Emanuel Tov, *Textual Criticism of the Hebrew Bible,* 2nd ed. (Minneapolis: Fortress Press, 2001) 258–85.

21. Engnell, *Gamla Testamentet* 2.60.

[22.] Tov, *Textual Criticism,* 313–50.

[23.] Tov, *Textual Criticism,* 295–96, 302–5.

24. Engnell, *Gamla Testamentet* 1.30.

25. Knut Liestøl, *Norske Aettesogor* (Oslo: Norli, 1922). See also idem, *The Origin of the Icelandic Family Sagas,* trans. A. G. Jayne (Cambridge: Harvard Univ. Press, 1930).

[26.] See Koch, *The Growth of the Biblical Tradition,* 132–48; and Aulikki Nahkola, *Double Narratives in the Old Testament: The Foundations of Method in Biblical Criticism,* BZAW 290 (Berlin: de Gruyter, 2001).

27. To mention only one example, it deprives us of the key to understanding the psalm and its cultic setting and nature when several exegetes (e.g., Buhl, Cheyne, and others) delete or completely rewrite and remove the last sentence in Ps 81:5b ("I hear a voice I had not known").

[28.] Michael Barnes, *Draumkvaede: An Edition and Study* (Oslo: Universitetsforlaget, 1974).

29. H. S. Nyberg, *Studien zu Hoseabuche: Zugleich ein Beitrag zur Klärung des Problems der alttestamentlichen Textkritik* (Uppsala: Almqvist & Wiksell) 128.

30. Nyberg mentions particularly Otto Eissfeldt, *The Old Testament: An Introduction,* trans. P. R. Ackroyd (New York: Harper & Row, 1965); but it applies to a greater extent to the older introductions and literary histories of the Old Testament. It also applies to a comparatively recent book like Johannes Hempel, *Die althebräische Literatur und ihr hellenistisch-jüdisches Nachleben* (Wildpark-Potsdam: Athenaion, 1930).

31. See Mowinckel, "Oppkomsten av profetlitteraturen," *NTT* 43 (1942) 69–79.

32. The evidence for this, provided by Hariton Tiktin (*Kritische Untersuchungen zu den Büchern Samuelis,* FRLANT 16 [Göttingen, Vandenhoeck & Ruprecht, 1922]), has not been reduced by anyone. [Ed.] See also P. Kyle McCarter Jr., *1 Samuel,* AB 8 (Garden City,

N.Y.: Doubleday, 1980); and idem, *II Samuel,* AB 9 (Garden City, N.Y.: Doubleday, 1984).

33. Nyberg, *Studien zu Hoseabuche,* 114–15.

34. See Mowinckel, "'Die letzten Worte Davids' in II Sam. 23,1-7," *ZAW* 45 (1927) 30–58.

35. As to the Norwegian tales, Prof. Knut Liestøl confirmed this to me in private communication concerning his own experience. He tells me that regarding one of the best storytellers (whom he personally met), the influence from the literary form given to the tales by Peter Christen Asbjørnsen and Jorgen Engebretsen Moe was quite clear. To convince oneself that the same is often the case with the Laplander tales, one need only read through those recorded by Quigstad and others in quite recent times. It is obvious that in many cases the real source is Asbjørnsen and Moe's *Norske Folkeeventyr.* Just Quigstad edited a complete edition of the Laplander (Samme) tales, *Lappiske eventyr og sagn,* 4 vols. (Oslo: Aschehoug, 1927–29). Letters sent to me by Dr. R. Christiansen (Feb. 21, 1947) and Rector J. Quigstad (Feb. 25, 1947) confirm the fact stated above.

3. The Original Units of Tradition

[1.] Hugo Gressmann, "Die literarische Analyse Deuterojesajas," *ZAW* 34 (1914) 254–97.

2. *Die Schriften des Alten Testaments in Auswahl, neu übersetzt und für die Gegenwart erklärt* (Göttingen: Vandenhoeck & Ruprecht, 1910–15).

[3.] For an overview of his method, see Ivan Engnell, "The Traditio-Historical Method in Old Testament Research," in *A Rigid Scrutiny: Critical Essays on the Old Testament,* trans. J. T. Willis (Nashville: Vanderbilt Univ. Press, 1969) 3–11.

4. The KJV obscures the identity of the heading in Jer 23:9a ("Concerning the prophets") by syntactically integrating these words into the sentence: "Mine heart within me is broken because of the prophets." [Ed.] The RSV and NRSV clarify the wording.

5. This chapter division in the MT has been "corrected" in English as well as Norwegian translations, where Isa 8:23 of the MT is labeled 9:1; therefore 9:1-6 in the MT is 9:2-7 in modern translations.

6. Compare the messenger and letter formula: "Thus says Yahweh: Say to X . . ." This is the typical introductory formula in prophetic sayings. See Ludwig Köhler, *Deuterojesaja (Jesaja 40–55) stilkritisch untersuch,* BZAW 37 (Giessen: Töpelmann, 1923) 102ff. [Ed.] See also James F. Ross, "The Prophet as Yahweh's Messenger," in *Israel's Prophetic Heritage: Essays in Honor of James Muilenburg,* ed. B. W. Anderson and W. Harrelson (New York: Harper, 1962) 98–107; Claus Westermann, *The Basic Forms of Prophetic Speech,* trans. H. C. White (Philadelphia: Westminster, 1967) 98–115; and Samuel A. Meier, *The Messenger in the Ancient Semitic World,* HSM 45 (Atlanta: Scholars, 1988).

7. Gunkel was the first to understand and state this clearly; see his "Prophets: Oral and Written," in *Water for a Thirsty Land: Israelite Literature and Religion,* ed. K. C. Hanson, FCBS (Minneapolis: Fortress Press, 2001) 85–133 (orig. German article, 1923). [Ed.] See Katheryn Pfisterer Darr, "Literary Perspectives on Prophetic Literature," in *Old Testament Interpretation: Past, Present, and Future. Essays in Honor of Gene M. Tucker,* ed. James Luther Mays et al. (Nashville: Abingdon, 1995) 126–43.

4. The Form-Critical Investigation

1. Hugo Winckler's "pan-Baylonianism" was quite one-sided, schematic, and artificial. But the truth in his perspective was the largely uniform ancient Near Eastern culture (parallel to medieval European culture or the contemporary Western culture). This uniformity, in a more concrete form, has been confirmed by recent archaeological research in the Near East.

[Ed.] On the interconnections of the Mediterranean region, see, for example: Morton Smith, "The Common Theology of the Ancient Near East," *JBL* 71 (1952) 135–48; Theodor H. Gaster, *Thespis: Ritual, Myth, and Drama in the Ancient Near East*, rev. ed. (Garden City, N.Y.: Doubleday, 1961); Cyrus H. Gordon, *The Common Background of Greek and Hebrew Civilizations* (New York: Harper & Row, 1962; reprinted New York: Norton, 1965); David D. Gilmore, editor, *Honor and Shame and the Unity of the Mediterranean* (Washington, D.C.: American Anthropological Association, 1987); and Peregrine Horden and Nicholas Purcell, *The Corrupting Sea: A Study of Mediterranean History* (Oxford: Blackwell, 2000).

2. See Hedwig Jahnow, *Das hebräische Leichenlied im Rahmen der Völkerdichtung*, BZAW 36 (Giessen: Töpelmann, 1923). [Ed.] Nancy C. Lee, *The Singers of Lamentations: Cities under Siege, from Ur to Jerusalem to Sarajevo*, BibIntSer 60 (Boston: Brill, 2002).

[3.] Mowinckel actually uses the terms "type research" and "type criticism" for *Gattungsforschung*. "Type," however, does not have the clarity in English of "genre," which has had more currency among contemporary scholars.

[4.] While many scholars have continued to use the label "lament psalm," since Gerstenberger's early studies, this genre has been more accurately identified as a "complaint psalm." On the form of the complaint psalm, see Hermann Gunkel, *Introduction to the Psalms: The Genres of the Religious Lyric of Israel*, completed by Joachim Begrich, trans. J. D. Nogalski (Macon, Ga.: Mercer Univ. Press, 1998) 121–98; Mowinckel, *The Psalms in Israel's Worship*, trans. D. R. Ap-Thomas (Nashville: Abingdon, 1962) 2.1–25; Erhard S. Gerstenberger, *Psalm Part 1, with an Introduction to Cultic Poetry*, FOTL 14 (Grand Rapids: Eerdmans, 1988) 11–14; and Patrick D. Miller, *They Cried to the Lord: The Form and Theology of Biblical Prayer* (Minneapolis: Fortress Press, 1994) 55–134.

5. For this important aspect of prophetic sayings, see Mowinckel, *Det Gamle Testamente* (Oslo: Aschehoug/Nygaard, 1929–55) 3.49, including bibliography.

6. See, for example, Gustav Hölscher, *Die Propheten: Untersuchungen zur Religionsgeschichte Israels* (Leipzig: Hinrichs, 1914) 396–99.

7. Mowinckel, *Det Gamle Testamente* 3.51–53.

8. Compare Walther Baumgartner, *Die Klagegedichte des Jeremiah*, BZAW 32 (Giessen: Töpelmann, 1917). [Ed.] See also William L. Holladay, *Jeremiah 2*, Hermeneia (Minneapolis: Fortress Press, 1989) 64–70.

9. The term "legend" does not, of course, imply that the narrative cannot have a historical core; it primarily expresses the religious and edifying intent of the narrative. Compare Mowinckel, *Hvordan det Gamle Testament er blitt til: Israelittisk-jødisk litteraturhistorie* (Oslo: Universitetsforlaget, 1934) 19–20. [Ed.] See also Mowinckel, "Legend," in *IDB* 3.108–10; Ronald M. Hals, "Legend," in *Saga, Legend, Tale, Novella, Fable: Narrative Forms in Old Testament Literature*, ed. George W. Coats, JSOTSup 35 (Sheffield: JSOT Press, 1985) 45–55; and Hermann Gunkel, *The Stories in Genesis*, trans. J. J. Scullion, (Vallejo, Calif.: Bibal, 1994; German ed. 1910).

10. On the other hand, the prose text in 2 Samuel 7 can be disregarded here, since it is not typical. In this late legend-formation, the brief message is embedded in a long, theological rationale that attempts to answer a purely theoretical question: Why was it not David who built the temple? The frequent attempts to separate a "genuine core" by means of literary criticism must be rejected in principle.

[11.] Mowinckel, *Psalmenstudien* 3; Hermann Gunkel, *Introduction to the Psalms*, 251–92; Mowinckel, *The Psalms in Israel's Worship* 2.53–73; Aubrey R. Johnson, *The Cultic Prophet and Israel's Psalmody* (Cardiff: Univ. of Wales Press, 1979); and W. H. Bellinger, *Psalmody and Prophecy*, JSOTSup 27 (Sheffield: JSOT Press, 1984).

12. Here one may clearly see the original relationship between the "oracle" of the seer-prophet and the instruction (*torah*) of the priest, which is also an oracle. Compare Gunnar Östborn, *Tora in the Old Testament: A Semantic Study*, trans. C. Hentschel (Lund: Ohlsson, 1945) 127ff. Östobern thinks that *torah* originally had the meaning "instruction," from which the meaning "law" developed. This is not correct, however; the original oracular connection of the word is quite clear. But the meaning "instruction" belongs also originally to the content of the conception, insofar as the oracle was very often an instruction about what to do in the special case, which the questioner put before the priest, the one imparting the oracle.

13. Mowinckel, *Psalmenstudien* 3.12–14.

14. Gustav Hölscher, *Die Profeten: Untersuchungen zur Religionsgeschichte Israels* (Leipzig: Hinrich, 1914) 87–88.

15. A brief survey of the artistic forms of the prophetic sayings (form and content) is available in Mowinckel, *Det Gamla Testamente* 3.38–56. For more detailed analysis of a single prophet, see Mowinckel, "Stilformer og motiver i profeten Jeremias diktning," *Edda* 36 (1926) 233–320. See also Gunnar E. Hylmö, *Gamla Testamentets Litteraturhistorie* (Lund: Gleerup, 1938) 72ff.

16. See, for example, Hermann Gunkel's "Prophets: Oral and Written," in *Water for a Thirsty Land: Israelite Literature and Religion*, ed. K. C. Hanson, FCBS (Minneapolis: Fortress Press, 2001) 88–93 (orig. German article 1923); and Hugo Gressmann, "Die literarische Analyse Deuterojesajas," *ZAW* 34 (1914) 259–60.

17. After he squares accounts with literary criticism, Julian Morgenstern believes that the preaching of Amos constitutes a single great speech that Amos made on a special occasion (*Amos Studies* [Cincinnati: Hebrew Union College Press, 1941] 10–11). This is in direct opposition to everything that form history has taught us about the preaching of the prophets and the transmission of their words. [Ed.] The composition of the Book of Amos has remained a controversial issue. See Hans Walter Wolff, *Amos, the Prophet: The Man and His Background*, trans. F. R. McCurley (Philadelphia: Fortress Press, 1973); idem, *Joel and Amos*, Hermeneia, trans. W. Janzen et al. (Philadelphia: Fortress Press, 1977); Robert B. Coote, *Amos among the Prophets: Composition and Theology* (Philadelphia: Fortress Press, 1981); Max E. Polley, *Amos and the Davidic Empire: A Socio-historical Approach* (Oxford: Oxford Univ. Press, 1989); and Shalom M. Paul, *Amos*, Hermeneia (Minneapolis: Fortress Press, 1991).

18. Mowinckel, "Oppkomsten av profetlitteraturen," *NTT* 43 (1942) 65–111.

19. Harris Birkeland, *Zum hebräischen Traditionswesen: Die Komposition der prophetischen Bücher des Alten Testaments* (Oslo: Dybwad, 1938) 5ff.

20. One also finds references to Coniah and Zedekiah later than 599 B.C.E.

21. For this interpretation, see my note on Jer 21:13-14 in *Det Gamla Testamente* 3.367,

with reference to similar use of the image in Isaiah. It is probably the conception of the "house of the forest of Lebanon" (1 Kgs 7:2) that was the pattern of this conception of thought. See further my notes on Jer 22:8-9 (ibid., 367–68) and on 22:20-22 (ibid., 369).

22. Examples of connecting words added by the collectors ("the tradition") are probably:

kî: Isa 3:1; 8:11; 30:9, 15; 31:4; 45:18; Jer 4:27; 9:19; 14:3; 15:5; 30:12; Amos 5:4
laken: Isa 28:14; Jer 18:13
wayyomer / we'amar / wa'omar: Isa 57:14; Mic 3:1
'al-zot: Mic 1:8
wehemmah: Hos 6:7

To these must be added longer connecting formulas such as "For Yahweh has said," "In that day it shall come to pass that," and the like; see, for example, Isa 7:18, 20, 23; 25:9; 26:1; Jer 13:17; 14:17; 17:5; 18:13; Mic 5:4, 9; Hab 2:6a; Zeph 1:8, 10, 12.

23. The connecting word (generally a *kî*) is missing in the LXX of Isa 8:11; Jer 4:27; 8:4; 14:3; 15:5; 17:5; 30:12; and possibly in other places as well.

24. Mowinckel, "Die Komposition des deuterojesajanischen Buches [2 parts]," *ZAW* 49 (1931) 87–112; 242–60.

25. Ivan Engnell, *Gamla Testamentet: En Traditionshistorisk Inledning* (Stockholm: Svenska Kykrans Diakonistyrelses, 1945) 1.45.

26. Hermann Gunkel, *Die Psalmen*, HKAT (Göttingen: Vandenhoeck & Ruprecht, 1929).

27. Still less of this is found in the Psalms commentary of Aage Bentzen, which also predominantly makes use of the form-critical approach. See Aage Bentzen, *Fortolkning til de gammeltestamentlige Salmer* (Copenhagen: Gad, 1932).

28. Engnell, *Gamla Testamentet* 1.45; also Engnell, "The Ebed Yahweh Songs and the Suffering Messiah in Deutero-Isaiah," *BJRL* 31 (1948) 54–93 (orig. art. in *SEÅ* 10 [1945] 31–65).

29. They are not numerous. The first is the article by Gressmann on Deutero-Isaiah (see note 16 above). See also Ludwig Köhler, *Deuterojesaja (Jesaja 40–55) stilkritisch untersuch*, BZAW 37 (Giessen: Töpelmann, 1923); Emil Balla, "Die Droh- und Scheltreden des Amos," Reformationfestprogram, Leipzig, 1926; Mowinckel, "Stilformer," 276ff.; Paul Humbert, *Problèmes du livre d'Habacuc*, Mémoires de l'Université de Neuchâtel 18 (Neuchâtel: Secrétariat de l'Université, 1944); Gunnar E. Hylmö, *Studier över stilen i de gammeltestamentliga profetböckerna*, Vol. 1: *De egentliga profetiska diktarterna*, LUÅ 25/4 (Lund: Gleerup, 1929). All new commentaries share this point of view, more or less.

30. On this question, see the detailed discussions in Mowinckel, "Die Komposition."

31. See, for example, Hermann Gunkel, "Prophets: Oral and Written," 85–133; Gunnar E. Hylmö, *De sakallade profetiska liturgierna I Jes. 25,1—26,21*, LUÅ 3 (Lund: Gleerup, 1938); Gunkel, "Jes. 33: Eine prophetische Liturgie," *ZAW* 42 (1924) 177–208; idem, "The Close of Micah: A Prophetical Liturgy," in *What Remains of the Old Testament and Other Essays*, trans. A. K. Dallas (London: Allen & Unwin, 1928) 115–49 (orig. German article, 1924); Paul Volz, *Der Prophet Jeremia*, KAT 10 (Leipzig: Deichert, 1922) XXXVIII, XLI–XLII. We may also make reference to the relatively large units into which Trito-Isaiah (Isaiah 56–66) has been divided. I have taken the eleven chapters as fourteen sayings of varying lengths (*Det Gamle Testamente*, vol. 3). And I have suggested the possibility that chapter 65 belongs to 63:7—64:11 based on the pattern of a lamentation day liturgy (276).

32. Engnell refers to Wilhelm Caspari's *Lieder und Gottessprāche der Rückwanderer*

(Jesaja 40–55), BZAW 65 (Giessen: Töpelmann, 1934); but Caspari's work is in no way typical of form criticism.

33. As does Engnell in "The Ebed Yahweh Songs" referring to Kissane: "The context is the guide to the interpretation, and disregard of the context leads to chaos" (Engnell, "The Ebed Yahweh Songs," 65). Of course this is true! But it is merely a truism.

34. It even comprises Isaiah 33, and possibly Isaiah 34; see Engnell, "The Ebed Yahweh Songs," 64.

35. I am aware of the "corporate thinking" of ancient Israel. I have always maintained this very strongly, but I also believe that this truth can be urged too strongly. Within one and the same mental and imaginative act of conception, with its view to concrete picture formation, a figure cannot simultaneously be painted on the retina as king and as people.

36. Or is it perhaps the opinion of the "tradition historian" that a text interpretation is not to be historical? Engnell sometimes employs the words "historicism" or "historicizing" in a deprecating way, which seems to indicate that by merely labeling an interpretation with this word he has proved it to be incorrect and unjustified. See Engnell, "The Ebed Yahweh Songs," 60, 66 n3, 87–88.

37. Mowinckel, *Psalmenstudien* 2.235–44.

38. Even if these sayings do not correspond to the original words of Deutero-Isaiah, they nevertheless remain valid as examples. This is true since in their present form they are new prophecies based on earlier promises and originate with the disciples of Deutero-Isaiah. I am now inclined to give up the doubt I expressed about the uniformity of Isa 48:1-11 (*Det Gamle Testament*, vol. 3). I am still doubtful about the originality of Isa 55:7.

39. See Mowinckel, *Jesaja-disiplene: Profetien fra Jesaja til Jeremia* (Oslo: Aschehoug/Nygaard, 1926) 145ff.; Mowinckel, *Det Gamle Testamente* 3.707–9 (unfortunately somewhat reserved). The interpretation of Habakkuk as a connected prophetic liturgy is also maintained very strongly by Paul Humbert in his thorough and valuable investigation, *Problèmes du livre d'Habacuc*.

40. Karl Budde in *Die heilige Schrift des Alten Testament*, 2 vols., ed. Emil Kautzsch and Alfred Bertholet, 4th ed. (Tübingen: Mohr/Siebeck, 1922-23) 1.653ff. See also Willy Staerk, *Die Ebed Jahwe-Lieder in Jes. 40ff.*, BWAT 14 (Leipzig: Hinrichs, 1913) 9ff.

41. Gressmann, "Die literarische Analyse Deuterojesajas," 254–58; Köhler, *Deuterojesaja*; and Mowinckel, "Die Komposition des deuterojesajanischen Buches."

42. Bentzen, *Fortolkning*. I have not had the opportunity to see Edward J. Kissane's commentary, *The Book of Isaiah*, 2 vols. (Dublin: Browne and Nolan, 1941–43). Based on comments by Engnell ("The Ebed Yahweh Songs"), however, it seems Kissane is headed in the older direction with respect to the issues I am discussing here.

43. Mowinckel, "Selvstendige enkeltutsagn eller storre taleenheter hos Deuterojesaja," *DTT* 9 (1946) 142–68.

44. Engnell's comments that the whole "Deutero-Isaian tradition complex" "constitutes a firm compositional unit," which may be "characterized as a great imitation of an anniversary liturgy" are merely a loose contention for which he offers no evidence ("The Ebed Yahweh Songs," [p. 41 in SEÅ]). Besides, how does this contention tally with the fact that Engnell himself recognizes that the sayings of Deutero-Isaiah are arranged according to catchwords? Liturgies are not arranged according to catchwords, but according to factual, liturgical-mythical-dramatic principles. It is quite another matter that the total

picture of the arrival of Yahweh (epiphany) and deliverance of Israel that is hovering in the mind of the prophet in its broad outlines has been taken from the ideas and forms of the annual throne-ascension festival. I have already pointed this out in *Psalmenstudien* 2.238–44, 251–54, 263–64, 273–76, 282–85, 288–90, 292–96.

45. Mowinckel, "Oppkomsten," 67–69.

5. Tradition and Writing

1. For this section, see Mowinckel, "Oppkomsten av profetlitteraturen," *NTT* (1942) 65–111. [Ed.] See the articles in Ehud Ben Zvi and Michael H. Floyd, editors, *Writings and Speech in Israelite and Ancient Near Eastern Prophecy,* SBLSymSer 10 (Atlanta: Scholars, 2000).

2. Mowinckel, "Oppkomsten," 71ff.

3. Humbert's division of the units, which connects Hab 2:5b to the following woe-exclamation, appears to me to conflict with both the tenets of form criticism and Hebrew syntax (Paul Humbert, *Problèmes du livre d'Habacuc,* Mémoires de l'Université de Neuchâtel 18 [Neuchâtel: Secrétariat de l'Université, 1944] 48). Verse 5b contains the necessary topical characterizations of "treacherous" (*bôgēd*) and "arrogant man" (*geber yahîr*), which apply the general sentence in v. 5a to the specific historical oppressor. [Ed.] See Michael H. Floyd, "Prophecy and Writing in Habakkuk 2,1-5," *ZAW* 105 (1993) 462–81; and idem, *Minor Prophets Part 2,* FOTL 22 (Grand Rapids: Eerdmans, 2000) 122–29.

4. Mowinckel, "Oppkomsten," 75ff. [Ed.] See R. L. Hicks, "*Delet* and *Megillah*: A Fresh Approach to Jeremiah xxxvi," *VT* 33 (1983) 46–66; Robert P. Carroll, *Jeremiah,* OTL (Philadelphia: Westminster, 1986) 656–68; William L. Holladay, *Jeremiah 2,* Hermeneia (Minneapolis: Fortress Press, 1989) 253–55.

5. On this determination of the narrative's purpose, see Mowinckel, *Zur Komposition des Buches Jeremia* (Oslo: Dybwad, 1913) 24–25.

6. Bernhard Duhm already maintained this in his commentary, *Das Buch Jeremia Erklärt,* KHC 11 (Tübingen: Mohr/Siebeck, 1901). I long ago abandoned my skepticism regarding this opinion (Mowinckel, *Zur Komposition,* 30); see also Mowinckel, *Det Gamle Testamente* (Oslo: Aschehoug/Nygaard, 1929-55) 3.289.

7. The chronological arrangement of the narratives is quite probable; see Mowinckel, *Zur Komposition,* 27; and Mowinckel, *Det Gamle Testamente* 3.289.

8. See Mowinckel, *Zur Komposition,* 14–17. [Ed.] See Robert P. Carroll, *Jeremiah,* OTL (Philadelphia: Westminster, 1986) 744–50; Marion Ann Taylor, "Jeremiah 45: The Problem of Placement," *JSOT* 37 (1987) 79–98; and Holladay, *Jeremiah 2,* 307–11.

9. See Mowinckel, *Det Gamle Testamente* 3.293–96; regarding the location in MT and LXX, see ibid., 289; also Harris Birkeland, *Zum hebräischen Traditionswesen: Die Komposition der prophetischen Bücher des Alten Testaments,* ANVAO (Oslo: Dybwad, 1938) 44–45. [Ed.] See Holladay, *Jeremiah 2,* 312–14.

10. Regarding these speeches, see especially: Duhm, *Jeremia,* XVI–XX; Mowinckel, *Zur Komposition,* 31–45; Birkeland, *Zum hebräischen Traditionswesen,* 42. The recognition in principle, held by Duhm and myself, of two different literary genres or tradition genres (prophetic sayings/oracles and speeches) is muddled, as usual, by Otto Eissfeldt, *The Old Testament: An Introduction,* trans. P. R. Ackroyd (New York: Harper & Row, 1965)

353–54. He makes the disastrous distinction between the first-person report ("Ichberichte") and the third-person report ("Fremdberichte") as the two "literary" types in the prophetic books. The tradition tended to let the prophets appear in the first person, though in certain cases, at least, we can prove that an original third person was changed to a first person; see Mowinckel, *Zur Komposition*, 58–59. [Ed.] See Robert P. Carroll, *Jeremiah*, 38–50; Holladay, *Jeremiah 2*, 10–24.

11. Mowinckel, *Zur Komposition*, 31–45. If one replaces the word "source" here with "tradition circle," most of what I said at that time still holds. The approach of my exposition there is in fact "traditio-historical."

12. Unfortunately, I did not make this sufficiently clear in my introduction to the Book of Jeremiah in *Det Gamle Testamente* (3.290). I allowed an unnecessary and unfounded partial concession to Duhm's view. In reality, however, this is not in agreement with the basic view underlying the argument in *Det Gamle Testamente*; nor is it in conformity with the facts stated there. I should have revised the passage on 290–91 in accordance with the argument above. In the same way, I should have distinguished between the speeches and the editorial notes that attach them to the book context.

13. Mowinckel, *Zur Komposition*, 6–10, 39–45; idem, *Det Gamle Testamente* 3.290.

14. See also Birkeland, *Zum hebräischen Traditionswesen*, 42.

15. See the argumentation in Mowinckel, *Zur Komposition*, 10–14; for the other speeches mentioned above, see the brief arguments in Mowinckel, *Det Gamle Testamente* 3. [Ed.] See Holladay, *Jeremiah 2*, 267–306.

16. See Mowinckel, *Det Gamle Testamente* 3 for the locations.

17. The connecting notes are, for example, "all the people who dwelt in Pathros in the land of Egypt" (Jer 44:15b); probably Jer 44:20-23 as well. See also the statement of time in Jer 19:14.

18. For Jer 32:2 see 37:1-16; for 32:3 see 37:21 and 38:18; for 32:4 see 34:3; 37:17; 38:23; and 39:5.

19. Jeremiah 52:28-30 is an independent tradition deriving from somewhere else. [Ed.] On this passage, see Carroll, *Jeremiah*, 868–70; Holladay, *Jeremiah 2*, 439–43.

20. Martin Noth, *The Deuteronomistic History*, trans. D. J. A. Clines et al., JSOTSup 15 (Sheffield: JSOT Press, 1981) 74.

[21.] On Hezekiah, see Iain W. Provan, *Hezekiah and the Books of Kings: A Contribution to the Debate about the Composition of the Deuteronomistic History*, BZAW 172 (Berlin: de Gruyter, 1988); and John H. Hull, "Hezekiah, Saint and Sinner: A Conceptual and Contextual Narrative Analysis of 2 Kings 18–20," Ph.D. dissertation, Claremont Graduate School, 2 vols., 1994. On the relationship of Isaiah 36–39 to 2 Kings 18:17—20:19, see: Peter R. Ackroyd, "An Interpretation of the Babylonian Exile: A Study of II Kings 20 and Isaiah 38–39," *SJT* 27 (1974) 329–52; A. K. Jenkins, "Hezekiah's Fourteenth Year: A New Interpretation of 2 Kings xviii 13—xix 37," *VT* 26 (1976) 284–98; Ronald E. Clements, "The Isaiah Narrative of 2 Kings 20:12-19 and the Date of the Deuteronomic History," in *Essays on the Bible and the Ancient World*, ed. Alexander Rofé and Yair Zakovitch (Jerusalem: Rubinshtain, 1983) 3.209–20; Peter Machinist, "Assyria and Its Image in First Isaiah," *JAOS* 103 (1983) 719–37; and Ehud Ben Zvi, "Who Wrote the Speech of Rabshekah and When?" *JBL* 109 (1990) 79–90.

22. Engnell contradicts himself when he declares Isaiah 36–39 to be "a tradition complex whose core is made up of the Hezekiah psalm in 38:9-20," and soon thereafter states that it is "a variant tradition to 2 Kings 18:1ff." ("The 'Ebed Yahweh Songs and the

Suffering Messiah in 'Deutero-Isaiah,'" *BJRL* 31 (1948) 64 n1 [54–93] (orig. art. in *SEÅ* 10 [1945] 31–65). It would be an odd "variant tradition" that lacked the very "core" of the tradition, the Hezekiah psalm! Now, as mentioned above, Isaiah 36–39 also contains a verse that no doubt derives from the Deuteronomistic History. Have parts of the saga work of the Deuteronomistic History existed then as floating "tradition complexes"? Using slogans like "tradition" and "complexes" one cannot explain away obvious facts. To raise the priority question regarding Isaiah 36–39 and 2 Kgs 18:17—20:19 is, therefore, not "wrong in principle," as Engnell contends. On the contrary, it would be a scientific and methodological error (thus an error in principle) not to raise it in this specific case. Of course there are plenty of parallel traditions where it is fundamentally wrong to raise such a priority question, for example: Psalm 18 and 2 Samuel 22; or Isa 2:2-5 and Mic 4:1-5. It is a foundational research principle, however, to recognize that not all cases are alike.

23. See Joachim Begrich, *Der Psalm des Hiskia: Ein Beitrag zum Verständnis von Jesaja 38,10-20*, FRLANT 42 (Göttingen: Vandenhoeck & Ruprecht, 1926). He attempts a reconstruction supported by the methods and results of form criticism and genre research. This is both justified in principle and may broadly have reached a correct result, even if it is, of course, impossible to obtain complete certainty in that way. [Ed.] On the Hezekiah psalm, see: William W. Hallo, "The Royal Correspondence of Larsa I: A Sumerian Prototype for the Prayer of Hezekiah," in *Kramer Anniversary Volume: Cuneiform Studies in Honor of Samuel Noah Kramer*, ed. B. L. Eichler, AOAT 25 (Kevelaer: Butzon & Bercker, 1976) 209–24; Marvin A. Sweeney, *Isaiah 1–39*, FOTL 16 (Grand Rapids: Eerdmans, 1996) 488–505; and Brevard S. Childs, *Isaiah*, OTL (Louisville: Westminster John Knox, 2001) 278–84.

6. The Growth and Development of Tradition

1. For the following, see Mowinckel, "Oppkomsten av profetlitteraturen," *NTT* 43 (1942) 65–111; and Mowinckel, *Det Gamle Testamente* (Oslo: Aschehoug/Nygaard, 1929–55) 3.33.

2. The prophecies of Amos and Hosea have been transmitted in Judean circles and partially altered to fit the Judean context; this is evidence for my point here. See Mowinckel, "Oppkomsten," 82–83; and Mowinckel, *Det Gamle Testamente* 3.569 and 621. Chapter 7 will also address this. [Ed.] See Hans Walter Wolff, *Amos, the Prophet: The Man and His Background*, trans. F. R. McCurley (Philadelphia: Fortress Press, 1973); idem, *Hosea*, trans. G. Stansell, Hermeneia (Philadelphia: Fortress Press, 1974).

3. See Mowinckel, *Jesajadisiplene: Profetien fra Jesaja til Jeremia* (Oslo: Dybwad, 1926).

4. See H. Ludin Jansen, *Die spätjüdische Psalmendichtung*, SNVAO (Oslo: Dybwad, 1937) 60, 63–64; Mowinckel, "Oppkomsten," 86, 88–92, 97, and 102; and Mowinckel, *Det Gamle Testamente* 3.36–37.

[5.] On these passages, see Gerhard von Rad, "The City on the Hill," in *The Problem of the Hexateuch and Other Essays*, trans. E. W. T. Dicken (London: Oliver & Boyd, 1966) 232–42; Hans Wildberger, *Isaiah 1–12*, CC (Minneapolis: Fortress Press, 1991) 81–96; and Brevard S. Childs, *Isaiah*, OTL (Louisville: Westminster John Knox, 2001) 28–31. On the larger issues of the connections between Isaiah and Micah, see Gary Stansell, *Micah and Isaiah: A Form and Tradition Historical Comparison*, SBLDS 85 (Atlanta: Scholars, 1988).

6. This is indeed the opinion of R. B. Y. Scott in "The Relation of Isaiah, Chapter 35 to Deutero-Isaiah," *AJSLL* 52 (1936) 178–91. But Scott's primarily linguistic-statistical argument simply proves the strongly "Deutero-Isaian" character of the chapter. The spirit of the chapter is considerably different. One finds little of the universalistic perspective of Deutero-Isaiah in Isaiah 34–35; and Deutero-Isaiah's interest was directed toward Babylon rather than Edom. See Wilhelm Caspari, "Jesaia 34 und 35," *ZAW* 49 (1931) 67–86. Isaiah 34–35 belongs to the circle of disciples stamped by Deutero-Isaiah, and who have been inadequately labeled "Trito-Isaiah" (Isaiah 56–66). Trito-Isaiah is not a single prophetic figure, as maintained by Karl Elliger (*Die Einheit des Tritojesaja: Jesaia 56–66*, BWANT 45 (Stuttgart: Kohlhammer, 1928), but a circle—the circle of Deutero-Isaiah. [Ed.] Claus Westermann agreed with Mowinckel's assessment of Trito-Isaiah as a collection from an Isaiah circle: *Isaiah 40–66*, trans. D. M. G. Stalker, OTL (Philadelphia: Westminster, 1969) 296–308. See also Paul D. Hanson, *The Dawn of Apocalyptic: The Historical and Sociological Roots of Jewish Apocalyptic Eschatology*, rev. ed. (Minneapolis: Fortress Press, 1979); idem, *Isaiah 40–66*, IBC (Louisville: Westminster John Knox, 1995); Odil Hannes Steck, *Studien zu Tritojesaja*, BZAW 203 (Berlin: Töpelmann, 1991); and Childs, *Isaiah*.

7. See note 6, and Mowinckel, *Det Gamle Testamente* 3.173–74. [Ed.] The relationship of Isaiah 34–35 to the rest of the book has remained a controversial issue; see Odil Hannes Steck, *Bereitete Heimkehr: Jesaja 35 als redaktionelle Brücke zwischen dem Ersten und dem Zweiten Jesaja*, SBS 121 (Stuttgart: Katholisches Bibelwerk, 1985); Craig A. Evans, "On the Unity and Parallel Structure of Isaiah," *VT* 38 (1988) 129–47; Marvin A. Sweeney, *Isaiah 1–39*, FOTL 16 (Grand Rapids: Eerdmans, 1996) 434–54; and Childs, *Isaiah*, 249–58.

8. How this fact can be "a major stumbling block" for literary criticism regarding the literary discrimination between Isaiah 1–39 and 40–66 is not easy to understand (Ivan Engnell, "The 'Ebed Yahweh Songs and the Suffering Messiah in 'Deutero-Isaiah,'" *BJRL* 31 (1948) 64 n1 [54–93] (orig. art. in *SEÅ* 10 [1945] 31–65). Even if the collection of sayings deriving from Isaiah and his circle of disciples, as well as from that circle in the post-exilic period (e.g., Isa 11:10-16; 13–14; 21:1-10) also contains sayings already stamped by the circle in its Deutero-Isaian forms of development, the collection in Isaiah 1–39 may very well have constituted a separate "book." Isaiah 1–39, as I indicated above, also contains chapters 24–27. Also included in this section are chaps. 34–35. Whether Isaiah 40–66 ever existed as a separate "book" is a separate question; nothing, however, prevents that from having been the case. [Ed.] On the development of the Book of Isaiah, see Rolf Rendtorff, *The Old Testament: An Introduction*, trans. J. Bowden (Philadelphia: Fortress Press, 1986) 198–200; idem, "The Book of Isaiah: A Complex Unity—Synchronic and Diachronic Readings," in *SBLSP 1991* (Atlanta: Scholars, 1991) 8–20; idem, "Isaiah 56:1 as a Key to the Formation of the Book of Isaiah," in *Canon and Theology*, trans. M. Kohl, OBT ((Minneapolis: Fortress Press, 1993) 181–89; and Christopher R. Seitz, *Zion's Final Destiny: The Development of the Book of Isaiah* (Minneapolis: Fortress Press, 1991).

9. See Isa 8:12, 16-19. Mowinckel, *Profeten Jesaja: En Bibelstudiebok* (Oslo: Dybwad, 1925) 19, 32; and Mowinckel, *Jesajadisiplene*. [Ed.] J. Ruck, "Isaiah and the Prophetic Disciple," *TBT* 21 (1983) 399–405.

[10.] See especially Klaus Baltzer, *Deutero-Isaiah*, trans. M. Kohl, Hermeneia (Minneapolis: Fortress Press, 2001); also Roy F. Melugin, *The Formation of Isaiah 40–55*, BZAW 141 (Berlin: de Gruyter, 1976).

[11.] See J. J. M. Roberts, "Isaiah in Old Testament Theology," *Int* 36 (1982) 130–43.

12. Karl Elliger, *Einheit;* idem, "Der Prophet Tritojesaja," *ZAW* 49 (1931) 112–41; idem, *Deuterojesaja in seinem Verhältnis zu Tritojesaja,* BWANT 63 (Stuttgart: Kohlhammer, 1933). Elliger is supported by Ernst Sellin, "Tritojesaja, Deuterojesaja und das Gottesknechtproblem," *NKZ* (1930) 73–93, 145–73.

13. Thus argues Engnell, "Ebed Yahweh Songs," 63. It is difficult to understand how it is possible to overlook the factual content of the arguments and methods of "literary criticism" and to fasten only on the formal side of the standpoint that they have assumed the natural idea of "books." This assumption has played no decisive role in the argument distinguishing Proto-Isaiah from Deutero-Isaiah. It is also difficult to understand the alleged abyss that separates Engnell's interpretation of the relation from my own (Engnell, 61–65). Perhaps Engnell forgets that even in the era of Hermann Gunkel and Hugo Gressmann the literary critics understood that oral transmission preceded the making of collections and books. I have stated this already in *Zur Komposition des Buches Jeremia,* SNVAO (Oslo: Dybwad, 1913) 26–27. Professor Simon T. Michelet discussed this new current in prophet research with conservative skepticism, but with some support in "Om literaer komposition i de gammel-testamentlige skrifter," *NTT* 18.2 (1917) 1–12.

14. Consult any major Isaiah commentary or Old Testament introduction for this issue. [Ed.] Recent discussions include: Ronald E. Clements, *Isaiah 1–39,* NCBC (Grand Rapids: Eerdmans, 1980) 2–8; Norman K. Gottwald, *The Hebrew Bible: A Socio-Literary Introduction* (Philadelphia: Fortress Press, 1985) 377–87; Christopher R. Seitz, "Isaiah, Book of (Third Isaiah)," in *ABD* 3.501–7; Childs, *Isaiah,* 1–5; and Hans Wildberger, *Isaiah 28–39,* trans. T. Trapp, CC (Minneapolis: Fortress Press, 2002).

15. See Mowinckel, *Die Erkenntnis Gottes bei den alttestamentlichen Profeten,* NTTSup 2 (Oslo: Grøndahl, 1941) 41–44, especially 41 n.2. For more detail, see Mowinckel, "Oppkomsten," 86, 94–97.

16. Mowinckel, "Oppkomsten," 92–93.

17. Mowinckel, *Det Gamle Testamente* 3.668 (§4a).

7. The Transformation of the Separate Prophetic Sayings

1. See above in chap. 6, and also Mowinckel, *Die Erkenntnis Gottes bei den alttestamentlichen Profeten,* NTTSup 2 (Oslo: Grøndahl, 1941) 41ff., especially 41 n2. For more detail, see Mowinckel, "Oppkomsten av profetlitteraturen," *NTT* 43 (1942) 86, 94ff.

2. See chap. 6 n2.

3. Note the "numerical sentences" where "two" and "three" are parallel terms in parallel lines; they actually mean the same thing: "two or three." [Ed.] See W. M. W. Roth, *Numerical Sayings in the Old Testament: A Form Critical Study,* VTSup 13 (Leiden: Brill, 1965); Meir Weiss, "The Pattern of Numerical Sequence in Amos 1–2," *JBL* 86 (1967) 416–23; Menahem Haran, "The Graded Numerical Sequence and the Phenomenon of 'Automatism' in Biblical Poetry," in *Congress Volume: Uppsala, 1971,* VTSup 22 (Leiden: Brill, 1972) 238–67; and Shalom M. Paul, *Amos,* Hermeneia (Minneapolis: Fortress Press, 1991) 27–30.

4. Peter Andreas Munch, *The Expression* Bajjom hahu': *Is It an Eschatological Terminus Technicus?* ANVAO 2 (Oslo: Dybwad, 1936). Munch, however, exaggerates his thesis and thinks that the expression is never an eschatological term.

5. In this case it even appears that we are dealing with an addition that is also secondary in relation to the first joining of the units into greater complexes. Isaiah 28:5-6, in fact, breaks the intended (and formally clear) joining of v. 7 to vv. 1-4. This joining, however, which combines a saying from the period before 722 B.C.E. with one spoken against the elites of Judah and in a different situation, is hardly that of Isaiah himself; rather, it comes from the tradition. If that is so, the insertion of vv. 5ff. may be much later, and perhaps belongs to the truly "literary" extensions of the book.

6. This is my interpretation of the divine epithet *Yhwh Sabaoth*. [Ed.] On this epithet, see: T. N. D. Mettinger, "Yahweh Zebaoth," in *DDD*², 920–24.

7. Bentzen's opinion is that the whole saying (Isa 31:4-9) dates from the period of King Ahaz and that it is an exhortation to keep silent, because Assur is also going to fall due to its pride (*Jesaja*). But this view is impossible. From that period, Judah's leading nobles express no fear of Assur at all in Isaiah 7. On the contrary, they had hopes of Assur as an ally, and the prophet and his disciples only experienced Assur's pride after they experienced its supremacy. At that time there was no question of Assur either falling or not falling.

8. This is always the meaning of *saba' val*, as seen by both August Dillmann and Frants Buhl (*Jesaja oversatt og fortolket* [Copenhagen, 1912]). Bentzen objects: "It is not necessary to think that *saba' val* always means struggle against"; but this objection cannot alter the facts.

9. See Mowinckel, *Psalmenstudien* 2.57–65.

10. This is also the meaning of Isa 18:1: a threat against the Ethiopians, not—as generally held—against the Assyrians; see Mowinckel, *Profeten Jesaja: En bibelstudiebok* (Oslo: Aschehoug/Nygaard, 1925) 46; *Det Gamle Testamente* (Oslo: Aschehoug/Nygaard, 1929–55) 3.130. My position stands over against that of W. Gesenius and F. Buhl, *Hebräisches und aramäisches Handwörterbuch über das Alte Testament*, 16th ed. (Leipzig: Vogel, 1915); and Paul Humbert, *Problèmes du livre d'Habacuc*, Mémoires de l'Université de Neuchâtel 18 (Neuchâtel: Secrétariat de l'Université, 1944) 19. Of the places where Humbert believes that the word is a particle of exclamation and exhortation, Isa 1:24 is a threat against "Yahweh's enemies"; in Isa 17:12, the prophet cries "woe" over the many peoples now making a noise against Jerusalem; in Jer 30:7, the meter shows that the LXX reading *hayu* is the correct one; in Jer 47:6, it is threatening—the prophet directs the woe-exclamation against those whom "Yahweh's sword" is going to strike; in Zech 2:10-11, the word predicts the unhappiness that is to befall "the northern land" and from which Zion is requested to save herself by flight. The only exception is Isa 55:1, which is marked with asterisks in the LXX, and where it may be presumed that the reading should be *hen* or *he'* "here!" [Ed.] On the woes in the biblical tradition, see K. C. Hanson, "How Honorable! How Shameful! A Cultural Analysis of Matthew's Makarisms and Reproaches," *Semeia* 58 (1994[96]) 83–114.

11. In this connection, the word is a designation of Jerusalem, whatever its original sense and content may have been; see Herbert G. May, "'Ephod' and 'Ariel,'" *AJSLL* 56 (1939) 61–62. In Isa 33:7, *'r'lm* should probably be pronounced *'ari'elim*, the Arielites, referring to the inhabitants of Jerusalem [contrast RSV: "the valiant ones"]. Regarding the original sense, see May's article and also Alfred Haldar, *Associations of Cult Prophets*

among the Ancient Semites, trans. H. S. Harvey (Uppsala: Almqvist & Wiksells, 1945) 130–34. [Ed.] See Richard D. Weis, "Angels, Altars and Angles of Vision: The Case of *'r'lm* in Isaiah 33:7," in *Tradition of the Text: Studies Offered to Dominique Barthélemy in Celebration of His 70th Birthday*, ed. G. J. Norton and S. Pisano, OBO 109 (Göttingen: Vandenhoeck & Ruprecht, 1991) 285–92.

12. Mowinckel, *Det Gamle Testamente* (Oslo: Aschehoug/Nygaard, 1929–55) 3.169.

13. I have understood the so-called "non-genuine sayings" in the books of Isaiah and Micah as evidence of the history and development of prophecy in the circle of Isaiah's disciples (Mowinckel, *Jesaja-disiplene: Profetien fra Jesaja til Jeremia* (Oslo: Aschehoug/Nygaard, 1926). This is true even if I did not make it sufficiently clear in my earlier work that one must also understand the disciples as transmitters of the tradition from and by their master.

14. Mowinckel, *Det Gamle Testamente* 3.33–38

15. Mowinckel, "Oppkomsten," 65ff.

8. The Trend of Tradition Development

1. See T. H. Robinson's statement in "Die prophetischen Bücher im Lichte neuer Entdeckungen," *ZAW* 45 (1927) 7. [Ed.] See also idem, "The Hebrew Prophets and Their Modern Interpretation," *ExpT* 50 (1929) 296–300.

2. Hugo Gressmann, *Ursprung der israelitisch-jüdischen Eschatologie*, FRLANT 6 (Göttingen: Vandenhoeck & Ruprecht, 1905) 238ff. See also Gressmann's *Der Messias*, FRLANT 43 (Göttingen: Vandenhoeck & Ruprecht, 1929) 77ff.

3. See the review of this material in August Freiherr von Gall, *Basileia tou Theou: Eine religionsgeschichtliche Studie zur vorkirchlichen Eschatologie*, RWB 7 (Heidelberg: Winter, 1926) 43ff., 48ff. One may find further references in Ivan Engnell, "The Ebed Yahweh Songs and the Suffering Messiah in Deutero-Isaiah," *BJRL* 31 (1948) 54–93. See also S. Luria, "Die ägyptische Bibel (Joseph- und Mosessage)," *ZAW* 44 (1926) 101.

4. See Lorenz Dürr, *Ursprung und Ausbau der israelitische-jüdischen Heilandserwartung: Ein Beitrag zur Theologie des Alten Testamentes* (Berlin: Schwetschke, 1925) 1ff. See also the thorough refutation of the theory of an eschatological scheme among the Babylonians and Egyptians in von Gall, *Basileia tou Theou*.

5. Von Gall, *Basileia tou Theou*, 81–82; Adolf Erman, *The Literature of the Ancient Egyptians: Poems, Narratives, and Manuals of Instruction, from the Third and Second Millennia B.C.* (London: Metheun, 1927) German ed., 1923, 151ff. [Ed.] See W. G. Lambert, *The Background of Jewish Apocalyptic* (London: Athlone, 1978); Christopher Rowland, *The Open Heaven: A Study of Apocalyptic in Judaism and Early Christianity* (New York: Crossroad, 1982); David Hellholm, editor, *Apocalypticism in the Mediterranean World and the Near East: Proceedings of the International Colloquium on Apocalypticism, Uppsala, August 12–17, 1979* (Tübingen: Mohr/Siebeck, 1983); and John J. Collins, "Apocalypses and Apocalypticism—Early Jewish Apocalypticism," in *ABD* 1.382–88.

6. See Alfred Haldar, *Associations of Cult Prophets among the Ancient Semites*, trans. H. S. Harvey (Uppsala: Almqvist & Wiksells, 1945) 129, 213. I will not comment on his "ritual" interpretation of Mal 3:1.

7. Haldar is completely justified in putting "prophetic" in quotation marks (*Associations*, 213). See also Haldar's example of the cult prophet's activity at the lamentation of

the dead god; this is almost the only material on pp. 58–59 that has anything to do with the issue; the text speaks of "lamentations," not "oracles." [Ed.] On lamenting the dying and rising deity, see Ezek 8:14 and Bendt Alster, "The Mythology of Mourning," *ActaSum* 5 (1983) 1–16; and idem, "Tammuz," in *DDD*[2], 828–34.

8. See Mowinckel, *Psalmenstudien* 2. [Ed.] See also: Mowinckel, *The Psalms in Israel's Worship,* trans. D. R. Ap-Thomas, 2 vols. (Nashville: Abingdon, 1962) 1.106–92; Thorkild Jacobsen, "Religious Drama in Ancient Mesopotamia," in *Unity and Diversity: Essays in the History, Literature, and Religion of the Ancient Near East,* ed. Hans Goedicke and J. J. M. Roberts, JHNES (Baltimore: Johns Hopkins Univ. Press, 1975) 65–97; W. G. Lambert, "Myth and Ritual as Conceived by the Babylonians," *JSS* 13 (1968) 104–12; Jacob Klein, "Akitu," in *ABD* 1.138–140; and Klaus Baltzer, *Deutero-Isaiah,* trans. M. Kohl, Hermeneia (Minneapolis: Fortress Press, 2001) 7–14.

9. See Mowinckel, *Jesaja-disiplene: Profetien fra Jesaja til Jeremia* (Oslo: Aschehoug/Nygaard, 1926) 89ff.

10. See Mowinckel in *Det Gamle Testamente* (Oslo: Aschehoug/Nygaard, 1929–55) 3.604–6. Whether the previously mentioned Egyptian prophecies after the event (*vaticinia ex eventu*), which—in the form of prophecy view history under the same scheme—are also influenced by similar cultic conceptions and experiences, I cannot discuss here. It is quite probable both regarding the Egyptian and Babylonian prophecies after the event of delivering ("savior") kings. It is not essential in this connection; the Israelite-Judean prophetic scheme receives its full explanation on the basis of Israelite-Judean conditions.

11. See Mowinckel, *Psalmenstudien* 2; and *Psalmenstudien* 3.30–63.

[12.] On the relationship of myth and ritual, see: J. R. Porter, "Myth and Ritual School," in *DBI* 2.187–88; S. H. Hooke, editor, *Myth and Ritual* (London: Oxford Univ. Press, 1933); idem, editor, *The Labyrinth* (London: SPCK, 1935); idem, editor, *Myth, Ritual, and Kingship* (Oxford: Clarendon, 1958); and Theodor H. Gaster, *Thespis: Ritual, Myth, and Drama in the Ancient Near East,* rev. ed. (Garden City, N.Y.: Doubleday, 1961).

13. See Hans G. Güterbock, "Die historische Tradition und ihre literarische Gestaltung bei Babyloniern und Hethitern bis 1200," *ZA* 8 (1934) 2–3; Johann Jakob Stamm, "Die kulturelle Leistungen der Sumerer," *TZ* 2 (1926) 14, 18–19. [Ed.] See also Samuel Noah Kramer, *The Sumerians: Their History, Culture, and Character* (Chicago: Univ. of Chicago Press, 1963); Jerrold S. Cooper, "Sumer, Sumerians," in *ABD* 6.231–34; and William W. Hallo, "Sumerian Literature," in *ABD* 6.234–37.

[14.] See Samuel Noah Kramer, *Sumerian Mythology: A Study of Spiritual and Literary Achievement in the Third Millennium B.C.*, rev. ed. (Philadelphia: Univ. of Pennsylvania Press, 1972).

15. The characterization of Amos and Hosea as "predominantly prophets of reaction and judgment" is correct and undeniable, even if one completely follows the "tradition" with regard to what they said. It is not inconceivable (as Engnell seems to believe) that a religious preacher, who assumes that the official religion of his time is wrong and more sinful than it is fear of God, may in certain circumstances have exclusively stated this and announced God's judgment upon his contemporaries (Engnell, *Gamla Testamentet: En Traditionshistorisk Inledning* [Stockholm: Svenska Kykrans Diakonistyrelses, 1945] 1.161 n1). On the contrary, the prophet in question does not, therefore, become a "religious monomaniac." One could only come to this conclusion if one is not aware of the seriousness of God's demands and of God's judgment of sin. It is a misunderstand-

ing to believe that we are concerned here with having "experienced only the angry aspect of God, not that of love" (Engnell). It is not a case of what the prophet experienced and recognized personally from and about God, but of what God told him to announce in a particular situation.

16. See Mowinckel, *Jesaja-disiplene*, 90ff.

17. This does not mean that the pattern is of "secondary origin in the circle of collectors," as Engnell maintains that Birkeland and I have argued (Engnell, "Ebed Yahweh Songs," 62). The scheme was there from the first moment the process of combination and transmission began. Whether it has already existed with "the prophets themselves" (Engnell, 61) depends on: (a) whether there is valid reason to assume that the master concerned has announced both kinds of prophecies; and (b) whether the process of transmission—and accordingly that of combination—started with the master. This issue must be investigated for each book separately, possibly without any certain results.

18. Thus Engnell, "Ebed Yahweh Songs," 62. In reality, this was covered already in Gressmann, *Der Messias*, 69–79.

19. One of these is also the investigation of the principle of collection and arrangement employed in the specific passage, for example, the principle of catchwords (see Mowinckel, "Die Komposition des deuterojesajanischen Buches [2 parts]," *ZAW* 49 (1931) 87–112; 242–60. It may be the case that the units within a larger complex have really been placed together according to catchword association, as is notoriously the case in the Deutero-Isaiah collection (Isaiah 40–55). But just because that is the case regarding one or the other saying does not mean it is possible to ascertain that this principle has been followed. This *may* be an indicator (but no more!) that the saying in question may have been placed where it is in the tradition-complex only at a later stage. But it is obviously wrong to contend without further detailed investigation that the catchword association has been used "in prophetic literature as a whole" (Engnell, "Ebed Yahweh Songs," 67–68 n3). And "the positive Messianic sayings are alternating there with judgment sayings exactly according to this principle." That is not always the case, as for example in Amos 9:8-15; Isa 9:2-7 [MT 9:1-6]; 11:1-9; and other passages. Even if this were the case, however, the principle of arrangement within tradition complexes and books is of course no proof that the promise of salvation discussed dates from the particular prophet himself.

9. The Prophets and the Tasks of Tradition History

1. Gustav Hölscher, *Hesekiel, der Dichter und das Buch: Eine literarkritische Untersuchung*, BZAW 39 (Giessen: Töpelmann, 1924); Nils Messel, *Ezechielfragen*, SNVAO (Oslo: Dybwad, 1945).

2. Charles Cutler Torrey, *Pseudo-Ezekiel and the Original Prophecy*, YOSR 18 (New Haven: Yale Univ. Press, 1930); and idem, "Certainly Pseudo-Ezekiel," *JBL* 53 (1934) 291–320.

[3.] The systematic traditio-historical approach has been carried out on the Book of Ezekiel by Walther Zimmerli in: *Ezekiel 1*, trans. R. E. Clements, Hermeneia (Philadelphia: Fortress Press, 1979); and idem, *Ezekiel 2*, trans. J. D. Martin, Hermeneia (Philadelphia: Fortress Press, 1983); see his article: "The Special Form- and Traditio-Historical

Character of Ezekiel's Prophecy," *VT* 15 (1965) 515–27. One finds a different position regarding tradition and redaction in Moshe Greenberg, *Ezekiel,* AB 22, 22A (New York: Doubleday, 1983–). Note also the helpful overview article: Lawrence Boadt, "Ezekiel, Book of," in *ABD* 2.711–22.

[4.] For a detailed analysis of Jesus sayings with a traditio-historical approach, see John Dominic Crossan, *In Fragments: The Aphorisms of Jesus* (San Francisco: Harper & Row, 1983).

[5.] William L. Holladay, in his masterful commentary, disagrees with Mowinckel's position here regarding Jer 23:1-4; see Holladay, *Jeremiah 1,* Hermeneia (Philadelphia: Fortress Press, 1986) 613–15. And Holladay distinguishes the problems in Jer 33:1-13 from those in vv. 14-26 (*Jeremiah 2,* Hermeneia [Philadelphia: Fortress Press, 1989] 221–31).

6. See, e.g., Ivan Engnell, "The Ebed Yahweh Songs and the Suffering Messiah in Deutero-Isaiah," *BJRL* 31 (1948) 60–61; idem, *Gamla Testamentet: En Traditionshistorisk Inledning* (Stockholm: Svenska Kykrans Diakonistyrelses, 1945) 1.157 n1. In a note on p. 199, Engnell admits, at the same time, the existence of different strata of tradition (*olika traditionskikt*). With great satisfaction, one is able to note his criticism of G. A. Danell's lack of any historical-critical discrimination of the source material. See the review of Danell's book, *Studies in the Name Israel in the Old Testament,* trans. S. Linton (Uppsala: Appelberg, 1946), in Engnell's paper, "Israel and the Law," *SymBU* 7 (1946) 16ff.

7. The older critical scholars since Wilhelm Vatke were influenced by the prevailing philosophy of history during their era (frequently Hegelianism) in their view of "the line of development" of the history of Israel (see Johannes Pedersen, "Die Auffassung vom Alten Testament," *ZAW* 49 [1931] 161–81). But this does not affect the necessity of attempting to elucidate "the lines of development" in the religious history of the Old Testament with all the means available. Labeling it "evolutionism" neither dismisses nor solves the problem. That one's view of the line is influenced to a certain degree by the interests and setting of the problems prevailing during the scholar's own era is not only an expression of the imperfection of human apprehension, but also evidence of the fact that the task is felt to be something topical and existential. See W. F. Albright, "The Ancient Near East and the Religion of Israel," *JBL* 59 (1940) 85–112. [Ed.] See also Albright, *Yahweh and the Gods of Canaan: A Historical Analysis of Two Contrasting Faiths* (Garden City, N.Y.: Doubleday, 1968).

8. For example, in Engnell, *Gamla Testamentet* 1.

9. This onesidedness is the main objection that can be raised against Joseph Coppens's otherwise very instructive survey of the history of research in *The Old Testament and the Critics,* trans. E. A. Ryan and E. W. Tribbe (Paterson, N.J.: St. Anthony Guild, 1942).

10. See Mowinckel, *Gamle Testamente* 3.14–23, to mention only a single expression of this understanding. See, however, Hugo Gressmann, *Der Messias,* FRLANT 43 (Göttingen: Vandenhoeck & Ruprecht, 1929) 82. [Ed.] Mowinckel, *He That Cometh,* trans. G. W. Anderson (New York: Abingdon, 1954).

11. See, e.g., Mowinckel, *Profeten Jesaja: En bibelstudiebok* (Oslo: Aschehoug/Nygaard, 1925) 66ff.

12. Already in 1926 I attempted to view "prophecy from Isaiah" as a whole from this point of view, and by so doing turned frequently and fairly decidedly against the "radical" literary criticism of older scholars; see Mowinckel, *Jesaja-disiplene: Profetien fra Jesaja til Jeremia* (Oslo: Aschehoug/Nygaard, 1926) 46ff., 89ff.; also Mowinckel, *Gamle Testament* 3.22–28.

13. As an expression of my own view, I would only refer to *Gamle Testament* 3.23–28. Otherwise it may be found in practically every account of the religion of Israel.

14. Harris Birkeland, *Zum hebräischen Traditionswesen: Die Komposition der prophetischen Bücher des Alten Testaments*, ANVAO (Oslo: Dybwad, 1938) 42.

15. As, e.g., Otto Eissfeldt, *The Old Testament: An Introduction*, trans. P. R. Ackroyd (New York: Harper & Row, 1965) 356–65. See also Paul Volz, *Der Prophet Jeremia*, 2nd ed., KAT 10 (Leipzig: Deichert, 1928) on Jer 11:1-4; 18:1-12; 19:2-9; etc.

16. See Mowinckel, *Gamle Testament* 3:321–28. See the same work on Jer 13:12-14; 16:1-15; 18:1-12; 19:1-13; 23:25ff.; and other places. Volz goes too far in this respect; he appears to think that if he merely prints the sentences in fairly equally long lines, the result is rhythmic-metrical prophetic style! He is not the only one to suffer from this lack of stylistic perception.

17. Thus Engnell, "The Ebed Yahweh Songs," [SEÅ 40]; and Engnell, *Gamla Testamentet* 1.30, 42. It is hardly correct that the interest to get hold of the exact words (*ipsissima verba*) of the prophet should be due to the fact that one still adheres to the old dogma of the verbal inspiration (*pace* Engnell, 30). A consistent fundamentalism maintaining literal inspiration is, in principle, indifferent about when and by whom the biblical words were spoken or written, for the real "author" is in any case the Holy Spirit, and the revelation is beyond time. According to the dogmatic view, therefore, Andre Rivet expressed a consistently Calvinistic dogma of verbal inspiration and rejected all special literary introductions to the separate books as nonessential and pointless (*Isagoge: Sev introductio generalis, ad Scripturam sacram Veteris et Novi Testamenti* [Lugduni Batavorum: Isaaci Commelini, 1627]); see Carl Heinrich Cornill, *Introduction to the Canonical Books of the Old Testament*, Theological Translation Library 23 (New York: Putnam, 1907).

10. The Spirit and the Word in the Prophets

1. The striking fact that the idea of Yahweh's spirit is wholly lacking in Jeremiah has often been noticed, and explanations have been suggested, among others by Friedrich Giesebrecht, *Die Berufsbegabung der alttestamentlichen Propheten* (Göttingen: Vandenhoeck & Ruprecht, 1897) 142; and Justus Köberle, *Die alttestamentliche Offenbarung*, 2nd ed. (Wismar: Bartholdi, 1908) 133, who gives the correct one. Paul Volz correctly recognizes that the reforming prophets in general do not employ this idea, and his suggested explanation is in the main along the right lines (*Der Geist Gottes und die verwandten Erscheinungen im Alten Testament und im anschliessenden Judentum* [Tübingen: Mohr/Siebeck, 1910] 62). But Volz is too one-sided because of his incorrect "animistic" view of the *ruaḥ* as an independent demon or spirit who originally had nothing to do with Yahweh. In this connection, Volz is certainly wrong in regarding the prophets to a large extent as "pneumatics" and uses their utterances regarding their consciousness of a call, their powers, and their relation to the deity as material for his account of the conception of the pneumatic in general, who according to Volz is the *ruaḥ*-endowed man (30ff., 72ff.).

2. The fact that Hosea attributes the immoral and faithless conduct of the people to a "spirit of harlotry" (Hos 4:12; 5:4) signifies, of course, nothing in this connection. There

can hardly be any allusion to a demon here (Volz, *Geist*). [Ed.] For an excellent discussion of this point, see Hans Walter Wolff, *Hosea*, trans. G. Stansell, Hermeneia (Philadelphia: Fortress Press, 1974) 84–85.

3. See Julius Wellhausen, *Die kleinen Propheten*, 3rd ed. (Berlin: Reimer, 1898) 143; Volz, *Geist*, 65; Mowinckel, "Mikaboken: Oversettelse med noter og tekskritisk kommentar," *NTT* 29 (1928) 33 [3–42]. Both the sign of the accusative (lacking before the other objects in the sentence) and the meter show that the words are interpolated. [Ed.] Wolff agrees that this is a later interpolation: *Micah*, trans. G. Stansell, CC (Minneapolis: Augsburg, 1990) 91–92.

4. The analogous Isa 19:14, on the contrary, is not from Isaiah; see Bernhard Duhm, *Das Buch Jesaia*, 4th ed. HAT (Göttingen: Vandenhoeck & Ruprecht, 1922); Karl Marti, *Das Buch Jesaja*, KHAT (Göttingen: Mohr/Siebeck, 1900); Gustav Hölscher, *Die Propheten: Untersuchungen zur Religionsgeschichte Israels* (Leipzig: Hinrichs, 1914) 366; Buhl, *Jesaja* (Copenhagen, 1912) 238ff.

5. To suggest that Yahweh's *ruaḥ* in this passage is the *ruaḥ* in Isaiah himself is impossible exegesis; see Volz, *Geist*, 65–66.

6. The passages that might be quoted here are Isa 11:2; 28:6; and 32:15. Regarding the last one, 32:15-20 is one of the clearest cases imaginable of spurious interpolation in a prophetic book. Verses 9-14 are a definite and unconditional threat of punishment to Jerusalem and its inhabitants (represented by the careless woman), ending with the statement that the city will forever be "a joy of wild asses, a pasture of flocks." To anyone with a fair psychological understanding of the prophets it will be evident that the abrupt continuation in v. 15 "until a spirit is poured upon us from on high," with the sudden occurrence of the 1st person pl. (the Judeans), which violates stylistic usage by changing into the 1st person sing. (Yahweh), and the different meter, cannot be the original continuation here. And "until" (*'ad*) in v. 15 is patently inconsistent with "forever" (*'ad 'olam*) in v. 14 (see Marti, *Jesaja*; and Buhl, *Jesaja*). Duhm, who maintains that the passage is genuine, is also compelled to admit that the passage is out of its context (*Jesaia*). But the opening "until" shows that this passage could never have existed by itself. It was obviously written as a continuation of vv. 9-14, to tone down the threat of punishment. And one can also see that it is an interpolation from the fact that a sentence in the middle of the passage (v. 19) clearly has nothing to do with vv. 15-20, but really belongs to vv. 9-14. [Ed.] On this passage, see Gary Stansell, "Isaiah 32: Creative Redaction in the Isaiah Traditions," in *SBLSP 1983* (Chico, Calif.: Scholars, 1983) 1–12; idem, *Micah and Isaiah: A Form and Tradition Historical Comparison*, SBLDS 85 (Atlanta: Scholars, 1988) 62–63; Marvin A. Sweeney, *Isaiah 1–39*, FOTL 16 (Grand Rapids: Eerdmans, 1996) 409–20; and Brevard S. Childs, *Isaiah*, OTL (Louisville: Westminster John Knox, 2001) 241–42.

7. In Haggai, Yahweh's *ruaḥ* (in the subjective, psychological sense) is an expression for his vigilant and protecting presence in the midst of the people, who have therefore no need to fear but can confidently set about rebuilding the temple (Hag 2:5). Zechariah uses the expression "spirit of Yahweh" of the dominating emotions of his mind (e.g., his passionate anger, Zech 6:8). But this expression is also used in a more outward sense of his active direction of the world's history, which causes Zerubbabel's pious undertaking to succeed. It is the medium of his wondrous power, as compared with the human power (*ḥayil* and *koaḥ*; Zech 4:6). In Zech 7:12 it is the power that inspired and taught the old prophets; but the passage is a redactional addition, expressing the view of later canonical Judaism (see Hölscher, *Die Propheten*, 447–48). [Ed.] On Hag 2:5, see: Hans

Walter Wolff, *Haggai*, trans. M. Kohl, CC (Minneapolis: Augsburg, 1988) 79–80; on Zech 7:12, see: David L. Peterson, *Haggai and Zechariah*, OTL (Philadelphia: Westminster, 1984) 292–93.

8. Several of these passages, however, do not derive from Ezekiel but to the editors of the book. And in Ezek 3:14; 8:3; 11:1; and 37:1, *ruaḥ* is a secondary gloss (see Hölscher, *Hesekiel: Der Dichter und das Buch*, BZAW 39 [Giessen: Töpelmann, 1924] 54–55, 69 n1, 75 n1, and 174 n2).

9. The same is true of Ezekiel 37 (see Hölscher, *Hesekiel*). [Ed.] Walther Zimmerli argues for attributing Ezekiel 37 to the prophet himself in *Ezekiel 2*, trans. J. D. Martin, Hermeneia (Philadelphia: Fortress Press, 1983) 258.

10. In Deutero-Isaiah, *ruaḥ* is the breath of life in living beings and given by Yahweh (Isa 42:5). Accordingly, Yahweh's *ruaḥ* means the power that brings life and fruitfulness (44:3). In addition, it is his powerful and wonder-working breath (40:7; the idea of the sirocco). On its psychological side, Yahweh's spirit is the content of his consciousness, his mind and intention, paralleling "counselor" (*'eṣah;* 40:13).

11. Contrary to the view of Sven Linder, *Studier till Gamla Testamentets föreställninger om Anden* (Uppsala: Almqvist & Wiksells, 1926) 68ff.

12. In Isa 48:16 the text is in disorder and the original meaning of the verse is quite uncertain; see Mowinckel, "Die Komposition des deuterojesajanischen Buches [part 2]," *ZAW* 49 (1931) 257–60. [Ed.] On this passage, see Klaus Baltzer, *Deutero-Isaiah*, trans. M. Kohl, Hermeneia (Minneapolis: Fortress Press, 2001) 293–96.

13. "Subjectively," *ruaḥ* is Yahweh's activating emotion (Isa 59:19; see 30:28), his mind and plans (63:10), the organ of his solicitous leading of Israel (63:14), and Moses' inspiration to display similar powers of leadership (63:11). Trito-Isaiah always shows a tendency to personify the "Spirit" and make it a hypostasis; 59:21 is a later prose interpolation (Duhm, *Jesaia*).

14. The same is true of Isa 48:16 in so far as the corrupted text refers to the special servant of Yahweh (see Mowinckel, "Komposition," 259–60). See note 12 above.

15. To give a general idea of what is meant, the passages may be quoted. To the apocalyptic editor of the original Joel's penitential liturgy, Yahweh's Spirit is the (eschatological) prophetic Spirit (Joel 2:28-32 [MT 3:1-5]). In the Daniel legends, it is "the spirit of the holy gods," a source of occult wisdom, especially the interpretation of dreams (Dan 1:17; 2:23; 4:5-6, 15; 5:11, 14), while to Deutero-Zechariah, the *nabi'* spirit is, on the contrary, a "spirit of uncleanness" (Zech 13:2). In Zech 12:10 the allusion is not to Yahweh's spirit, but to the repentant state of mind Yahweh will someday arouse in the people.

16. For the interpretation of the passage, see Mowinckel, "Profeternes forhold til nebiismen," *NTT* 11 (1910) 133. The text is very defective, but the general sense is clear. This passage (Hos 9:7-9) is a typical prophetic reproof, the beginning and end of which are clearly indicated by the threats in v. 7a and v. 9b. It is usual to take "prophet" (*nabi'*) and "man of the spirit" (*'iš ha-ruaḥ*) as referring to the prophet Hosea and his kind, and to interpret the passage as if Hosea were quoting a popular objection to the prophets in order to turn it against the people themselves: yes, we are "mad" and "fools" (as you say), but that is on account of sorrow and despair at your many sins. But "fool" (*'ewil*) and "mad" (*mešugga'*) are such strong expressions that the prophet would hardly accept them as descriptions of his state of mind, even if he applied the thought in a fashion altogether opposed to what the people meant. And they are never used in the sense of sorrow and despair. The word *'ewil* can never denote anything but the intellectually,

religiously, and morally degraded fool in the sense of miscreant and sinner (*raša'*). When we consider how often the prophets cry out against the *nebi'im*, there can be no doubt that the reproof in this case is addressed to the class which is most frequently mentioned here—the *nebi'im*, "the men of the spirit," "Ephraim's watchmen"—and that the "great wickedness" of v. 7 is the wickedness of the *nebi'im*. It is "Ephraim's watchmen" who "set snares for him, namely for Ephraim, in all his (Ephraim's) ways" (v. 8). The poetic form is that of *qinah*-periods, originally 4 strophes of 2 periods each: vv. 7a; 7b; 8; 9. In v. 7a the second line of the first period has dropped out. In v. 7b, "his iniquity" (*'awono*) must be read for "your iniquity" (*'awonekah*); either before or after this word the predicate of the sentence has dropped out; probably there was a statement that the wickedness of the *nabi'* led the people astray. The last line—*werabbah maśṭemah* "and great is the snare(?)" (or "the persecution"?)—is neither grammatical nor suitable; but what the original text contained is impossible to say. In v. 8 "with my God" (*'im elohai*) makes no sense. The context requires a verb expressing the misdeeds of the *nabi'*; and the rest of the second line is wanting after *nabi'*. In v. 9a, we must read *šaḥath we [...]* for *šiḥethû*, but the synonymous word after *we* has dropped out. In v. 9b, which parallels 8:13, we must read the 1st person sing. of the verbs to make the period suitable here, assuming that the period is original. The speaker is Yahweh himself: it is he who will "remember" and "punish" the sins of the *nebi'im*. [Ed.] On Hos 9:7-9, see Wolff, *Hosea*, 149–59.

17. This expression in Mic 2:11a was also probably in Mic 3:5 originally (see Mowinckel, "Mikaboken," 33). [Ed.] On these two passages in Micah, see Wolff, *Micah*, 84–85, 101–3.

18. Isaiah 28:9-10 cannot very well be taken to be the drunkards' scornful mimicry of Isaiah's words. For the interpretation, see Mowinckel, *Profeten Jesaja: En Bibelstudiebok* (Oslo: Aschehoug/Nygaard, 1925) 38–39. [Ed.] See Sweeney, *Isaiah 1–39*, 363; Childs, *Isaiah*, 207. On ecstasy, see: Robert R. Wilson, "Prophecy and Ecstasy: A Re-examination," *JBL* 98 (1979) 321–37; and Simon B. Parker, "Possession Trance and Prophecy in Pre-exilic Israel," *VT* 28 (1978) 271–85.

19. See Mowinckel, "Profeternes forhold," 126–38; 333–57. The unfriendly relation of the prophets to nebi'ism is to some extent exaggerated there, inasmuch as it is probably incorrect to say that none of the reforming prophets were *nebi'im*. Only Amos expressly refuses to be called a *nabi'* (Amos 7:14). [Ed.] On Amos 7:14, see Hans Walter Wolff, *Joel and Amos*, trans. W. Janzen et al., Hermeneia (Philadelphia: Fortress Press, 1977) 311–14; and Shalom M. Paul, *Amos*, Hermeneia (Minneapolis: Fortress Press, 1991) 243–48.

20. Deutero-Isaiah makes a couple of allusions to auditions (Isa 40:3, 6); but here we may equally well have a traditional mannerism. [Ed.] On prophetic visions and auditions, see Johannes Lindblom, *Prophecy in Ancient Israel* (Philadelphia: Fortress Press, 1973) 122–37; Walther Zimmerli, "Visionary Experience in Jeremiah," in *Israel's Prophetic Tradition: Essays in Honour of Peter Ackroyd*, ed. Richard J. Coggins et al. (Cambridge: Cambridge Univ. Press, 1982) 95–118; Lester L. Grabbe, *Priest, Prophets, Diviners, Sages: A Socio-Historical Study of Religious Specialists in Ancient Israel* (Valley Forge, Pa.: Trinity Press International, 1995) 107–12; and Francis Landy, "Vision and Poetic Speech in Amos," in *Beauty and the Enigma: And Other Essays on the Hebrew Bible*, JSOTSup 312 (Sheffield: Sheffield Academic, 2001) 159–84.

21. See Hölscher, *Die Propheten*, 82–88. Zechariah's visions of the night do not seem to be real dream or half-dream visions but more artificial allegories in vision form. At

any rate, the ideas in them have been worked over and given a more finished form. [Ed.] On Zechariah's visions, see: Paul D. Hanson, *The Dawn of Apocalyptic: The Historical and Sociological Roots of Jewish Apocalyptic Eschatology*, rev. ed. (Philadelphia: Fortress Press, 1979) 248–56; David L. Peterson, "Zechariah's Visions: A Theological Perspective," *VT* 34 (1984) 195–206; *idem, Haggai and Zechariah 1–8*, OTL (Philadelphia: Westminster, 1984) 111–20; and Michael H. Floyd, *Minor Prophets, Part 2*, FOTL 22 (Grand Rapids: Eerdmans, 2000) 352–54.

22. See Hölscher, *Die Propheten*, 248–53; Bernhard Duhm, *Israels Propheten* (Tübingen: Mohr/Siebeck, 1916) 391ff.

23. See Hölscher, *Die Propheten*, 181–85, and on Amos, 197.

24. Regarding these, see Hölscher, *Die Propheten*, 79–128. On Isaiah and the seers, see Ivar Hylander, "War Jesaja Nabi?" *Monde Oriental* (1931) 53ff.

25. The old Arab seers spoke of their "whisperer" *hatif*, a demon (god) who whispered their revelations to them. [Ed.] On the traditions of Arab prophets, see: Jaakko Hämeen-Anttila, "Arabian Prophecy," in *Prophecy in Its Ancient Near Eastern Context: Mesopotamian, Biblical and Arabian Perspectives*, ed. M. Nissinen, SBLSymSer 13 (Atlanta: Society of Biblical Literature, 2000) 115–46.

26. See Ludwig Köhler, *Deuterojesaja (Jesaja 40–55) stilkritisch untersucht*, BZAW 37 (Giessen: Töpelmann, 1923) 102ff. [Ed.] On the prophets and the divine word, see: Gerhard von Rad, *Old Testament Theology*, Vol. 2: *The Theology of Israel's Prophetic Traditions*, trans. D. M. G. Stalker (New York: Harper & Row, 1965) 80–98.

27. See Mowinckel, "Der Ursprung der Bileamsage," *ZAW* 48 (1930) 265–66.

28. Johannes Lindblom summarizes the cases where these formulas occur in the prophets in *Die literarische Gattung der prophetischen Literature*, UUÅ (Uppsala: Lundequistska, 1924) 97ff. He provides the statistics. [Ed.] For a list and discussion of prophetic formulas, see Sweeney, *Isaiah 1–39*, 544–47.

29. See Walter Jacobi, *Die Ekstase der alttestamentlichen Propheten*, Grenzfragen des Nerven- und Seelenlebens 108 (Munich: Bergmann, 1920) 48ff. [Ed.] On *ruaḥ* in Ezekiel, see Zimmerli, *Ezekiel 2*, 566–68.

30. Compare Hans Wilhelm Hertzberg, *Prophet und Gott: Eine Studie zur Religiosität des vorexilischen Prophetentums*, BFCT 28 (Gütersloh: Bertelsmann, 1923) 83ff.

31. See, however, Lindblom, *Die literarische Gattung*.

[32.] On the prophetic call narratives, see: James F. Ross, "The Prophet as Yahweh's Messenger," in *Israel's Prophetic Heritage: Essays in Honor of James Muilenburg*, ed. Bernhard W. Anderson and W. Harrelson (New York: Harper, 1962) 98–107; Norman C. Habel, "The Form and Significance of the Call Narrative," *ZAW* 77 (1965) 297–323; von Rad, *Old Testament Theology*, 2.50–69; Klaus Baltzer, "Considerations regarding the Office and Calling of the Prophet," *HTR* 61 (1968) 567–81; Rolf Knierim, "The Vocation of Isaiah," *VT* 18 (1968) 47–68; Walther Zimmerli, *Ezekiel 1*, trans. R. E. Clements, Hermeneia (Philadelphia: Fortress Press, 1979) 97–100; and Klaus Koch, *The Prophets*, Vol. 1: *The Assyrian Period*, trans. M. Kohl (Philadelphia: Fortress Press, 1983) 108–13.

33. Jeremiah 5:13 cannot very well refer to what the people say about Jeremiah and the prophets who agree with him. The majority of the "prophets" at the time were in full accordance with the superficial optimism of the people (see Jer 23:9-12). The imperfect *yihyeh* implies, moreover, something future—in other words, a threat of punishment, not a lasting state. Verse 13 is, therefore, in the wrong place before the introductory formula in v. 14a. The verse is part of Jeremiah's own words (vv. 14-17), not of the people's,

and it refers to his opponents the *nebi'im*. [Ed.] On the complexities of this passage, see: William L. Holladay, *Jeremiah 1*, Hermeneia (Philadelphia: Fortress Press, 1986) 183–89; and Robert P. Carroll, *Jeremiah*, OTL (Philadelphia: Westminster, 1986) 182–84.

34. What follows is in essential agreement with Hertzberg, *Prophet und Gott*, 11–139, though the emphasis on the various points is not quite the same. [Ed.] On Yahweh's word, see Klaus Koch, "The Language of Prophecy: Thoughts on the Macrosyntax of the *debar YHWH* and Its Semantic Implications in the Deuteronomistic History," in *Problems in Biblical Theology: Essays in Honor of Rolf Knierim*, ed. H. T. C. Sun et al., 210–21 (Grand Rapids: Eerdmans, 1997).

35. See Johannes Pedersen, *Israel: Its Life and Culture*, 4 vols. (London: Oxford Univ. Press, 1926) 1.167–70.

36. Hertzberg, *Prophet und Gott*, 121–22. [Ed.] On Isa 55:10-11, see Baltzer, *Deutero-Isaiah*, 480–84. On Jer 20:9 and 23:29, see Holladay, *Jeremiah 1*, 553–55, 644.

37. In Exod 34:28, *dabar* means "commandment."

38. See Hölscher, *Die Propheten*, 148 n2; Hertzberg, *Prophet und Gott*, 93ff. But Hertzberg rather overestimates the importance of the formal distinction.

39. For what follows, see Hertzberg, *Prophet und Gott*, 108ff. [Ed.] For an analysis of altered states of consciousness (ASCs) and prophetic experience, see John J. Pilch, "Visions in Revelation and Alternate Consciousness: A Perspective from Cultural Anthropology," *Listening: Journal of Religion and Culture* 28 (1993) 231–44; and idem, "Altered States of Consciousness: A 'Kitbashed' Model," *BTB* 26 (1996) 133–38.

40. See the accounts of visions in Isaiah 6; Jeremiah 1; 24; 38:21-23; Amos 7:1-3; 9:1-4; etc. In addition to these, see: Isa 8:11; 21:1-5; 22:14; Hab 2:1-2. [Ed.] See the books and articles listed in n. 32.

41. See Jacobi, *Die Ekstase*, 58ff.

42. Giesebrecht, *Die Berufsbegabung*; Hertzberg, *Prophet und Gott*, 109–10.

43. See Paolo Mantegazza, *Die Ekstase des Menschen* (Jena, 1888); Hölscher, *Die Propheten*, 1–78; Jacobi, *Die Ekstase*, 58ff.

44. Compare Jeremiah's declaration: "I have not pressed you" (Jer 17:16). [Ed.] On the difficulties of this verse, see Holladay, *Jeremiah 1*, 505–6.

45. The Greeks were not the only ones who understood poetry to be the "speech of the gods"; the ancient Semites also attributed the *mana* (power) and art of poetry to the influence of higher powers; see Mowinckel, *Psalmenstudien* 3.26.

46. This is correctly pointed out by Hertzberg, *Prophet und Gott*, 122–23. Note also Rudolf Otto's phrase "the wholly Other" ("der ganz Andere") in *The Idea of the Holy*, trans. J. W. Harvey, 2nd ed. (New York: Oxford Univ. Press 1950).

47. Jeremiah 32:7 anticipates v. 8b and makes it impossible (Hertzberg, *Prophet und Gott*, 124–25), and is therefore a redactional addition. Originally the opening words of v. 6 were: "The word of Yahweh came to Jeremiah thus," which is Baruch's form of introduction. For *wayyomer yirmeyahu haya*, Syriac and LXX[A] read: *wayehi*, and for *'elai* LXX and Syriac read *'el yirmeyahu*, both of which are correct. [Ed.] For the text-critical and form-critical issues in Jer 32:6-8, see William L. Holladay, *Jeremiah 2*, Hermeneia (Philadelphia: Fortress Press, 1989) 203, 210, 213–14.

48. Compare the sexual sense of the word "know," which goes back directly to the sense of intimate mutual fellowship and unity. See Pedersen, *Israel* 1.237ff.

49. The same idea is found in Babylonian: "a king whom the deity knows" = a king chosen by the deity.

50. Compare Gustav Hölscher, *Geschichte der israelitischen und jüdischen Religion* (Giessen: Töpelmann, 1922) 85–86. Paul Volz somewhat exaggerates this trait in the Yahweh of later times; *Das Dämonische in Jahwe: Vortrag auf dem Alttestamentlertag in München,* Sammlung gemeinverstandlicher Vortrage und Schriften aus dem Gebiet der Theologie und Religionsgeschichte 110 (Tübingen: Mohr/Siebeck, 1924).

51. Otto, *The Idea of the Holy.*

52. As this conviction underlies the whole prophetic message, it is not susceptible of proof by quoting single passages. The prophets themselves never furnish evidence of it, for they do not go out of their way to say what is obvious. See, however, in more intellectual circles, the attempts made by cult-liturgical "epiphany formulas" to express this element of law inherent in the nature of Yahweh: "I am Yahweh your God, who led you out of Egypt (Exod 21:2; Deut 4:6; Ps 50:7; 81:10; 95:6); see Mowinckel, *Le Decalogue,* EHPR 16 (Paris: Alcan, 1927) 7ff. "Yahweh, Yahweh, a God merciful and gracious, slow to anger, and abounding in steadfast love and faithfulness, keeping steadfast love for thousands, forgiving iniquity and transgression and sin, but who will by no means clear the guilty, visiting the iniquity of the fathers upon the children and the children's children, to the third and fourth generation" (Exod 34:6-7). "I Yahweh your God am a jealous God, visiting the iniquity of the fathers upon the children to the third and the fourth generation of those who hate me, but showing steadfast love to thousands of those who love me and keep my commandments" (Exod 20:5-6; Deut 5:9-10). [Ed.] See the important essays relating to these self-revelation formulas in Walther Zimmerli, *I am Yahweh,* ed. W. Brueggemann, trans. D. W. Stott (Atlanta: John Knox, 1982).

53. Since the Israelites avoided abstract definitions of a person's nature, preferring to see the expression of a person's "nature" in conduct and standards, there are not very many passages that expressly predicate Yahweh as "righteous." The righteousness of his nature is preferably expressed by the passages that say that right action is what he expects of people (for example, Amos 5:24). Accordingly, it is unnecessary to use the word "righteousness"; right conduct can be expressed by synonyms or simply by giving a concrete list of right actions, as in Isa 1:17; Hos 6:6; Mic 6:8; Jer 5:3; and so on.

54. See Nelson Glueck, *Das Wort ḥesed,* BZAW 47 (Giessen: Töpelmann, 1927); Pedersen, *Israel,* 1.238–39; *idem, Der Eid bei den Semiten in seinem Verhältnis zu verwandten Erscheinungen sowie die Stellung des Eides im Islam,* Studien zur Geschichte und Kultur des islamischen Orients (Strasburg: Trubner, 1914) 35. [Ed.] See Hans-Jürgen Zobel, "Ḥesed," in *TDOT* 5 (1986) 44–64; and Hans Joachim Stoebe, "Ḥesed," in *TLOT* 2 (1997) 449–64.

55. Hertzberg provides the correct interpretation of this passage: *Prophet und Gott,* 23–24.

56. On this topic, see my article on the prophets' message: Mowinckel, "Profetenes forkynnelse," *NTT* 33 (1932) 1–37.

57. The other passages mentioned in Gesenius-Buhl[16] under *torah* 3a refer partly to the current religious and moral laws (written and unwritten) and partly to the written book of the law: Deuteronomy.

58. The term *nebûah* does not occur at all. *Maśśa'* is only found in the secondary headings (Isaiah 13–23; 30:6) and in the very late headings (Zech 9:1; 12:1; Mal 1:1), and also in the headings in Nahum and Habakkuk, which *may* be somewhat later as well. Jeremiah has recourse to the word once in order to use it for a play on words in a threat (Jer 23:33); and a later interpolator has added some remarks on this in Jer 23:34-40. [Ed.]

See Richard D. Weis, "A Definition of the Genre *maśśa'* in the Hebrew Bible," Ph.D. dissertation (Claremont Graduate School, 1986).

59. The saying here is not necessarily addressed to the *nebi'im.*

60. Hertzberg, *Prophet und Gott,* 119.

61. In the targums, *ruaḥ gebura'* is the normal term for the spirit of Yahweh when it is regarded as the source of miraculous capacities and powers.

62. Pedersen, *Israel* 1.349–52; Hans Wilhelm Hertzberg, "Die Entwicklung des Begriffes *mišpaṭ* im Alten Testament," *ZAW* 40 (1922) 256–87. Hertzberg wrote without acquaintance with Pedersen's book, and he therefore "modernizes" the content of the word too much.

63. Pedersen, *Israel* 1.142–45; see Ps 72:1-2.

11. THE PROPHETS AND THE TEMPLE CULT

1. This raises the question, for example, of whether this religion was originally "prophetic" or not.

2. Mowinckel, *Psalmenstudien* 2.19–35. Mowinckel, *The Psalms in Israel's Worship,* trans. D. R. Ap-Thomas, 2 vols. (Nashville: Abingdon, 1962) 1.165–66, 181–82.

3. Mowinckel, *Ezra den skriftlaerde* (Kristiania: Dybwad, 1916) 98, 102, 111. [Ed.] See also Joachim Begrich, "Die priestliche Tora," in *Gesammelte Studien zum Alten Testament,* ThBü 21, ed. W. Zimmerli (Munich: Kaiser, 1964) 232–60 (orig. article 1936).

4. Mowinckel, "Om nebiisme og profeti," *NTT* 10 (1909) 192–227.

5. The Hebrew verb *nb'* means "to speak," "to proclaim"; from this Semitic root comes the name of the Mesopotamian god Nabi'u or Nabû. [Ed.] See A. R. Millard, "Nabû," in *DDD*[2], 607–10.

6. One should not say magic wand; Mowinckel, *Psalmenstudien* 1.59–63.

7. Mowinckel, "*Kmr, Komer,*" *ZAW* (1916) 238–39.

8. Here I refer simply to the material that Gustav Hölscher has collected and examined in "Zum Ursprung des israelitischen Prophetentums," in *Alttestamentliche Studien: Rudolf Kittel zum 60. Geburtstag dargebracht,* ed. A. Alt et al., BWAT 13 (Leipzig: Hinrichs, 1913) 88–100. In my 1909 article ("Om nebiisme og profeti"), I examined much of the material presented by Hölscher and drew the same conclusions as he.

9. See "Om nebiisme og profeti," 203–4, 227–37. It is still customary among modern-day dervishes to make the dervish's emblems of office out of the sheep's wool that is brought by the novice and used as the initiation sacrifice; see Hölscher's article (n. 8 above).

10. Contrary to Bernhard Stade, *Biblische Theologie des Alten Testaments,* 2 vols. (Tübingen: Mohr/Siebeck, 1905–11) 1.67.

11. In an earlier work—in which I exaggerated somewhat—I emphasized the distinction between the *nebi'im* and the "literary prophets," and I dealt with the most important passages: Mowinckel, "Profeternes forhold til nebiismen," *NTT* 11 (1910) 126–38.

12. In opposition to Hans Schmidt, "The Earliest Israelite Prophecy before Amos," in *Twentieth-Century Theology in the Making,* Vol. 1: *Themes of Biblical Theology,* ed. Jaroslav Pelikan, trans. R. A. Wilson (New York: Harper & Row, 1969) 38–48 (orig. German article in *RGG*[2]). One should not build too much on the Ahijah legend in 1 Kgs 11:29-40. The account

is deuteronomistic; we know nothing about Ahijah's actual motives. At any rate, one *nabi'* or another could be secured for any revolutionary or political act. An Israelite nationalistic stance against Judah's rule may perhaps have been at work in Ahijah.

13. Compare Mowinckel, "Om nebiisme og profeti," 224–27.

14. Ibid., 220–21, 224–25.

15. Without revealing a trace of doubt, Rudolf Kittel translates it "the chief bearer"; and just as uncritically, he claims that *maśśa'* can mean "carrying" as well as a "(musical) instrument" (HKAT). Immanuel Benzinger also allows "carrying"; but he quite correctly knows that *maśśa'* has never meant, and can never mean, a presentation. And he has also noted that, in this context, one would hardly expect a notice about carrying or carriers (KHC). The wisest is Frants Buhl, who in his Danish translation of the Old Testament considers the words untranslatable. [Ed.] See now, Richard D. Weis, "A Definition of the Genre *maśśa'* in the Hebrew Bible," Ph.D. dissertation (Claremont Graduate School, 1986).

16. See Mowinckel, *Psalmenstudien* 2.94–107; Mowinckel, *The Psalms in Israel's Worship* 1.127–29, 175–76.

17. Mowinckel, *Psalmenstudien* 2.117 and throughout; Mowinckel, *The Psalms in Israel's Worship* 1.132.

[18.] On prophets and prophecy in the ancient Near East, see, for example: William L. Moran, "New Evidence from Mari on the History of Prophecy," *Bib* 50 (1969) 15–56; James F. Ross, "Prophecy in Hamath, Israel, and Mari," *HTR* 63 (1970) 1–28; Moshe Weinfeld, "Ancient Near Eastern Patterns in Israelite Prophetic Literature," *VT* 27 (1977) 178–95; Abraham Malamat, "A Forerunner of Biblical Prophecy: The Mari Documents," in *Ancient Israelite Religion: Essays in Honor of Frank Moore Cross*, ed. P. D. Miller et al. (Philadelphia: Fortress Press, 1987) 33–52; Maria deJong Ellis, "Observations on Mesopotamian Oracles and Prophetic Texts: Literary and Historiographic Considerations," *JCS* 41 (1989) 127–86; Herbert B. Huffmon, "Prophecy, Ancient Near East," in *ABD* 5.477–82; Simon B. Parker, "Official Attitudes toward Prophecy at Mari and in Israel," *VT* 43 (1993) 50–68; Simo Parpola, *Assyrian Prophecies*, SAA 9 (Helsinki: Neo-Assyrian Text Corpus Project, 1997); Martti Nissinen, *References to Prophecy in Neo-Assyrian Sources*, SAAS 7 (Helsinki: Neo-Assyrian Text Corpus Project, 1998); Lester L. Grabbe, "Ancient Near Eastern Prophecy from an Anthropological Perspective," in *Prophecy in Its Ancient Near Eastern Context: Mesopotamian, Biblical and Arabian Perspectives*, ed. M. Nissinen, SBLSymSer 13 (Atlanta: Society of Biblical Literature, 2000) 13–32; and Karel van der Toorn, "Mesopotamian Prophecy between Immanence and Transcendence: A Comparison of Old Babylonian and Neo-Assyrian Prophecy," in *Prophecy in Its Ancient Near Eastern Context*, 71–87.

19. This is the solution for the apparent contradiction between Zech 1:1 and Ezra 5:1; 6:14. Iddo is not the prophet's personal grandfather, but the family from which he comes, identical with Iddo in Neh 12:4. [Ed.] For a discussion of these problems, see John W. Wright, "Iddo," in *ABD* 3.376.

20. See Paul Volz, *Die Biblischen Altertümer*, 2nd ed. (Stuttgart: Calwer, 1925) 162ff.

[21.] Mowinckel, *The Psalms in Israel's Worship* 2.214; Mowinckel, *Psalmenstudien* 4.29–33.

[22.] On Mesopotamian extispicy, see: Frederick H. Cryer, *Divination in Ancient Israel and its Near Eastern Environment: A Socio-Historical Investigation*, JSOTSup 142 (Sheffield: JSOT Press, 1994); Ulla Jeyes, *Old Babylonian Extispicy: Omen Texts in the*

British Museum, Uitgaven van het Nederlands Historisch-Archaeologisch Instituut te Istanbul 64 (Istanbul: Nederlands Historisch-Archaeologisch Instituut te Istanbul, 1989); and Ulla Koch-Westenholz, *Babylonian Liver Omens,* CNI Publications 25 (Copenhagen: Carsten Niebuhr Institute of Near Eastern Studies/University of Copenhagen, 2000).

[23.] "The Journey of Wen-Amon to Phoenicia," in *ANET,* 26; trans. John A. Wilson. Wilson dates this document to the 11th century B.C.E., and it was discovered in el-Hibeh, Egypt.

24. Mowinckel, *Psalmenstudien* 1.72, 145.

[25.] See also the Akkadian "Prayer to the Gods of the Night": "Stand by, and then, in the divination which I am making, in the lamb which I am offering, put truth for me" (*ANET,* 391; trans. Ferris J. Stephens). See Mowinckel, *Psalmenstudien* 1.145.

26. Compare the images of Amos (for example, the basket of fruit; Amos 8:1-3) and of Jeremiah (the almond tree; Jer 1:11-12).

27. Compare the article "Traum," in *RGG*[2]. [Ed.] See also: A. Leo Oppenheim, *The Interpretation of Dreams in the Ancient Near East, with a Translation of an Assyrian Dream-Book,* TAPS 46.3 (Philadelphia: American Philosophical Society, 1956); J. Oberman, "How Daniel Was Blessed with a Son: An Incubation Scene in Ugarit," JAOSSup 46 (1946); Isaac Mendelsohn, "Dreams," in *IDB* 1.868–69; and Robert Karl Gnuse, *The Dream Theophany of Samuel: Its Structure in Relation to Ancient Near Eastern Dreams and Its Theological Significance* (Lanham, Md.: University Press of America, 1984).

28. Mowinckel, *Psalmenstudien* 1.154–57.

29. Mowinckel, *Psalmenstudien* 4.5–7; Mowinckel, *The Psalms in Israel's Worship* 2.94, 209.

30. Mowinckel, *Psalmenstudien* 4; idem, *The Psalms in Israel's Worship* 2.94, 209.

[31.] For a current discussion of Habakkuk 3, see Michael H. Floyd, *Minor Prophets: Part 2,* FOTL 22 (Grand Rapids: Eerdmans, 2000) 79–161. Mowinckel also wrote a later essay on this passage: "Zum Psalm des Habakkuk," *TZ* 9 (1953) 1–21.

[32.] Mowinckel, *Psalmenstudien* 2.44–80.

33. I completely agree with Karl Budde in his interpretation of the Book of Habakkuk; see Budde, *Das prophetische Schrifttum,* Religionsgeschichtliche Volksbücher 2/5 (Tübingen: Mohr/Siebeck, 1906).

[34.] Mowinckel, *Psalmenstudien* 4.17–22; Mowinckel, *The Psalms in Israel's Worship* 2.212–13.

35. Hermann Gunkel, *The Psalms: A Form-Critical Introduction,* trans. T. M. Horner, FBBS 19 (Philadelphia: Fortress Press, 1967). [Ed.] See also Mowinckel, *The Psalms in Israel's Worship* 1.197.

Bibliography

The Works of Sigmund Mowinckel in English

Books

1937 *The Two Sources of the Predeuteronomic Primeval History (JE) in Genesis 1–11.* ANVAO. Oslo: Dybwad.

1946 *Prophecy and Tradition: The Prophetic Books in the Light of the Study of the Growth and History of the Tradition.* Oslo: Dybwad.

1956 *He That Cometh.* Translated by G. A. Anderson. Rev. ed. Nashville: Abingdon. Norwegian ed. 1951.

1957 *Real and Apparent Tricola in Hebrew Psalm Poetry.* ANVAO. Oslo: Dybwad.

1959 *The Old Testament as Word of God.* Translated by R. B. Bjornard. Nashville: Abingdon. Norwegian ed. 1938.

1962 *The Psalms in Israel's Worship.* 2 vols. Translated by D. R. Ap-Thomas. Nashville: Abingdon. Norwegian ed. 1951. Reprinted Sheffield: JSOT Press, 1992.

1981 *Religion and Cult.* Translated by J. F. X. Sheehan. Milwaukee: Marquette University. Norwegian ed. 1950.

Articles

1934 "The 'Spirit' and the 'Word' in the Pre-exilic Reforming Prophets." *JBL* 53:199–227.

1935 "Ecstatic Experience and Rational Elaboration in Old Testament Prophecy." *AcOr* 13:264–91.

1936 "Ecstatic Experience and Rational Elaboration in Old Testament Prophecy." *AcOr* 14:319.

1939 "The Babylonian Matter in the Predeuteronomic Primeval History (JE) in Gen. 1–11." *JBL* 58:87–91.

1950–51 "Traditionalism and Personality in the Psalms." *HUCA* 23:205–31.

1953 "The Hebrew Equivalent of *Taxo* in *Ass. Mos.* ix." In *Congress Volume: Copenhagen, 1953*, 88–96. VTSup 1. Leiden: Brill.

1955 "Psalms Criticism between 100 and 1935." *VT* 5:13–33.

1956 "Some Remarks on Hodayoth 39:5-20." *JBL* 75:265–76.
1957 "The Copper Scroll—An Apocryphon?" *JBL* 76:261–65.
1959 "General Oriental and Specific Israelite Elements in the Israelite Conception of the Sacral Kingdom." In *The Sacral Kingship*, 283–93. Studies in the History of Religions 4. Leiden: Brill.
1959 "Notes on the Psalms." *StTh* 13:134–65.
1961 "The Name of the God of Moses." *HUCA* 32:121–33.
1961 "The Verb *śiaḥ* and the Nouns *śiaḥ* and *śiḥa*." *StTh* 15:110.
1962 "Drive and/or Ride in the O.T." *VT* 12:278–99.
1962 "Legend." In *Interpreter's Dictionary of the Bible*, edited by G. A. Buttrick, 3:108–10. Nashville: Abingdon.
1962 "Literature." In *Interpreter's Dictionary of the Bible*, edited by G. A. Buttrick, 3.139–43. Nashville: Abingdon.
1962 "Tradition, Oral." In *Interpreter's Dictionary of the Bible*, edited by G. A. Buttrick, 4:683–85. Nashville: Abingdon.
1963 "Israelite Historiography." *ASTI* 2:4–26.
1963 "*Šaḥal*." In *Hebrew and Semitic Studies: Presented to Godfrey Rolles Driver in Celebration of his Seventieth Birthday, August 20, 1962*, edited by D. W. Thomas and W. D. McHardy, 95–103. Oxford: Clarendon.
1967 "Mowinckel's Letter." *Luther Theological Seminary Review* 5/2:41–44.

Complete Bibliography

Kvale, Dagfinn, and Dagfinn Rian. "Sigmund Mowinckel: A Bibliography." *SJOT* 2 (1988) 95–168.

Assessments of Sigmund Mowinckel's Work

Ap-Thomas, D. R. "An Appreciation of Sigmund Mowinckel's Contribution to Biblical Studies." *JBL* 85 (1966) 315–25.

Barr, James. "Mowinckel, the Old Testament, and the Question of Natural Theology (The Second Mowinckel Lecture—Oslo, 27 November 1987)." *StTh* 42 (1988) 21–38.

Barstad, Hans M. "Some Aspects of Sigmund Mowinckel as Historian." *SJOT* 2 (1988) 83–91.

Clements, Ronald E. "Sigmund Mowinckel." In *Historical Handbook of Major Biblical Interpreters*, edited by D. K. McKim, 505–10. Downers Grove, Ill.: InterVarsity, 1998.

Dahl, Nils A. "Sigmund Mowinckel: Historian of Religion and Theologian." *SJOT* 2 (1988) 8–22.

Gnuse, Robert K, and Douglas A. Knight. "Foreword to the Reprint Edition." In Sigmund Mowinckel, *The Psalms in Israel's Worship*, xxi–xxviii. Biblical Seminar 14. Sheffield: JSOT Press, 1992.

Hauge, Martin Ravndal. "Sigmund Mowinckel and the Psalms—A Query into His Concern." *SJOT* 2 (1988) 56–71.

Hygen, Johan B. "Sigmund Mowinckel: The Man and the Teacher." *SJOT* 2 (1988) 1–7.

Jeppesen, Knud. "The Day of Yahweh in Mowinckel's Conception Reviewed." *SJOT* 2 (1988) 42–55.

Kapelrud, Arvid S. "Sigmund Mowinckel and Old Testament Study." *ASTI* 5 (1967) 4–29.

———. "Sigmund Mowinckel's Study of the Prophets." *SJOT* 2 (1988) 72–82.

Knight, Douglas A. *Rediscovering the Traditions of Israel.* Rev. ed. SBLDS 9. Missoula, Mont.: Scholars, 1975. 221–24; 250–59; 275–81.

Rian, Dagfinn. "'The Insights I Have Gained': Prof. Sigmund Mowinckel as He Saw Himself." In *Text and Theology: Studies in Honour of Professor Dr. Theol. Magne Saebø, Presented on the Occasion of His 65th Birthday,* edited by Arvid Tångberg, 228–36. Oslo: Verbum, 1994.

———. "Mowinckel, Sigmund Olaf Plytt." In *Dictionary of Biblical Interpretation,* edited by John H. Hayes, 166–68. Nashville: Abingdon, 1999.

Ringgren, Helmer. "Sigmund Mowinckel and the Uppsala School of Old Testament Study." *SJOT* 2 (1988) 36–41.

Saebø, Magnes. "Mowinckel, Sigmund." In *TRE* 23 (1994) 384–88.

———. "Sigmund Mowinckel and His Relation to the Literary Critical School." *StTh* 40 (1986) 81–93.

———. "Sigmund Mowinckel in His Relation to the Literary Critical School." *SJOT* 2 (1988) 23–35.

Select Bibliography on Tradition History

Alster, Bendt. "Interaction of Oral and Written Poetry in Early Mesopotamian Literature." In *Mesopotamian Epic Literature: Oral or Aural?* edited by Marianna E. Vogelzang and Herman L. J. Vanstiphout, 23–55. Lewiston, N.Y.: Mellen, 1992.

Brueggemann, Walter. *David's Truth in Israel's Imagination and Memory.* 2nd ed. Minneapolis: Fortress Press, 2002.

Campbell, Antony F. *The Ark Narrative, 1 Sam 4–6, 2 Sam 6: A Form-Critical and Traditio-Historical Study.* SBLDS 16. Missoula, Mont.: Scholars, 1975.

Carlson, R. A. *David, the Chosen King: A Traditio-Historical Approach to the Second Book of Samuel.* Translated by Eric J. Sharpe and Stanley Rudman. Stockholm: Almqvist & Wiksell, 1964.

Childs, Brevard S. *Memory and Tradition in Israel.* SBT 1/37. Naperville, Ill.: Allenson, 1962.

Coats, George W. "Tradition Criticism, OT." In *IDBSup,* edited by Keith Crim. Nashville: Abingdon, 1976. 912–14.

Coote, Robert B. "Tradition, OT, Oral." In *IDBSup,* edited by Keith Crim. Nashville: Abingdon, 1976. 914–16.

Culley, Robert C. "Oral Tradition and Biblical Studies." *Oral Traditions* 1 (1986) 30–65.

De Vries, Simon J. *From Old Revelation to New: A Traditio-Historical and Redaction-Critical Study of Temporal Transitions in Prophetic Prediction.* Grand Rapids: Eerdmans, 1995.

Engnell, Ivan. *A Rigid Scrutiny: Critical Essays on the Old Testament.* Translated by John T. Willis. Nashville: Vanderbilt Univ. Press, 1969.

Gressmann, Hugo. *The Tower of Babel.* New York: Jewish Institute of Religion Press, 1928.

Groves, Joseph W. *Actualization and Interpretation in the Old Testament.* SBLDS 86. Atlanta: Scholars, 1987.

Gunkel, Hermann. *The Folktale in the Old Testament.* Translated by Michael D. Rutter. HTIBS 6. Sheffield: Sheffield Academic, 1987.

———. "The Influence of Babylonian Mythology upon the Biblical Creation Story." In *Creation in the Old Testament,* edited by Bernhard W. Anderson, 25–52. IRT 6. Philadelphia: Fortress Press, 1984.

———. *Introduction to the Psalms: The Genres of the Religious Lyric of Israel.* Completed by Joachim Begrich. Translated by James D. Nogalski. MLBS. Macon, Ga.: Mercer Univ. Press, 1998.

———. *The Stories of Genesis.* Translated by John J. Scullion. Berkeley: BIBAL, 1994.

———. *Water for a Thirsty Land: Israelite Literature and Religion.* Edited by K. C. Hanson. FCBS. Minneapolis: Fortress Press, 2001.

Hendel, Ronald S. *The Epic of the Patriarch: The Jacob Cycle and the Narrative Traditions of Canaan and Israel.* HSM 42. Atlanta: Scholars, 1987.

Jeppesen, Knud, and Benedikt Otzen, editors. *The Productions of Time: Tradition History in Old Testament Scholarship.* Translated by Frederick H. Cryer. Sheffield: Almond, 1984.

Knierim, Rolf. "Criticism of Literary Features, Form, Tradition, and Redaction." In *The Hebrew Bible and Its Modern Interpreters,* edited by Douglas A. Knight and Gene M. Tucker, 123–65. Philadelphia: Fortress Press, 1985.

Knight, Douglas A. *Rediscovering the Traditions of Israel.* Rev. ed. SBLDS 9. Missoula, Mont.: Scholars, 1975.

———, editor. *Tradition and Theology in the Old Testament.* Philadelphia: Fortress Press, 1977.

———. "Tradition History." In *ABD,* edited by David Noel Freedman. New York: Doubleday, 1992. 6:633–38.

Laessøe, Jørgen. "Literary and Oral Tradition in Ancient Mesopotamia." In *Studia Orientalia Ioanni Pedersen septuagenario A.D. VII id. nov. anno MCMLIII,* 205ff. Hauniae: Munksgaard, 1953.

Mowinckel, Sigmund. *He That Cometh.* Translated by G. W. Anderson. Nashville: Abingdon, 1954.

———. *The Psalms in Israel's Worship.* 2 vols. Translated by D. R. Ap-Thomas. Nashville: Abingdon, 1962.

———. "Tradition, Oral." In *IDB,* edited by George A Buttrick, Nashville: Abingdon, 1962. 4:683–85.

Niditch, Susan. *Oral World and Written Word: Ancient Israelite Literature.* LAI. Louisville: Westminster John Knox, 1996.

Nielsen, Eduard. *Oral Tradition: A Modern Problem in Old Testament Introduction.* SBT 1/11. Chicago: Allenson, 1954.

———. *Shechem: A Traditio-Historical Investigation.* 2nd ed. Copenhagen: Gad, 1959.

Noth, Martin. "The Background of Judges 17–18." In *Israel's Prophetic Heritage: Essays in Honor of James Muilenburg,* edited by Bernhard W. Anderson and Walter Harrelson, 68–85. New York: Harper, 1962.

———. *The History of Pentateuchal Traditions.* Translated by Bernhard W. Anderson. Englewood Cliffs, N.J.: Prentice Hall, 1972.

———. *The Laws in the Pentateuch and Other Studies.* Translated by D. R. Ap-Thomas. Philadelphia: Fortress Press, 1967.

Rad, Gerhard von. *Old Testament Theology.* Translated by David M. G. Stalker. 2 vols. Edinburgh: Oliver & Boyd, 1962–65. Reprinted OTL. Louisville: Westminster John Knox, 2001.

———. *The Problem of the Hexateuch and Other Essays.* Translated by E. W. Trueman Dicken. New York: McGraw-Hill, 1966.

Rast, Walter E. *Tradition History and the Old Testament.* GBS. Philadelphia: Fortress Press, 1972.

Stansell, Gary. *Micah and Isaiah: A Form and Tradition Historical Comparison.* SBLDS 85. Atlanta: Scholars, 1988.

Zimmerli, Walther. "The Special Form- and Traditio-Historical Character of Ezekiel's Prophecy." *VT* 15 (1965) 515–27.

Select Bibliography on Prophecy

Baltzer, Klaus. *Deutero-Isaiah: A Commentary on Isaiah 40–55.* Translated by Margaret Kohl. Hermeneia. Minneapolis: Fortress Press, 2001.

Barstad, Hans M. "Comparare necesse est: Ancient Israelite and Ancient Near Eastern Prophecy in a Comparative Perspective." In Nissinen 2000:3–11.

Ben Zvi, Ehud, and Michael H. Floyd, editors. *Writings and Speech in Israelite and Ancient Near Eastern Prophecy.* SBLSymSer 10. Atlanta: Scholars, 2000.

Blenkinsopp, Joseph. *A History of Prophecy in Israel.* Rev. ed. Louisville: Westminster John Knox, 1996.

Brennemann, James E. *Canons in Conflict: Negotiating Texts in True and False Prophecy.* New York: Oxford Univ. Press, 1997.

Brueggemann, Walter. *Hopeful Imagination: Prophetic Voices in Exile.* Philadelphia: Fortress Press, 1986.

———. *The Prophetic Imagination.* 2nd ed. Minneapolis: Fortress Press, 2001.

———. *Texts That Linger, Words That Explode: Listening to Prophetic Voices.* Edited by Patrick D. Miller. Minneapolis: Fortress Press, 2000.

Carroll, Robert P. "Prophecy and Society." In *The World of Ancient Israel*, edited by R. E. Clements, 203–25. Cambridge: Cambridge Univ. Press, 1989.

———. *When Prophecy Failed: Cognitive Dissonance and the Prophetic Traditions of the Old Testament.* New York: Seabury, 1979.

Chaney, Marvin L. "Bitter Bounty: The Dynamics of Political Economy Critiqued by the Eighth-Century Prophets." In *Reformed Faith and Economics*, edited by Robert L. Stivers, 15–30. Lanham, Md.: University Press of America, 1989.

Clements, Ronald E. "Patterns in the Prophetic Canon." In *Canon and Authority: Essays in Old Testament Religion and Theology*, edited by George W. Coats and Burke O. Long, 42–55. Philadelphia: Fortress Press, 1977.

———. "The Prophet as Author: The Case of the Isaiah Memoir." Ben Zvi and Floyd 2000:89–101.

Coggins, Richard, Anthony Phillips, and Michael Knibb, editors. *Israel's Prophetic Traditions: Essays in Honour of Peter Ackroyd.* Cambridge: Cambridge Univ. Press, 1982.

Crenshaw, James L. "Transmitting Prophecy across Generations." In Ben Zvi and Floyd 2000:31–44.

Culley, Robert C. "Orality and Writtenness in the Prophetic Texts." In Ben Zvi and Floyd 2000:45–64.

Culley, Robert C., and Thomas W. Overholt, editors. *Semeia* 21: *Anthropological Perspectives on Old Testament Prophecy*, 1982.

Darr, Katheryn Pfisterer. "Literary Perspectives on Prophetic Literature." In *Old Testa-*

ment Interpretation: Past, Present, and Future. Essays in Honor of Gene M. Tucker, edited by James Luther Mays et al., 127–43. Nashville: Abingdon, 1995.

Davies, Philip R. "'Pen of iron, point of diamond' (Jer 17:1): Prophecy as Writing." In Ben Zvi and Floyd 2000:65–81.

de Moor, Johannes C., editor. *The Elusive Prophet: The Prophet as a Historical Person, Literary Character and Anonymous Artist.* OtSt 45. Leiden: Brill, 2001.

Dempsey, Carol J. *The Prophets: A Liberation-Critical Reading.* Minneapolis: Fortress Press, 2000.

Ellis, Maria deJong. "Observations on Mesopotamian Oracles and Prophetic Texts: Literary and Historiographic Considerations." *JCS* 41 (1989) 127–86.

Floyd, Michael H. *Minor Prophets: Part 2.* FOTL 22. Grand Rapids: Eerdmans, 2000.

———. "Prophecy and Writing in Habakkuk 2, 1-5." *ZAW* 105 (1993) 462–81.

———. "'Write the revelation!' (Hab 2:2): Re-imagining the Cultural History of Prophecy." In Ben Zvi and Floyd 2000:103–43.

Gitay, Yehoshua. "The Individual versus the Institution: The Prophet versus His Book." In *Religion and the Reconstruction of Civil Society: Papers from the Founding Congress of the South African Academy of Religion, January 1994,* edited by J. W. de Gruchy and S. Matrin. Miscellania Congregalia 51. Pretoria: Univ. of South Africa, 1995.

———, editor. *Prophecy and Prophets: The Diversity of Contemporary Issues in Scholarship.* SBLSS. Atlanta: Scholars, 1997.

Gordon, Robert P., editor. *The Place is Too Small for Us: The Israelite Prophets in Recent Scholarship.* SBTS 5. Winona Lake, Ind.: Eisenbrauns, 1995.

Gottwald, Norman K. "The Biblical Prophetic Critique of Political Economy: Its Ground and Import." In *The Hebrew Bible in Its Social World and in Ours,* 349–64. Semeia Studies. Atlanta: Scholars, 1993.

———. "Were the 'Radical' Prophets also 'Cultic' Prophets?" In *The Hebrew Bible in Its Social World and in Ours,* 111–17. Semeia Studies. Atlanta: Scholars, 1993.

Grabbe, Lester L. "Ancient Near Eastern Prophecy from an Anthropological Perspective." In Nissinen 2000:13–32.

———. *Priests, Prophets, Diviners, Sages: A Socio-Historical Study of Religious Specialists in Ancient Israel.* Valley Forge, Pa.: Trinity, 1995.

Gunkel, Hermann. "The Israelite Prophecy from the Time of Amos." In *Twentieth Century Theology in the Making,* edited by Jaroslav Pelikan, translated by R. A. Wilson, 48–75. New York: Harper & Row, 1969.

———. "The Prophets: Oral and Written." In *Water for a Thirsty Land: Israelite Literature and Religion,* edited by K. C. Hanson, 85–133. FCBS. Minneapolis: Fortress Press, 2001.

Hämeen-Anttila, Jaakko. "Arabian Prophecy." In Nissinen 2000:115–46.

Hanson, Paul D. *The Dawn of Apocalyptic: The Historical and Sociological Roots of Jewish Apocalyptic Eschatology.* Rev. ed. Philadelphia: Fortress Press, 1979.

Huffmon, Herbert B. "A Company of Prophets: Mari, Assyria, Israel." In Nissinen 2000:47–70.

Hutton, Rodney R. *Charisma and Authority in Israelite Society.* Minneapolis: Fortress Press, 1994.

Koch, Klaus. *The Prophets.* Translated by Margaret Kohl. 2 vols. Philadelphia: Fortress Press, 1983–84.

Lang, Bernhard. *Monotheism and the Prophetic Minority: An Essay in Biblical History and Sociology.* SWBA 1. Sheffield: Almond, 1983.

Lindblom, Johannes. *Prophecy in Ancient Israel.* Philadelphia: Fortress Press, 1973.

Long, Burke O. "Prophetic Authority as Social Reality." In *Canon and Authority: Essays in Old Testament Religion and Theology*, edited by George W. Coats and Burke O. Long, 3–20. Philadelphia: Fortress Press, 1977.

March, W. Eugene. "Prophecy." In *Old Testament Form Criticism*, edited by John H. Hayes, 141–77. TUMSR 2. San Antonio: Trinity Univ. Press, 1974.

Miller, Patrick D. "The World and Message of the Prophets: Biblical Prophecy in Its Context." In *Old Testament Interpretation: Past, Present, and Future. Essays in Honor of Gene M. Tucker*, edited by James Luther Mays et al., 97–112. Nashville: Abingdon, 1995.

Moran, William L. "New Evidence from Mari on the History of Prophecy." *Bib* 50 (1969) 15–56.

Nissinen, Martti, editor. *Prophecy in Its Ancient Near Eastern Context: Mesopotamian, Biblical and Arabian Perspectives.* SBLSymSer 13. Atlanta: Society of Biblical Literature, 2000.

———. "The Socio-Religious Role of the Neo-Assyrian Prophets." In Nissinen 2000:89–114.

———. "Spoken, Written, Quoted, and Invented: Orality and Writtenness in Ancient Near Eastern Prophecy." In Ben Zvi and Floyd 2000:235–71.

Overholt, Thomas W. *Channels of Prophecy: The Social Dynamics of Prophetic Activity.* Minneapolis: Fortress Press, 1989.

———. *Prophecy in Cross-Cultural Perspective.* SBLSBS 17. Atlanta: Scholars, 1986.

Parker, Simon B. "Possession Trance and Prophecy in Pre-exilic Israel." *VT* 28 (1978) 271–85.

Peckham, Brian. *History and Prophecy: The Development of Late Judean Literary Tradition.* ABRL. New York: Doubleday, 1993.

Peterson, David L. "Defining Prophecy and Prophetic Literature." In Nissinen 2000:33–44.

———, editor. *Prophecy in Israel: Search for an Identity.* IRT 10. Philadelphia: Fortress Press, 1987.

———. *The Roles of Israel's Prophets.* JSOTSup 17. Sheffield: JSOT Press, 1981.

Rad, Gerhard von. *Old Testament Theology.* Vol. 2: *The Theology of Israel's Prophetic Traditions.* Translated by David M. G. Stalker. Edinburgh: Oliver & Boyd, 1965. Reprinted OTL. Louisville: Westminster John Knox, 2001.

Redford, Donald B. "Scribe and Speaker." In Ben Zvi and Floyd 2000:145–218.

Stansell, Gary. *Micah and Isaiah: A Form and Tradition Historical Comparison.* SBLDS 85. Atlanta: Scholars, 1988.

Steck, Odil Hannes. *The Prophetic Books and Their Theological Witness.* Translated by James D. Nogalski. St. Louis: Chalice, 2000.

Sweeney, Marvin A. "Formation and Form in Prophetic Literature." In *Old Testament Interpretation: Past, Present, and Future. Essays in Honor of Gene M. Tucker*, edited by James Luther Mays et al., 113–26. Nashville: Abingdon, 1995.

———. *Isaiah 1–39; with an Introduction to Prophetic Literature.* FOTL 16. Grand Rapids: Eerdmans, 1996.

Toorn, Karel van der Toorn. "From the Oral to the Written: The Case of Old Babylonian Prophecy." In Ben Zvi and Floyd 2000:219–34.

———. "Mesopotamian Prophecy between Immanence and Transcendence: A Comparison of Old Babylonian and Neo-Assyrian Prophecy." In Nissinen 2000:71–87.

Tucker, Gene M. "Prophecy and Prophetic Literature." In *The Hebrew Bible and Its Modern Interpreters*, edited by Douglas A. Knight and Gene M. Tucker, 325–68. Philadelphia: Fortress Press, 1985.

Weinfeld, Moshe. "Ancient Near Eastern Patterns in Israelite Prophetic Literature." *VT* 27 (1977) 178–95.

Westermann, Claus. *Basic Forms of Prophetic Speech*. Translated by Hugh Clayton White. Philadelphia: Westminster, 1967.

Wildberger, Hans. *Isaiah*. 3 vols. Translated by Thomas H. Trapp. CC. Minneapolis: Fortress Press, 1991–2002.

Wilson, Robert R. "Prophecy and Ecstasy: A Re-examination." *JBL* 98 (1979) 321–37.

———. *Prophecy and Society in Ancient Israel*. Philadelphia: Fortress Press, 1980.

Wolff, Hans Walter. *Amos the Prophet: The Man and His Background*. Translated by Foster R. McCurley. Philadelphia: Fortress Press, 1973.

———. *Micah the Prophet*. Translated by Ralph D. Gehrke. Philadelphia: Fortress Press, 1981.

Zimmerli, Walther. "From Prophetic Word to Prophetic Book." In Gordon 1995:419–42. (German article 1979.)

———. *I Am Yahweh*. Edited by Walter Brueggemann. Translated by Douglas W. Stott. Atlanta: John Knox, 1982.

———. "Prophetic Proclamation and Reinterpretation." In *Tradition and Theology in the Old Testament*, edited by Douglas A. Knight, 69–100. Philadelphia: Fortress Press, 1977.

———. "The Special Form- and Traditio-Historical Character of Ezekiel's Prophecy." *VT* 15 (1965) 515–27.

Index of Authors

Editor's Note: Dates have been supplied for authors of earlier generations in order to provide historical context.

Index of Ancient Sources

The Quest of the Historical Jesus
First Complete Edition
Albert Schweitzer

Water for a Thirsty Land
Israelite Literature and Religion
Hermann Gunkel

Jesus and the Message of the New Testament
Joachim Jeremias

The Spirit and the Word
Prophecy and Tradition in Ancient Israel
Sigmund Mowinckel

Parable and Gospel
Norman Perrin